INVADING AMERICA
1943
AMBASSADORS AT LARGE

CLIFFORD COLE

EDITED BY SARA GOODWINS

Loaghtan Books
17 Onslow Avenue
Sutton
Surrey
SM2 7ED

Published by Loaghtan Books

First published: January 2012

Typesetting and origination by:
Loaghtan Books

Printed and bound by:
Lavenham Press Ltd

Website: www.loaghtanbooks.com

ISBN: 978 1 908060 02 0

For Mrs Louise Cole
with thanks

Front cover: The Battery parades in New York

Rear cover: Clifford Cole in 1943 and 2006

Front/rear background: The Capitol from Pennsylvania Avenue, 1943 (see also page 18)

Title page: The officers and sergeants of the 1st Composite Demonstration Battery Royal Artillery. Captain Cole is centre front

CONTENTS

CLIFFORD COLE, 1912-2008

Born 22 June 1912 Clifford Cole was brought up in Goole, Yorkshire. He was the youngest of six, with three brothers and two sisters, and attended Goole Grammar School. Their father was a captain in the merchant navy and the seventh generation to be so. Cole's great love was spending time on his father's boat with the family on the River Derwent. Later in life Cole has his own boat, a six-berth conversion moored at Tewkesbury.

When he left school Cole became a trainee manager at Woolworths and, aged 24, became the company's youngest manager in over 700 stores in Britain. When war broke out Cole joined the army and, between 1940 and 1960, served in England, Nigeria, Egypt, Greece and Cyprus.

In 1943 Cole spent the six months in the US which are the subject of this book. Shortly after his return he gave a talk on his American experiences to interested service personnel. In the audience was Patricia Louise Bates, a subaltern in the Auxiliary Territorial Service (ATS) who was working as a plotter on a gun site.

They married in February 1946; Cole family legend states that Cole was on a boat in Africa when be proposed – by letter – and only just got back to England in time for the wedding. Over the next ten years they had three children, Andria, Sarah and Graham.

While in the army Cole met Don Perry who had started his own surveying and estate agency business in Cheltenham. Perry offered Cole a job if he studied and qualified. Cole left the army in 1960 with the rank of major and not only completed the three-year course in thirteen months but also won the medal for top student in the exams. He then joined D.N. Perry & Co as a chartered surveyor. Three years later he stated his own practice in Cheltenham and, after a few years, also opened branches in Tewkesbury, Worcester and Bishop's Cleeve.

By January 1975 all their children were working so Cole took a sabbatical and he and his wife spent fourteen months travelling the world. In their compact motor caravan they visited every continent except Antarctica.

Shortly after their return to the UK Cole retired from business. During the summer he concentrated on his hobbies of bowling and stamp collecting while winters were spent by the Coles in visiting North America and touring every American state and Canadian province. In later years they spent the winters in Portugal which had a warmer climate.

Eventually the day came when Cole's eyesight began to fail and the long drive became a little too much. Even so he remained actively involved with his hobbies and, with a second-hand computer which he bought and taught himself to use, managed to continue with his writing.

In his tribute to Clifford Cole his son Graham said: 'he wanted to live until he was 100, not to get a letter from the Queen but so that he could write to the English Cricket team to tell them that if he could get 100, why couldn't they...' Unfortunately Cole was bowled out for 96.

Clifford Cole died in 2008 before preparation for this book had begun. Nevertheless it is his work; we can only hope that he would have been pleased with it.

Editor's notes

Although he finished his army career as a major, at the time of his visit to America, Clifford Cole held the rank of captain. To avoid possible confusion this book uses the rank he held during his US tour.

The text was written by Captain Cole either during his tour of America or shortly after he returned to Britain. It therefore dates from 1943 and early 1944. The editorial input has been limited to providing the biography and footnotes, inserting information which Cole had suppressed under wartime censorship, writing captions for the photographs and occasionally explaining references within the text, such explanations being enclosed in square brackets [ ].

The photographs were taken while the Battery was in America, by the Battery's official photographer and others, and collected by Captain Cole to use as illustration to his book.

THE TOUR AND ITS PURPOSE

The first phase of the Battery's stay in America covered its demonstration work in Camp Davis. During this time the Battery developed what it needed to do to entertain and educate the public and US troops about the British war effort, specifically its anti-aircraft capability.

The radar equipment brought from England was still largely at the development stage, and few people had even seen it, never mind become familiar with its operation. It gave continual problems, partly because of lack of adequate training in its use, and partly due to shortage of spares and lack of skilled maintenance. I was therefore detailed to take on more of the administrative work of the Battery, specifically as director of programmes. All information regarding the demonstrations and social activities of the battery came to me and I forwarded them in good time and with detailed instructions to the right personnel.

Leaving Camp Davis the Battery, divided into various detachments, embarked on a coast-to-coast tour, necessitating a lot of movement, short stays at appointed camps, and long periods of demonstrations. It also included parades in the cities and towns near the camps, and more than the average publicity.

The Battery had been given a taste of this publicity, but it was expected that anything we had experienced was as nothing to the extensive publicity scheduled for us. As the Battery moved on its way, it was preceded at each step by an advance party consisting of one officer belonging to the Battery, one officer and a sergeant belonging to the escort detachment, possibly an officer of the public relations office, and any other named personnel considered needful for particular destinations or conditions. Their duty was to arrange for the Battery's arrival, prepare the publicity, survey the area and choose the best positions for adequate demonstration, and generally ensure that the best facilities were available for a good show by the visitors.

The general lines along which the publicity was to be put over was as follows:
- Fostering of good relations with the public in the nearby towns.
- Fostering of good relations with the camp personnel.
- Publicity over a wider area via local radio.
- National publicity over nationwide networks.
- National appeal of the cinema networks using the medium of the newsreel.

Camp Edwards, **ANTIAIRCRAFT ARTILLERY TRAINING CENTER** *Massachusetts*

Vol. I No. 1   Antiaircraft Training Center, Camp Edwards, Mass.   September 7, 1943

Welcome! British Ack-Ack

Largest Army Installation in New England

Thousands of Troops Have Received Rigorous AAATC Training Program Here

The Antiaircraft Artillery Training Center, Camp Edwards, Mass., commanded by Brigadier General M. C. Handwerk, is one of the installations where fighting elements of the Army Ground forces are trained in the highly specialized techniques of destroying enemy planes and tanks, physically toughened for battle and moulded into close knit, cohesive combat teams.

Trained in hard rigorous methods of warfare, these soldiers-in-training not alone learn how to fire the powerful 90 mm AA guns; the roaring 40 mm weapons; the crackling 50 cal. machine guns,

AA MEN SALUTE "TOMMIES"

An American 90 millimeter gun crew in training during the dead of winter at Scorton Neck, AAATC firing range, where the "Tommies" will display their AA technique.

Neck, the No. 1 firing range, permanent installations are a feature. Some 36 buildings, which include housing for a full battalion as

sive operations that they have managed to destroy once and for all the time-worn notion that antiaircraft is used exclusively as

Antiaircraft Artillery Training Center Proud To Entertain British

American AA Men Eager to Make "Tommies" Visit a Memorable One

Greetings Tommy! In accents representing every one of the forty-eight United States, the Commanding General, every officer and enlisted man in the Antiaircraft Artillery Training Center at Camp Edwards, welcomes you, the members of the British 1st Composite Antiaircraft Battery, Royal Artillery.

From Brigadier General Morris C. Handwerk, commanding general of the AAATC, down to the greenest recruit in the newest battery, we are proud to salute you, our battle-scarred brothers in arms.

Here on Cape Cod you will be closer home than at any other point in your trip around America. And by the same token we

features of garrison life. But also some other entertainment has been arranged.

The publicity plan, determined in advance, was prepared with following aims in mind:
- Bringing anti-aircraft defence to the forefront of the minds of the people of America.
- Fostering good relations between services.
- Playing up the angle of the veteran troops teaching the novices, i.e. the experienced teaching the inexperienced.
- Fostering good relations between peoples.
- Fostering Anglo-American relations generally.

The method employed to achieve those aims was to be carried out in general as follows:
- A parade was to be arranged in the nearest town to the camp on a date soon after the Battery's arrival. This was to help foster good public relations.
- Advanced newspaper publicity was to be prepared and issued to make the public conscious of the fact that the British were coming.
- Social events such as a public dance and a camp dance were to be arranged in advance. This enabled the Tommies to mix and the public and camp personnel to meet them.
- Radio programmes on the local and national networks were to be arranged in advance, using two main themes behind the programmes: firstly the Battle of Britain, Dunkirk and the North African campaign were to be re-enacted, so that people would hear the facts from the men who went through the campaigns. Secondly, the social side, where the battery would provide singers, pianists, etc. to appeal to the lighter mood of the public.
- In addition, wherever possible, demonstrations were arranged whereby the public saw the British soldier at play for example outdoor games such as soccer, rugby, cricket, and indoor games such as darts.
- Visits to war plants were to be arranged wherever possible, with the idea of showing the soldier where his weapons may have come from and showing the war worker the man who used the weapons they make.

It was hoped by these means to make the most of the brief stay of the men at each camp. Naturally, this would necessitate a great deal of hard work on the part of the Battery. They would work a full day doing army demonstrations as trained soldiers, and 'work' a further period in the evening in the interests of good relations. Simultaneously, it would give each member of the Battery an excellent idea of the different customs of the different states and the different reactions of the people.

The Battery on its arrival in New York

CHAPTER 1

BRIEFING – THE LUCKY FEW

It was 0845 hours on 4 May 1943, and I had just returned to Brigade Headquarters. It had been a hard day in a 'utility' driving 120 miles visiting the gun sites and searchlight sites which made up the units of the 64th Anti-Aircraft Brigade. I'd been checking, advising and inspecting the new radar equipment being secretly installed in the Middle Wallop Sector. The work was hurried as we had to maintain the preparedness of the anti-aircraft defences covering most of the counties of Dorset, Wiltshire and Oxfordshire.

As I returned I could see signs of Group Captain John 'Cats Eyes' Cunningham getting his Beaufighters into the air from the nearby airfield[1]. I sat down to my 'midday' meal at 2100 hours; yet another warmed up dinner but not the less appreciated. I also persuaded myself that an after-dinner drink in the small officers' mess would go down well.

The rest of the brigade's staff officers were around the piano being entertained by Tony Forwood, the Entertainments Officer. Tony had recently married Glynis Johns[2], the up and coming young star of stage and screen. The officers were involved in what passed for singing, while Staff Captain Arthur Harris helped along the melody on his banjo-cum-ukulele. It was easy to join in and round off another day of preparing for the next attack by enemy bombers, another day in a long war.

The Brigade Commander came in unannounced. The music stopped, courtesies were exchanged and then the music started up again, if perhaps a shade less noisily. Brigadier C.B.S. Morley TD[3], was known by some of the more senior officers in the Brigade as 'Scrubbing Brush Morley' as any officer not pulling his weight was unlikely to remain in the Brigade for long. Nicknames are endemic in the army; they called me 'The Boffin'.

The Brig called me over. Nothing unusual, I felt, as he always had a point or two arising out of his own day's intensive activity. I was therefore not at all prepared for the news that I'd been posted to a captain's appointment in a new Battery to be formed. I was even less prepared for the news that the Battery would be going to America. The Brig could not however enlighten me as to what I was to do there; nor could he say how I would go to America, or when. He could only add that I had two days to prepare to leave. I had a thousand questions but had to remain in a state of excited ignorance.

I had been a captain in the 64 Ack Ack Brigade, on special duties connected with radar for a year and a half, and it seemed odd that I would be leaving. However, I had no time to stop and think as two days was hardly long enough to hand over to an officer who had to continue along the same specialised lines. Nevertheless, I was ready to proceed to my new unit, stationed somewhere in East Anglia, by the set times.

My goodbye to the Brigade Commander was a sad

Vickers predictor in action

affair. No man outside my own family had ever meant so much to me before. Having only recently buried my young wife [who died of tuberculosis] after a mere six months of married life, he had become almost a father figure and a man I could turn to in times of need. No man had ever been the cause of such a great change in my personal affairs, well being or ideals as he had. For no man would I have worked harder or given more – or in whom would I always have had more faith. But the moment passed and, with an assurance that when I came back to England I should contact him among my very first duties, I turned my back on my army home and left for my new station.

After a long and difficult journey, as anyone who tried to get to the north coast of East Anglia in wartime knew

---

1   Middle Wallop was home to night-fighter unit 604 Squadron RAF. The Bristol Beaufighters were equipped with a very early form of radar which enabled them to detect and hit enemy aircraft. Radar was a military secret so, to explain Cunningham's success, the press dubbed him 'Cats Eyes' and attributed his good night vision to his consumption of carrots. The airfield is now home to the Museum of Army Flying.
2   Anthony Forwood married Glynis Johns in 1942; they divorced in 1948. Later in life he became the manager and companion of Dirk Bogarde and shared his house. Glynis Johns was born in 1923 in South Africa where her Welsh parents were on tour, By 1943 when Cole was writing Johns had appeared in nine films. One of her best known film roles was in 1964 in Mary Poppins, when she played Winifred Banks, the children's suffragette mother.
3   TD stands for Territorial Decoration and is a long-service award for officers in the Territorial Army. Until 1949 the TD indicated twenty years' service, with war years counting double; after 1949 the number of years required for the award were reduced to twelve.

only too well, I arrived at Weybourne Camp[4] at 0215 hours on 6 May 1943 to find I was among the first of many who were expected there. I presented my posting orders to the adjutant and was taken to see the camp commandant, Colonel Westover. He asked me many pertinent questions, a number of which I was unable to answer, not being in full possession of the facts. Nor could I find out from him what my duties were to be, but merely that I was to report to Major Thomas Metcalf TD[5], who was to command the new Battery and who had already arrived. I duly contacted the OC [Officer in Charge] and his admin officer, Captain Derek Scorer and was told that I'd been appointed the instructor in fire control (IFC) of the new Battery. I would be working closely with the OC who was himself a qualified instructor in gunnery (IG).

Lieutenant Colonel Thomas C. Metcalf RA commanding the 1st Composite AA Demonstration Battery RA. Major Metcalf was promoted to Lieutenant Colonel during the American tour

I was told that I was to be a specialist member of a new anti-aircraft battery that was being formed for the purpose of demonstrating British methods of AA defence to an ally. I was also informed that the Battery was to be issued with the very latest radar equipment – so new, in fact, that it hadn't yet come off the production line. And finally I was reminded that, although I was one of the few who knew of the new unit's destination, it was still an official secret and should not even be hinted to anyone who was not entitled to know. In point of fact, not even Major Metcalf had official information as to our eventual destination, and, although we both knew in general terms, neither of us mentioned it. Derek Scorer was up to his eyes in work – the formation of a new unit always puts a great initial strain on the administrative staff – so I didn't see much of him for days.

Thinking about the new radar I could well understand the reason for providing the latest model, for radar was developing so fast it was almost out of date before it was deployed. What I found disturbing was that I'd never even seen the equipment, or the specification, so it looked as though I could be in for a very trying time even though there was scope to make a good show.

There was intense activity in the next two weeks. Officers and men were continuously arriving, being interviewed and going through their paces on local equipment in an endeavour to select 346 officers and men capable of forming a Battery which would be a credit to the thousands of anti-aircraft gunners in the British army. Almost all those already selected had served in North Africa or other intense actions, the exception being a few, like myself, whose secret equipment had not been in general use overseas. Clothes and stores kept arriving and additional instructions were being constantly received. And through all this turmoil, anti-aircraft equipment kept coming in for the Battery, some of which was in poor condition or incomplete and had to be repaired. The GL[6] arrived in pretty poor shape but was repaired by 2 AA Workshop Company. A generator also arrived in poor shape and I took a dim view of a unit supplying a demonstration Battery with a piece like that. The LW[7] was not working, yet was set up; I found it necessary to ask for an additional cable length and labelled which aerial was which as there was no indication on the equipment. I also devoted some days to fine tuning the equipment and training the men.

Five days after my arrival at Weybourne I left camp in the early morning to go to London to see AA Command. I'd been concerned about LW operations but when I pressed it with Colonel Porritt from AA Command I was assured that the necessary equipment and information would be forthcoming. I also talked to Colonel Harris the USA Liaison Officer, but he didn't know anything about their radiolocation.

While I was in London I also made time to organise my personal equipment and kit and went to Moss Bros[8] to order those items of my tropical kit which were not issued. My order was delivered to camp on 29 May and I had the various articles washed to shrink them a little.

---

4   Weybourne Camp on the north Norfolk coast was first used in 1935 by the Anti Aircraft (AA) Division of the Territorial Army as a temporary summer camp, becoming permanent in 1937. Weybourne (pronounced 'Webbun') along with a complementary camp along the coast at Stiffkey (often pronounced 'Stewkey') were the main live-firing training ranges for Ack-Ack Command. It continued in use until 1958 and is now home to the Muckleburgh Collection of military vehicles.
5   Major, later Lieutenant Colonel, Thomas Metcalf was in the Army Reserve in England before the war. He entered active service as a captain and was one of the most experienced anti-aircraft gunners in the British Army. He had been instructor for the London defences and had also been involved in organising the defences of major cities including Coventry, Birmingham and Liverpool.
6   GL (gun laying or ground locating) radar was developed to provide accurate targeting for AA guns. First called GL Mark I it later became known as Equipment Radar AA No. 1 Mk. 1.
7   Light Warning Set. Transportable early warning and/or locating radar used to direct artillery.
8   Situated in King Street, Covent Garden, as early as 1910 Moss Bros had set up its Military Department to supply uniforms to the services.

Major R Hoare, AA Command. Responsible for much of the British publicity

Back in camp visitors helped or hindered, experts from all commands arrived to offer their advice, and through constant trial and retrial a team was gradually chosen. The four main considerations to be taken into account in the selection of these men were:

1   that they were efficient at their job;
2   that they had seen some action against an enemy;
3   that they were respectable in appearance;
4   that they were physically fit.

At this stage, Major Metcalf having personally selected each and every officer and man, the 1st British Anti-Aircraft Demonstration Battery RA, as it was to be called, was ready to begin training as a team – although it might be better to say four teams for it was split into four parts. We had a Heavy AA Gun Troop, a Light AA Troop, a Searchlight (Radar Controlled) Troop, and the Battery Headquarters Staff, each with their own OC. In addition, a detachment of REME [Royal Electrical and Mechanical Engineers] personnel with its own OC was permanently attached, to maintain the equipment, including my own radar equipment. Then followed three weeks of intensive training; a very hard three weeks, which seemed to flash by like three days. The preparation culminated in a Press Day and inspection by the General Officer Commanding in Chief (GOC in C) of Anti-Aircraft Command General Sir Frederick Pile[9].

No one felt that a total of six weeks was long enough, yet almost everyone was in good heart. Our preparations had been as thorough as the time permitted and most of us felt we should be a credit to the army and to our country. We had had little time for social activities, although I did receive a letter which, by mentioning air raids, reminded me of the excited interest we took in the activities, night after night and day after day, of large formations of RAF and USAAF bomber aircraft which flew over our camp. In what was otherwise a quiet retreat from civilisation it was strange to lie in bed at night – when we were able to be in bed – listening to these hordes of bombers, some dropping a few of their bombs in order to gain height over the coast, going out and then, at some time later, returning in different formation to their bases.

Officially our destination was still unrevealed so it was rather disconcerting to hear from one of the officers that he had been told by the landlord of the only pub within miles, that the lads at Weybourne Camp were going to America. Needless to say the officer in question reminded the landlord of the penalties for passing on rumours, much to that gentleman's surprise and consternation. But all doubts were put on one side when an advance party was detailed and

Maintenance of 3.7 inch heavy AA gun by REME personnel

9   General Pile saw action in the First World War and held the position of GOC in C AA Command throughout the Second. He strongly supported the use and importance of radar.

Colonel J.S. Muirhead. Formerly in charge of AA Defences in Tobruk, then with the British Army Staff in Washington (BASW) and the man who talked Secretary of State for War Stimson into the tour

the question of destinations, marks, pay and the thousand and one things it became necessary to deal with, inevitably revealed America as the destination.

I'd been appointed Battery Entertainment Officer, which I thought might be fun, and had put out an appeal for men to form a Concert Party to entertain us. In the meantime concert party duties were allocated to key personnel: our producer was Lieutenant Dix, assistant producer Bombardier Stomer. I came up with a name for it – The Bowmen of England – and held a controlling interest, but wanted to act as a free agent and liaison officer between American and British Entertainment. I also hoped to free up an Ack Ack Beer Beer[10] broadcast from America but things didn't turn out quite as I expected.

Major Metcalf arranged for a trial inspection of the Battery along the lines that it was thought the GOC in C's inspection would take. During our training it had become apparent that, as well as being ack ack gunners, we were all being trained to be capable of putting on a representative display of marching drill, a ceremonial parade, rifle drill, and all the drills usually associated with infantry. This not only called for the complete reorganisation of our training but it meant a total reorientation of our minds. Surprisingly it all went much better than most of us thought might be the case.

It was at this stage that we were told we should have a job of work to do on our voyage out. We were detailed to act as voyage guard to a large number of German prisoners of war being sent to Canada. As the main radar equipment was to be sent directly from factory to ship and would therefore not be available for training, I was the obvious choice to be appointed acting adjutant of the POW guard. On 11 June therefore I went to a POW camp at a big mill in Oldham[11], accompanied by the Battery sergeant major (BSM) plus eight sergeants, my staff sergeant and three bombardiers to receive the necessary instruction about the correct methods of dealing with prisoners of war. Handling of prisoners in accordance with the Geneva Convention[12] turned out to be quite a business and great care was needed to ensure that all the relevant instructions sent out by the War Office were correctly followed. This necessitated quite an extra amount of work and I could see we were going to have a busy voyage.

The voyage guard contingent returned from Oldham on 17 June 1943 in time for the press day and inspection by the GOC in C AA Command, scheduled for the following day. The morning was very bright, but as the day advanced it began to cloud over and the threat of rain was constantly hanging over us. The band of the Royal Norfolks arrived to play incidental music during inspection and the men were on parade by 1045 hours having spent almost an hour being inspected by the troop commanders. It was to be our great day, a grand finale to a very intensive six weeks' work.

I could not help thinking, as we all stood there in our new battle dress, newly painted steel helmets, immaculately polished boots and khakied gaiters, how much attention had been paid to us since my arrival six weeks ago. I wondered what it was all leading to and what the Eighth Army[13] would say if they could see us. However, I didn't have much time for ruminating, because at that juncture, the GOC in C arrived.

---

10 Ack Ack Beer Beer was a show developed by the BBC Forces Programme specifically for personnel working at anti-aircraft and barrage balloon stations. Barrage Balloons were sometimes called 'Beer Beers', developed from an alliteration of the double B.

11 Almost certainly the POW camp at Glen Mills, Wellyhole Street. It was an old cotton mill with the capacity to hold 5,000 POWs and, for a while, was a transfer point and holding depot for German POWs being sent to Canada. At the time when Captain Cole was writing it contained many ranking soldiers from the Afrika Korps; Cole refers to this in chapter 2.

12 Officially called the Convention Relative to the Treatment of Prisoners of War, the third Geneva Convention, as it's usually known, was signed at Geneva on 27 July 1929. It covered the treatment of POWs during the Second World War. The UK ratified it in June 1931, the US in February 1932, Canada in February 1933 and Germany in February 1934.

13 The Eighth Army was formed of men from many nationalities but commanded by British officers. It fought in the North African and Italian campaigns and got its name from the fact that the French had fielded seven previous armies in the same territory. Many of the demonstration battery's men were drawn from the Eighth Army.

To the strains of martial music, General Pile carried out his inspection. He was accompanied by three other generals one of whom was a brigadier general in the American army, plus six brigadiers from AA Command. Shaking hands with nearly everyone and asking some little question from each about their history, their beliefs, their opinions, the General passed from file to file. He was the smallest man on parade, yet quite obviously the most dominating, his personality so vibrant, that I couldn't help feeling proud to serve under him. Yet when he arrived at where I stood stiffly to attention, I felt almost petrified. I answered some little question which to this day, I do not remember, and the next minute he was gone.

Microphones, moving pictures for future editions of Movietone News [international cinema newsreel], photographers, stenographers – they were all there at the dais, especially erected so that the General could address the Battery. It was our first experience of publicity and rather overawed us when we heard that twenty-five papers were represented. Most of us felt there was some mistake. Not one of us realised that the GOC in C's speech was being recorded by the BBC for a broadcast. It wasn't until he began to speak that we realised that his speech was not only meant for us but was being targeted at the world. He coined such stirring phrases as, 'you are to be the representatives of the British army to the American people'; 'each and every one of you will be an ambassador'; 'through you will the American people not only judge the British army, but British people as a whole'; 'let the American people know by your example that you are one of the races that held on, even after Dunkirk'. And it was only after listening to the General's speech that we began to realise the magnitude of our task, and at the same time the honour that had been bestowed on us by our assignment as ambassadors at large.

The Battery headquarters in Camp Davis, North Carolina

Overleaf: the ticker tape parade welcoming the Battery to New York (see chapter 4). Note the gentleman standing outside the window on the building ledge five floors up!

11

CHAPTER 2

DEPARTURE AND ARRIVAL

The General had told us that we would be away for approximately six months, so we all had leave first. I arrived back on 26 June to find that I'd been detailed for the advance party. That meant leaving the same day and travelling to an 'unknown' destination by rail 'somewhere in the north'. In fact it was Glasgow. Major Toomey commanding the prisoners voyage guard met me at the camp in the morning, a resplendent figure in tartan trews, and we were soon ready to depart.

It was a very strange feeling, realising that your destiny, your whole life might in six short months undergo a complete change without your being able to have any say in the matter. Here was I preparing to visit a country I had heard so much of, read so much about, yet knew so little of that I felt a peculiar nervousness as to how I was going to react to

On Ile de France; *the British Battery arrives in New York*

it all. If I had been given to nightmares, I felt sure that I should have a nightmare that would have a predominancy of men chewing gum, bootleggers, gangsters, film stars, divorce, skyscrapers, vast machines and vast production, Southern hospitality, tobacco and cotton. I was desperately wanting to shout out to the world 'I'm going to America' but couldn't in the interests of security. In any case, I kept telling myself, one fence at a time; you have a whole crowd of German prisoners to escort safely across.

My thoughts turned to the prisoners. I had just spent a week getting myself used to mixing with, or rather handling, large numbers of prisoners. I reflected on an evening, two weeks previously, when I had asked the commandant's permission to go to a POW concert. I wanted, for my own enlightenment, to study the German *en masse* while he wasn't studying me. I will always remember the *Obergefreiter* [lance corporal] on the stage rousing his audience into almost a frenzy of sentimental passion by his *lieder*[1] singing; the audience swaying in sympathy with the music until it positively

---

1   Songs, often ballads and usually of a sentimental nature.

frightened me to see the effects. The thought flashed through my mind that this susceptibility to mass hypnotism was a clear indication of how Hitler gained his popularity.

The possibility of mass violence on board ship, especially when they got to know, as they obviously would, that they were to cross the dreaded Atlantic and brave all Hitler's U-boats, made me think. The miles slipped by and despite the uncomfortable nature of the journey (a long one) and an occasional doze, I stayed in this form of reverie until we reached our destination. I had not been very companionable, I realised. Major Toomey and the other members of the advance party were all there, but I'd not helped them and in fact pitied them in my rather superior way. They had the misfortune to be going to America only for the voyage and with an immediate return journey in front of them. Fortunately I hadn't time to think any more along those lines, because we arrived at the embarkation staff officer's (ESO) office.

The ESO examined our papers and told us that we were embarking by tender onto the *Ile de France*[2]. We just had time to have our last meal ashore – our last meal under Britain's wartime conditions for some time. We ordered a last beer too, as we had been told that the ship was 'dry'. Looking back on these things later, it seemed that if I were going into the unknown, then at least I was clinging to the last remnants of the known in a rather quaint way – the last this, last that, etc.

Once on board, things were different. I was plunged into a maelstrom of scurrying figures; sailors, soldiers, stevedores and the multitude of other people, each no doubt having some vital duty to perform. My pass, along with the passes of all the other members of our party, was examined, scrutinised, franked and checked until I felt that everybody must know we had arrived. A public address system throughout the ship kept calling Captain so-and-so or Mr somebody-or-other. It took me hours to collect my wits and really get down to the job of preparing the way for guard and prisoners alike. I had an office to set up, but where, I had not the faintest notion. However, a concerted effort by Major Toomey and I gradually pinpointed the ship's staff captain as the man who could help and we began to see daylight. By then it was time to get to our own quarters and retire to bed, ready for a heavy day the next day. We only had twenty-four hours advance on the main party and a lot of organising to do before their arrival.

I could not get a clear picture of the happenings that next day. I was more than somewhat overawed by the vast preparations that were necessary to allow a ship conveying troops to sail. I vaguely realised that the ship was under the supreme command of the master, that the troops on board were under the command of lieutenant colonel OC troops; that there were baggage masters responsible for all baggage; stevedores responsible for all loading of stores; gunnery officers responsible for the defence of the ship; and that we who were to guard the prisoners abroad were only a small part in the whole scheme of things, almost a minor incident in a day's work. Nevertheless, arrangements went ahead for the housing of the guard and for securing the prisoners in a compound especially built to enable them to be segregated from the rest of the ship's company. This compound was a labyrinth of passages, quarters and stairways and I had to keep my wits about me in order not to lose myself down there.

On Ile de France. *Captain Clifford Cole (left) with Lieutenant Colonel OC Troops. Unfortunately we don't know the name of the OC, but what has he done to his hands?*

The time just flew and in what seemed to be an hour or so after arrival on board but what was in reality twenty-eight hours, we were told that the Battery was coming alongside. In one hour they were safely billeted in their quarters, and within two hours had all had a hearty meal after their journey, a meal that included white bread and oranges. It was like something out of another world in those days of austerity, for we hadn't seen such things for years. And soon, in our own little section of this vast organisation, peace and quietness reigned.

It had always been a source of extreme satisfaction to me, this flair that the British Tommy had for settling down in strange surroundings. Here was no exception, as I had occasion to note at 0500 hours the next day, when, tired of working through the night, I stole quietly through their quarters to make certain that they had settled down as comfortably as possible. Men who had never before even seen a hammock slung were contentedly sleeping, heads in, feet out of

2   Built by the French Line in conjunction with the French government, the *Ile de France* was launched in 1926 and famed as the first ship fitted out in *Art Deco* style. Used as a troop and cargo carrier by the British during the war she served with distinction first in the Indian Ocean and then from April 1943 in the Atlantic. In the autumn of 1945 she was returned to the French Line.

hammocks slung so close together that it was impossible to squeeze between them. Strange devices had been adopted for hanging clothes, strange methods devised for making certain blankets remained in the hammock and didn't end up heaped on the deck with the first move of the occupant in his sleep. Some were sleeping in shirts, some in vests and some in their original birthday suits. I stole out very quietly, retired to my own bunk and slept until 0830 hours.

We embarked the prisoners on the morning of 29 June. They came in four groups and their embarkation was without incident and without anyone hardly even noticing that 2,500 prisoners of war were now on board. Interpreters arrived and soon we had the prisoners sorted into groups for meals, discipline and recreation. Guards were posted using the ship's main deck as our barrack square, and the organisation for escorting to meals was rehearsed. We soon settled into almost domestic routine, with each man doing his appointed if unusual task as though he had been doing it for years. The men's reaction to the fact that these were the noted Afrika Korps prisoners was perhaps a little disappointing. At that stage, they seem to be weighing each other up in a rather one-sided sort of way; a guard with a sten gun having an obvious advantage.

The fun started when one of the prisoners developed serious internal pains. The ship's medical officer diagnosed peritonitis. Two hours after the first notification, the prisoner was back on shore on his way to hospital in an ambulance. That seemed simple enough, but Major Toomey had signed for so many live prisoners and it was his responsibility to deliver that number to authorities on the other side. We therefore had to get a signed chit for this man which said 'receipt for 1 Body (Live)'! I often wondered what happened to the POW after he left the ship. Did he live? Was he repatriated? Was he thankful for such swift medical arrangements? I never knew.

There was a big sick parade the morning we embarked, although Lieutenant Thorns the medical officer (MO) was a good lad and did a stout job. We had another serious case reported, this time of sceptic blood poisoning, which we thought might have meant another shore job, but it was not as serious as we first thought. During that same day all POWs were fingerprinted by an officer and five other ranks from the American army staff aboard ship, with the British guard providing the discipline.

Recreation for the POWs was not easy to arrange with the limited deck space; facilities were somewhat restricted but, by dint of a little squeezing, we managed to get half the prisoners out at once. They were allowed two periods of two hours each day – and as we discovered later, the more time they had out, the better health they maintained; sickness was reduced and heat rashes, etc., almost eliminated, but it meant continuous movement to fit meals and recreation for so many into twelve hours.

Getting a lot of prisoners into a mess hall and out again three times a day, when the mess hall had got to be used for two further shifts at each meal, was no mean business, especially when the merchant navy happened to be the next shift into a meal. They were inclined to make things difficult for the guard (who were only doing their duty) by causing scenes if their shift was even two or three minutes late. If that happened they cursed the prisoners, railed against the guards etc., etc. It was a difficult problem but the OC troops came to our rescue, and after that all went well.

We did have one or two very amusing episodes.

Tommies buying fruit; not only would the British soldiers have been unfamiliar with US currency, they would also probably not have experienced a supermarket before. And in America there was little or no rationing. Big changes!

Sergeant Chandler, one of the provosts [an army specialist in custody and detention], checking that the prisoners were in bed at the right time, found one wandering about in the bathroom. Not having an interpreter, he tried to tell him to go to bed but failed in English and thereupon tried his hand in French. It was at that moment that I came upon him saying: *'Dormez vous ici?'* [Are you sleeping here?]. As the bathroom was unfortunately an inch deep in water through a tap having been left running he would have a wet sleep, I thought. Another incident which lightened the strain of guard duty occurred during one of the innumerable counts we had to make to see that no one had escaped,. We got a count of one prisoner too many. It turned out later that one of the warders had been counted as a prisoner.

Not so very amusing was the constant discovery of portholes being forced open for fresh air. Unfortunately, they also let light out on dark nights and, as we had no wish to be torpedoed, we had to redouble our checks as a preventative to this sort of business; we punished persistent offenders by refusing them their first recreational period. The conditions below deck for the POWs were pretty bad – terribly hot, crowded and airless – and the *Lagerfuhrer*[3] requested that we allow portholes to be opened. As the weather was very calm I allowed them to be opened during the hours of recreation in exchange for a promise that he would ensure they were closed during the hours of darkness. The MO took the temperature of the POW quarters, particularly No 1 Section, and monitored it. The boys were Afrika Korps and had been trained in hothouses however, so, rather callously I suppose, I thought they should have been used to it. As we neared our destination the heat became intense and at one period we had many men fainting through lack of air. This set up a real problem and we had to resort to a recreation period in the evenings in the mess hall.

I felt constantly grubby aboard ship, partly because the plumbing was lousy and partly because there was no time to deal with things such as cleanliness of kit, etc. After four days without a batman[4] I finally found one on 1 July, the day we put to sea

On 4 July the OC ship gave orders that all ranks would sleep fully dressed as we were entering the 500-mile belt of danger zone. Rumour had it that the RDF (Radio Direction Finding, called Radar in America) picked up something, although nothing was said about what it might have been. I slept in everything except shoes and jacket but there were no incidents.

Bill Harrison, the guard commander, was an absolute brick, but I was sorry in a way that he wouldn't let someone else take some of his duties for him as he was almost continuously on duty. A week into our voyage we had a political fracas among the prisoners. One requested to be taken into protective custody as he had anti-Nazi tendencies and an attempt had been made to beat him up. We put him in the Brig [a military prison on board ship] and then moved him into another section the next day.

Harrison also brought two cases up before Major Toomey towards the end of the voyage. The sense of discipline the Germans had even went so far as to make the *Lagerfuhrer* charge two of his clan; one for insubordination; the other for stealing dishcloths to make a vest. The *Lagerfuhrer* seemed to know all about procedure, as I suppose he ought, being their equivalent of our regimental sergeant major. His charges were neatly and precisely worded. As punishment the Major stopped recreation for the two men for the remainder of the voyage, a serious matter as their quarters were at a temperature of 90°F.

It was an astonishing fact that the only trouble we had on the voyage was from merchant seaman. The insubordinate POW was a merchant seaman, as were the men from the allied merchant navy who caused the problems we had at first with messing. They resented being ordered about, yet followed one of their own leaders almost to mutiny. The POW had exactly the same idea; he refused to carry out any order given to him. It was a good job it wasn't a longer stay on the ship or he would have tasted a cell.

No one admitted it but guarding the POWs was more of a strain than we expected. I tried to find out why the guard detail was on edge for no apparent reason and came across an interesting sidelight in the general reaction to the prisoners. Each was exceptionally well disciplined, his reactions to orders quick, his bunk spotless, his hygiene good, his clothes always clean and as neat as can be expected under difficult circumstances.

Captain Derek Scorer

In fact it would appear that he should have been an ideal prisoner to handle. The average POW in this particular crowd was flaxen haired, young, healthy and vigorous to such an extent that the great danger was that our men, being human, would say: 'why this man doesn't look as though he would harm anyone'. Judging by the remarks and the many attempts made to do deals in cigarettes for watches, etc., an initial leniency was the exact and very dangerous reaction of our men. However by the end of the voyage, the guards had noticed a number of instances of mean little happenings,

---

3   Literally 'camp leader', he was the senior ranking POW who acted as a spokesperson for the group and was to a certain extent responsible for discipline within the POW ranks.
4   British term for a ranking soldier assigned to one or more commissioned officers as a servant; the job came with a number of perks so was not generally unpopular. The role largely fell into disuse after the Second World War.

dumb insolence and robot behaviour which, after a number of days, tended to cause people to mistrust even the apparent innocent little things like congregating in bunches to swap yarns. One officer stated: 'by the end of the voyage I felt I would just as soon kill a German as guard one', despite the fact that he had never been in contact with the Germans as battle opponents, nor had any particular reason privately to hate them. There seemed to be great relief among the men when the job of work of guard duty was over.

At least in one way, the prisoners had been fortunate on their voyage. They had not been pestered with bedbugs and other small insects. The guards on the other hand had been troubled with them the whole way across; I myself was bitten on the chest, neck and arms and found it a most unpleasant experience. I understood from an amateur bug hunter that he'd spotted seven varieties of cockroach. Transports that had little or no time for anything other than transporting troops were bound to suffer over a period of time. This ship was one of the worst.

We landed on 9 July 1943 after nine days at sea and eleven on board. Extra precautions had to be observed, cases having frequently happened before where prisoners had made an attempted escape. Additional provosts and warders were on duty as porthole guards and we also arranged extra guards for meals. The day the POWs disembarked we were up at 0350 hours and prisoners were detailed to stow all lifebelts, hammocks, etc. in D10 and D11. Careful watch was kept to see that no one made this large pile a hideout. All POWs had to have washed, shaved and decks swept by 0600 hours. They were given a last meal aboard and then

Captain Robert Dunlop

disembarked in batches onto ferries where American guards were waiting with automatic Thompson sub-machine guns. All was over by 1130 hours, and it was a moment of great relief when the last prisoner left the ship. Initially no-one wanted to sign for the POWs, but all was finally done, the documents in order, Bill Harrison and I breathed a sigh of relief and the OC troops gave us a pat on the back.

Once the Germans were under the charge of their new guards I had an opportunity of going on deck and taking my first view of America as we watched the entry into New York harbour. There's no need to describe what I saw. It's been described a million times but there was no question about it, it was just a magnificent sight, skyscrapers and all. The number of ships in harbour was outstanding. What a look of curiosity, there was stamped on all the spectators' faces as they lined up on the ship's rail as we docked at Pier 4.

However, I had not much time for further speculation. Captain Derek Scorer, Colonel Muirhead, Major Greville Steele and Major Jeffries the quartermaster came aboard to greet us, tell us plans, shepherd us through the customs, change our money and in fact do the thousand and one other things that I never realised were part of getting on or off a ship. There was great disappointment when we heard we were having to stay on board another night. Major Metcalf fought hard to get permission for the Battery to stay in New York for the evening but to no avail. There had been great bustle and movement going on all day, but we were not part of it and, as reveille was to be at 0345 hours, there was a mass move to an early bed.

As his cabin was free from bugs I was sharing for that night with Captain Robert Dunlop who was to do the early publicity for us. My batman failed to wake me the next morning and it wasn't until I heard a lot of movement going on at around 0600 hours that we awoke. Captain Winder came to our cabin to say that everyone was on the buses. I was so fuddled that I put on the Major's shirt and then his pants, discarded both and tried to wash, all in a desperate haste. Looking back, it seems extremely funny, but then, oh dear! We had not time for any breakfast, just dressed, grabbed our bags and disembarked into one of a large number of fine looking buses that were drawn up on the quayside ready to take us to the railhead.

We travelled by bus to a big army depot at Brooklyn where we boarded a special train. The first stop where we could stretch our legs was Washington DC where we managed to buy fruit and magazines, and get a glimpse of the Capitol.

The country we saw was magnificent and we passed through places with such magic names as Pennsylvania, Delaware, Virginia, Baltimore and Richmond. The dim out[5] of the cities was brilliancy to us who were used to the stygian gloom at home. How nice it was to see the lights again.

The train was very comfortable, with two dining cars where the food was very good. The extra little comforts intrigued us to such an extent that the journey passed remarkably quickly. The single fact that we could see a newspaper after days without one helped enormously. And it was an American newspaper, which was of course a book in disguise and could fill in a lot of time.

We arrived at Camp Davis, North Carolina at 0200 hours of 11 July 1943. The amazing spectacle that greeted us will ever live in my memory. Imagine having lived in a blacked-out country for four years, and then suddenly arriving at a railway siding and stepping out of the train into the glare from forty lorries with headlights, spotlights and side lights all blazing. It took us some moments to realise what it all meant. However, we gathered that the lorries were there to transport the men and kit to the camp, so in they all piled. Ten jeeps and six sedan cars were there for the officers and their kit, and in no time at all, we were on our way to a breakfast of real orange juice, bacon and two eggs, jam and toast. You can well imagine how much it was appreciated. To see two eggs on one plate was almost a dream come true after the rationing in England[6].

It was a very well satisfied body of men that retired to prepared bunks at 0400 hours, with the prospect of a good eight hours sleep ahead of us; reveille being fixed for midday. It was a not-so-well-satisfied group of men who woke up after a very hot night, during which most of us had discarded covers, to find our bodies covered with mosquito bites. We were all fed up; first bugs, then mosquitoes – what next? However, we had arrived in America. Our worries, if any, about the Atlantic crossing were over. Before us lay glorious uncertainty and a lot of hard training and work.

---

5   In Britain 'dim out' was officially called 'half lighting' and became generally legal at sundown on 17 September 1944, i.e. more than a year after Captain Cole was writing. Under half lighting regulations those living within five miles of the coast and anyone with skylights had to maintain the blackout, but everyone else needed only to use ordinary curtains unless a siren sounded in which case blackouts needed to be reinstalled.

6   One egg per week, occasionally one per fortnight, was the usual ration for a civilian adult in Britain at the time; rationing for those on active service was much more generous, but eggs were still in very short supply.

CHAPTER 3

WILMINGTON, NORTH CAROLINA AND CAMP LIFE

To help them to understand a little more of what to expect, each man was presented with a little handbook called *Hello America*. Written by a US army officer, it contained a lot of useful information, written in an easy intelligible style. To quote:

'In which we learn a little of what to expect – and a lot more of what not to expect.

'George Bernard Shaw has said that England and America are two countries separated by a common language. Through this epigram runs a rather disconcerting vein of truth.' Then followed a list of words which had a double meaning, good in one country and bad in the other.

'However, language differences just symbolise rather than represent the difference between the two countries. Actually the things which we have in common are far more numerous and far more important than our differences, which… are more humorous than antagonising.

'Forget what you have learned of America from the cinemas. You can be quite certain that you will encounter no gang warfare and see not a single tommy-gun in the entire city of Chicago.

'Don't expect to meet a real-life Indian; few Americans ever do.

'Remember, if the average American playgoer took Noel Coward at his word he would picture England as a place where everybody had a town and country home with countless servants, and where the average man spent all his waking (and presumably his sleeping) moments in drawing rooms or in the boudoir of someone else's wife.

'You have been at war for four years; we, one year. Don't give way to resentment if you find that the war has not, apparently, hit the American as hard as it has hit your people.

'America appreciates what Britain went through in the days of the air Blitz and cheers her accomplishments in North Africa. In America as well as in Britain, 'I fought with the British Eighth Army' is a ticket to immortality.

'We hope that you will find your stay in America pleasant and that this booklet will start you off on the right foot.'

The Battery bathing in the sea

Such information was very pleasant reading and a happy start to the men's stay in the country. The application of large doses of orange juice, tomato juice, ice cream, real fruit drinks, etc., helped considerably to make this, their first contact with America, a very pleasant one. Gunnery and related matters occupied most of our days, except when we were doing some form of public demonstration or parade, and many of our evenings were filled with social events which our kind hosts organised for us and which made our visit so memorable.

The domestic arrangements, mosquitoes aside, were superb. We were allotted a corner of the camp to set up our offices, quarter officers and men, and house our equipment. In another part of the camp we were to train, organise and eventually commence demonstrations to the American units. We also had to have our photos taken with our name and number in front of us for an American-style pass.

Cartoon of the American escort detachment drawn by T/Sgt Keyser

The place where the officers slept was a two storey wooden hut; I had a bottom corner room. We messed with the American officers – their officers' club is the equivalent of our officers' mess – and paid 30c (1/6d) for each meal, settling the bill monthly. Unfortunately the beer was almost undrinkable so we spent our time drinking coca cola which we grew to like. I asked for a cup of tea and they brought me hot water and a thing known as a tea ball. You dipped it in the hot water – not boiling – and it's supposed to mash like that. I learned to be careful ordering tea in America.

We were being allowed $3.33 (16/6d) per day whilst we were in America and paid for meals, etc., out of that. We expected only $1 but were lucky enough to get the extra allotment, particularly as things were dearer than in England. Papers for example were 3c and 5c (2d and 3d)[1].

On the day of the men's arrival, they had their first bathing parade at a place called Sears Landing, five miles from the main post itself. It was a long stretch of unbroken coastline, with quite big Atlantic rollers coming into the shore. Bathing huts were laid on for officers and men with freshwater showers in the huts for after the bathe. The temperature was about 90°F [32°C] and five minutes uncovered gave you a sunburn you didn't forget in a hurry; just another worry to add to the mosquitoes, bugs and ray fish[2] which appeared in those waters. Yet the combination of the sun, sand and all those facilities was absolutely tremendous and suited the men down to the ground.

One of the first conferences we had was to introduce the escort detachment to the Battery officers. The escort detachment was almost as big as the Battery with eleven officers and 127 other ranks, mostly drivers. In addition to the escort detachment, several officers were attached to us from the camp HQ to facilitate our work. Everything was done that could be done to help us make our arrangements a success, and no trouble seemed too great for our hosts.

Brigadier General Bryan L Milburn commanding the Anti-Aircraft Artillery (AAA) School paid a surprise visit to us and welcomed us to the camp, which I thought very nice. The camp was divided into four parts:

1. The US AAA Board which is the equivalent of our ADRDE Trials wing[3];
2. The School of AAA which is equivalent to Manorbier and Watchet;
3. The Officer Cadet School – our Shrivenham;
4. The AAA Training Center (TC) – which is our firing camp.

In the Battery the three instructors, Lieutenants Ray Dix, Philip Mollett and Robert Dunlop were charged with forming the detail of the demonstration programme. I visited the American Red Cross[4] where I asked them for information on Betty Hutton, the girl film star who was coming along to see us[5]. I also wanted music publications plus all the information I could get about theatre organisations who might be the equivalent of the British Drama League[6]. They arranged for me to meet a nurse whom they said was interested in producing amateur drama and Dixie and I duly went along. We found that they were most kind but that they hadn't the faintest idea really of what we wanted.

Most of my social activities were centred around the town of Wilmington. From the start we had facilities for getting in and out of the town. Jeeps were plentiful and I found that I had a jeep to myself. Because the distance from the camp to civilisation was approximately thirty-five miles, the men in camp were given extra petrol (which the Americans called

1   The wartime exchange rate was roughly four dollars to the pound.
2   Probably electric rays which generate an electric current to immobilise prey and which can be strong enough to stun people.
3   Cole here was giving the British equivalents to American organisations. ADRDE is the Air Defence Research and Development Establishment; the official title for Manorbier was Pilotless Aircraft Unit (PAU) RAF and specialised in radio-controlled drones; a gunnery range was established at Watchet for anti-aircraft practice – teams shot at unmanned aircraft which were either towed or catapulted over the sea; Shrivenham was and is a training centre for commanders and staff officers.
4   As well as nursing, the American Red Cross provided entertainment for troops.
5   Betty Hutton had co-starred with Bob Hope in the film *Let's Face It*, due for release in the US on 5 August 1943, three weeks or so after Cole was writing (see also chapter 6).
6   An organisation promoting the theatre as entertainment for everyone, encouraging amateur dramatic societies and canvassing for a national theatre.

The Battery quarters in Camp Davis

gas) to enable them to make the trip into town once a week in their own cars. The number of officers and men who had cars and ran them surprised me, but I soon got used to that and was glad of the many lifts I was offered. Officers giving lifts usually arranged to pick us up and bring us back too, and on very many occasions I had the offer to stay the night and return the next morning.

Camp Davis itself was interesting, but mainly as a remarkable engineering achievement. It was built in 1941, at a cost of about $20 million. The camp proper, including more than a thousand buildings, occupied 9,000 acres; the firing point a further 1,340 acres; and it had access to 44,800 acres for manoeuvres. The land it occupied was nothing but swampland, and more than one million tons of earth had to be moved to create irrigation and clear mosquito-infested swamp for habitation by anything up to 80,000 people. When the camp was made, a forty-mile road had to be built. The road was made out of a mixture of sand and tar and was laid, after foundations had been dug, at the rate of one mile a day; it was not affected by the heat and was very serviceable.

Roanoke Island nearby was the site of the first English settlement in America[7]; Kitty Hawk, and Kill Devil Hills are made famous by the achievements in aviation of the Wright brothers[8]. Bath, oldest town in the state, was at one time the HQ of the notorious Bluebeard[9]. Closer still to Camp Davis, there was the old HQ of Lord Cornwallis, one of the leading British Generals in the American War of Independence, and Woodrow Wilson's tablet was in the Presbyterian church in which he worshipped as a boy[10]. Down the Cape Fear River from Wilmington was Fort Fisher, where later we went to stay in another camp [see chapter 14]. That was the scene of a tremendous naval bombardment in the Civil War. When it fell, Wilmington, then the last great seaport of the Confederacy, was throttled. Much evidence of the South's bygone grandeur – so often brought to life in films – could be seen in the plantations adjoining the river.

Barrack interior in Camp Davis

---

7   Sir Walter Raleigh tried to establish a permanent English settlement there in 1585 and 1587. Both failed.
8   Kitty Hawk is frequently cited as the location of the Wright brothers' first powered aeroplane flight, but it actually occurred in Kill Devil Hills.
9   Cole probably means Blackbeard, the piratical name of Bristol-born Edward Teach who lived in Bath for a time.
10 US President from 1913 to 1921, Wilson was a deeply religious Presbyterian.

Wilmington itself was settled over 210 years ago by Englishmen, I was told. It was named after the Earl of Wilmington and its ties with England had always been strong. When we made our first visit, it was a town of about 130,000 people, but fewer than four years previously, its population was no more than 50,000. That influx of so many strangers was caused by the shipbuilding industry and led almost to embarrassment; houses were at a premium. More than a ship a week was being built there in shipyards which, although in production during the last war, had been closed in 1919 and remained idle until this new conflagration.

Our arrival was soon known in the district and, before long, we had to appoint an officer to deal with the mass of telephone calls and correspondence we were getting. Invitations out to dinners, weekends, public functions and private homes, dances and socials kept pouring in. Before long, we found that we had enough invitations for all the men

Arranging the Wilmington parade with the town authorities. Left to right: Wilmington Chief of Police, Colonel J.S. Muirhead, BASW, Lieutenant Colonel Howard Hunter, commanding the American escort detachment

to spend Saturday evening and Sunday away from camp, and it was so arranged. First we had to fulfil our first public duty after our arrival in the States. A parade through the streets of Wilmington.

17 July opened fine and hot and the Battery moved into Wilmington in convoy – the first of many hundreds of convoys that we were to undertake during our visit. The escort department transport officer was responsible for all arrangements and we found that our sole duty was to sit in the Jeeps, trucks or sedans, which formed the convoy of thirty vehicles in all.

At the outskirts of Wilmington, we had our first experience of a motorcycle escort. I must confess to a strange elation as we moved through the outskirts of the town with all its traffic brought to a standstill by the peculiar wail of the sirens fitted to the motorcycles of the police. Many of us just couldn't imagine what all the fuss was about, but accepted it as part of our new life.

We arrived at our destination, and got out of the trucks. The men formed up in three troops in column of three and carried out troop inspection; we wanted to look our best in the somewhat strange shorts, bush shirts, hosetops, puttees, boots and steel helmets. The men certainly looked a credit to the British army as they were brought to attention and, to the accompaniment of an American band, moved off for the two-mile parade through winding streets to the City Hall.

Publicity had been working overtime it appeared, because crowds lined the streets. As the men marched with the characteristic arm-swing and precision, the public showed their appreciation with applause, cheering and clapping the whole way along the route. It was certainly a change from routine AA gunnery. It was very hot by this time; none of the men had a dry garment on them, and a half an hour's marching and a further three-quarters of an hour's stay in front of City Hall being welcomed to the city, did not add to their comfort.

The mayor was most kind in his speech of welcome, and made us feel as though the city really was glad to see us. Despite the heat, which was most trying after our rapid change of climactic conditions, we felt

The parade by the British Battery through the streets of Wilmington

very elated and ready to enjoy a good weekend. The men were fallen out at this juncture and cold drinks and sandwiches distributed to them by many of the friendly ladies who'd come up with this very welcome idea. Afterwards the men were sorted out and attached to their respective hosts, and away they went for their first American weekend.

I had been invited, along with three of my fellow officers, Harrison, Winder and Mollett, to stay the weekend with a Mrs Inglis Fletcher an authoress and traveller[11] who had a house on a plantation bordering on the Cape Fear River. We had, of course, no conception of what a plantation might be like except from seeing the film *Gone with the Wind*, which might or might not have been accurate. Mr Fletcher, our host, was there to meet us and shepherded us to his waiting car. There followed a car ride of twelve miles along winding roads and sandy lanes where it seemed impossible that a car could travel. On the way we collected films, beer and, because of the chance remark of one of my friends, a melon, before we arrived at the plantation. Our hostess greeted us on the steps, looking very picturesque in an extra-large straw hat. Our host and hostess, both in their early sixties were kindness itself from the start and, as the weekend progressed, we learned to appreciate their thoughtfulness. But I could probably best describe the weekend by selecting parts of the letter I sent home, while I was there:

Dear Mother and Father,

I felt it was an appropriate moment to write to you as I'm in the middle of enjoying a stay in an American home and thought you'd like to know what Mr & Mrs America do at weekends.

First without being platitudinous I hope, let me remind you that there is not a typical American home. There may be a 'typical Southern white man's home' or a 'typical Southern black man's home' or a 'typical New York home', but they differ by a far greater degree, so I'm told, then does the typical English home in the north, south, east or west of England...

We'd been on a parade through Wilmington, North Carolina. We were hot, we'd perspired, we were sticky, and we were somewhat confused after the grand reception the Wilmington people gave us, and withal we had to meet our host after the parade. The control of troops, collection of our weekend clothes and collection of our wits, took up a lot of his time, but he was most patient and we knew from then on that we were going to enjoy our weekend.

Our first impression of the plantation was of a large house with a predominance of French windows screened by mosquito screens, but otherwise reminiscent of many of the fairly large English mansions in their park settings.

The setting here is an overgrown rice plantation; overgrown with shrubs, trees, bushes and long grasses. The trees are all covered with Spanish moss, a type of creeper that in outline is somewhat like the weeping willow, but most unlike it in appearance, being dull grey and rather ethereal. It is a magnificent sight at night when the moon shines through the trees.

A small stream, reputed to contain alligators and certainly containing plenty of mullet, which were leaping continuously, runs like an avenue in front of the main portico. What a pity the mosquitoes prevent full appreciation of this delightful scene.

Inside the house is an atmosphere of space and coolness. Pale shades of distemper, white window frames, polished light oak floors, polished tables with ornaments of delicate crystal; beautiful hand-worked table linen which reminds me of the many hours given over to this occupation at home; and above all the paintings, of the scenes around the house and the plantation. Easy chairs with gay and colourful chair covers completed the scene.

---

11 Born on 20 October 1879, Inglis Clark Fletcher wrote extensively about North Carolina and is particularly noted for the historic accuracy of her works of fiction.

The first impression of the house was most favourable. It would have been disappointing, however, if it had all been just right... Maybe it is the plumbing, which is in a state of almost complete chaos, because water is pumped from a well outside by a petrol engine that is in its last stages of decay; or the lighting, which is fitted in the house but when switched on glows dimly as if in protest against its installation in this house of old-world grandeur.

This focal point of the household was the icebox. In the icebox were the candles for emergency lighting; they had to be there or they would melt away. In addition there was just everything that makes the world go round, stacked carelessly in this massive wooden box.

I had never before realised just what an icebox meant to a family in this climate, with the humidity such that your clothes are wet and limpid on you for the main part of the day. I had always imagined that the icebox was to the American what the vacuum cleaner is to the English household; a luxury to be attained only after countless demonstrations by door-to-door salesman. But of course it's not. Without it the household be faced with a crisis indeed. Butter would not be available ten minutes of the day; meat would go bad; drinks would be hot; many things would be sour and so on ad infinitum.

This was old icebox. No electric modern machine would mean to this house what this box has meant to it for a great many years. I'm sorry to have to spend so much time in its company but to me it was a revelation and I just couldn't get over my discovery. The sight of the contents was like a glutton's dream.

Second in my list of discoveries, however, were the showers, one to every bedroom. What a pity they didn't work! We did manage a change and a good cold sluice down though, and a brief rest in the bedroom we had been allocated helped to cool us down, before we joined the rest of the household.

About five o'clock we had tea and cakes. This was our first cup of tea in America, and it was served so correctly according to our standards, and at such an opportune moment, that we felt this was a great moment. After tea, a long chat with our host and hostess. I found them most interesting to talk to, our hostess being a well-known American authoress. She writes historical novels, mainly about the area we are in now. She intrigued me by her desire for knowledge about ourselves. I say intrigued because I had been led to believe that as an American she would first of all tell us all about her achievements, her desires and ambitions, and then as a sort of sideline say 'And how about yourself?'

Dinner was excellent.

Maybe it was appreciated the more because it was served at the time we have been accustomed to. We have been trying, since we landed, to appreciate an early evening meal, but we have not yet had the time to do so. Or maybe it was because the meal was served on a beautifully polished table by candlelight. Or it could be that we had, for the first time, a dish which for really excellent flavour is hard to beat – southern fried chicken.

After dinner a stroll onto the porch, which terminated quickly as an invasion of mosquitoes began to form up. A pleasant chat in the lounge and then to bed, our host insisting that we rub our legs, arms and neck with vinegar as an anti-heat precaution before retiring.

I stood for some time at the bedroom window, watching the magnificent view of the stream, the trees in the cloak of Spanish moss and in the far distance the twinkling lights of the shipyards, working at full pressure twenty-four hours a day, day in day out. I could not help thinking about the men who were working in the intense heat of the riveting and welding shops. How can they stand it when it has taken me all my time to keep my energy alive without manually working? I hadn't realised that natural obstacles like that had to be overcome in this intense drive on production. My admiration for them increased tremendously.

It was late when I got to sleep, but it was fairly early when I woke to find a small and very picturesque negro boy holding out a large cup of coffee for me. Without a word he slipped out of the bedroom and left me with the coffee, wide awake and thoughtful.

I fancied a bath, but realised that the water situation prevented it. I learned later that it was only due to negligence on the part of the negro man-of-all-work that the water system was not functioning. Manpower is difficult here, just as much as it is at home. This negro servant had got himself a job in the shipyard at a comparatively fabulous wage, and 'did' for the family he had been with for some time, in his spare time. On this occasion he had let the work of the house go in his desire for money, and had failed to set the pump working to fill the house tanks. Our host fetched him back from the shipyards to teach him a lesson.

This household, like many others, so I was informed, rarely eats the hearty breakfasts that I have been used to. A little grapefruit juice, coffee, toast and marmalade is a standard morning meal, but on this occasion they had catered for the visitors, and how we enjoyed it!

As we finished breakfast fairly late, we had little time to do anything except sit down and recuperate until more guests arrived for lunch.

The extra guests, a major and his wife, arrived about noon. The major was a quiet, unassuming, but intensely interesting man when roused; his wife made up in vivaciousness what her husband lacked in robustness of manner. They were a delightful couple and the type of people one would expect to be friends of our hosts.

We were all a happy family. We helped to prepare the little extras for lunch and helped to set the table, chattering all the while about our own homes, likes, dislikes, differences and things in common. The Major's wife had brought over a bottle of dry martini made to her own recipe. We found it excellent, all the more because North Carolina is a dry state and liquor or wines have to be obtained on a special licence.

Lunch is worth recording, not because I want your mouths to water any more than they possibly already have done, but merely to show the attention paid to the small details, even in a normal household. We had soup, chicken with curried egg, corn-on-the-cob (a delicacy I have not yet learned to appreciate but without which a meal in the South is not complete), gherkins, mangos, sweet pickle – all the appetisers which I found not even necessary – potatoes, salad with cucumber – I'm told that salad served on a small separate plate is inevitable at every lunch or dinner – white bread rolls and butter, and to finish off a real fruit salad.

Our hostess invited us to look into the kitchen, warning us to be as unobtrusive as possible. I did so and was charmed with the sight of three little negro children sitting at a small table having their lunch, while their mother was finishing the washing-up. They looked so picturesque in their gaily coloured cotton frocks, but acted shy on the sight of me. I felt rather like an intruder, but was glad I had seen this very homely sight, this other side of the picture. They certainly did not look oppressed nor badly done by.

After lunch we had a bout of photography. Cameras came out and we had our pictures taken in various groups on the main portico.

Taking life very gently – it just doesn't pay to rush in this heat – we spent quite the biggest part of the afternoon souvenir hunting. The remainder was spent in the beautifully appointed sitting room, quietly discussing the inter-country and inter-state politics, habits, customs and armies. They were literally puzzled about our

Two Tommies as guests in a Wilmington home

attitude to the Irish[12]. We were puzzled about their attitude to the John L. Lewis situation[13]. As we were both equally puzzled about our own problems, we could not reach a satisfactory conclusion and both agreed that armchair strategy was unwise anyway, so problems were amicably shelved.

Teatime jogged us out of this rather introspective mood. I'm sure at heart we didn't really want to become serious on this placid afternoon, but there had been a rather natural tendency to explore each other's realms. I believe that after a period we realised that nothing could really come out of our endeavours to solve the problems of state, but that as a safety valve we had done our duty and could now relax and continue with our immediate problem of tea and cakes.

I had to leave at 5.30 to fulfil another appointment in lieu of one of the other officers who had not been feeling quite up to the mark, so tea was my last meal.

The parting was typical of the weekend. A strong handshake, an invitation to visit any time I wanted, an invitation to the launching of a liberty ship at the shipyard (where our host had come out of retirement to take charge of training[14]), and a drive back into Wilmington by yet another unexpected guest who had just turned up with a hundredweight of ice (a commodity becoming increasingly difficult to get).

I wish you were here and could be introduced to Mr and Mrs America – you'd like them.

Your loving son…

As a contrast I spent the evening with Al Schierenbeck, a second lieutenant in the US Army, at his home in Orleander a suburb of Wilmington. Schierenbeck was living with friends in one of many white-painted houses which seemed to be

---

12 Ireland was officially neutral during the Second World War. It had little military might and a history of troubled relationships with the UK. Britain feared that a German invasion of Ireland might be successful and would lead to Britain being surrounded by hostile troops. In addition the Irish Republican Army (IRA) wanted Northern Ireland, which had chosen to remain part of Britain, to be subsumed into a unified Ireland and was using terrorist activities to try to force the merger. The IRA was known to be in contact with German intelligence.
13 John L. Lewis was president of the United Mine Workers of America. In April 1943 he defied the wartime no-strike pledge and brought half a million workers out in industrial action. Steel mills closed for weeks and power shortages crippled production as a result. Only intervention by President Roosevelt on 2 May ensured that coal mining was resumed.
14 Mr Fletcher, Cole's host, was a retired mining engineer, which probably accounts for his interest in the doings of John L. Lewis.

used for the summer season only; they were all spring cleaned each year before occupation. The inside was decorated in pale shades – pale distemper, pale linen covers, pale painted doors and windows and light furniture. Everything seemed so spotless that I was almost afraid to sit down.

Captain Roger Keys, another of our officers, was already safely ensconced in a large armchair drinking highballs and being bombarded with questions by a curious group of neighbours. 'What do your insignia mean?' 'What is the red flash for?' 'Why do you wear a coloured side cap?' 'What is your rank?' 'Where is your home?' 'Are

Demonstration baseball game arranged for the British, Camp Davis

you married?' were a few of the many questions I helped him to answer, while others: 'How do you like our country?' 'When do you think the war will end?' 'What you think of the weapons we're sending you?' I found more difficult. My brother officer had already lost two pips as souvenirs and I was in danger of losing my hat as the evening wore on to the accompaniment of a succession of iced water, iced drinks, chicken sandwiches, cookies (biscuits), and yet more drinks.

This sensation of being the centre of attraction was at first quite embarrassing, but as it never slackened, we began to get used to it. Being on show twenty hours a day was not something we had bargained for when we left England, but so far it was a terrific novelty to us and we could still say 'three pips stand for captain, two pips first lieutenant, one pip second lieutenant; a major wears a crown…' and so on as though we were eager to let them into the secret.

Transport had been laid on to take us back to camp and we thanked our lucky stars that it was a closed car because the evening turned stormy. As we swung out onto the main road, the storm broke and thunder, lightning and rain, such as I had never before experienced, accompanied us the whole thirty miles back.

The following day, 19 July, there occurred in the camp guardroom one of those inexplicable things that make life the thing it is. One of the British gunners was shot through the eye and killed; an awful business. The inquest found that he

Lieutenant John Hale

committed suicide in a moment of temporary insanity. There appeared to be no reason, no justification, no logic for it whatever. Enquiry revealed no possible cause for such an act. Naturally, no publicity was given to it, but many of us tried for own peace of mind to find some clue to the man's state of mind. Despite all our investigations we were forced to let the matter remain as the inquest had recorded. After the usual notifications to parents and high authority no one talked about the incident. A certain air of restraint and gloom pervaded the camp, but no tangible connection to this event was discernible until maybe two to three weeks later when, overnight, one of the 3.7 inch guns was found to have the gunner's name painted on it. Such is the comradeship of the army.

I had been struck with the unanimous friendliness of all ranks towards us. Wherever we went about the camp we were treated with kindliness and civility. I had occasion to visit the dentist and, much as I dislike it, I found that here too this friendly spirit was very noticeable. When I left the chair, it was minus two pips and an AA command sign, but with two invitations to dinner and/or a weekend, and an invitation to a deershoot, all in the short space of an hour. The dental clinics were marvels of modern practice, with all very latest equipment and the most modern methods. Before I left the clinic I was taken round by the colonel in charge and shown the various branches of dentistry practised there. They included the complete manufacture of dentures on the spot, using only a small number of key personnel backed up with trainee intakes and female civilian nurses.

John Hale and I discovered an officers' club in Wilmington, which proved to be an excellent meeting place, especially as it was not dry and drinks were cheap. Started and run by Colonel McKnight, an officer in the Engineers, the Colonel personally welcomed us to the club. During the course of the evening, another officer, Major Eugene Edwards, invited us for a sixty-mile weekend cruise on one of the motor cruisers doing national service 'spotting' along the coast, an invitation we gladly accepted [see end of chapter].

On first arriving in America I spent a lot of my time writing two short books, the first about British radar training methods and the second on the maintenance of equipment. They saved me a lot of talking as they were a kind of handbook for the American radar people. I had several sessions with US personnel working with radar and found it best to give them something to read and then answer their questions afterwards. I had some difficulty getting the typing done so I approached the staff at the Training School, who mimeographed and bound the books for me[15]. The set up in the school

THE NORTH CAROLINA SHIPBUILDER

was good. They had huge safe rooms for secret documents and two stages of security, confidential and secret. For the first time in my life I had my fingerprints taken for identification purposes and was then provided with a standard American identification card, the only alteration being the word 'attached' added in front of 'the US Army', this in addition to the pass I was given when I first arrived. I also met Major Heineman who was the head of the radar section of the school; Major Willis does guns, Captain Clanton searchlight radar.

24 July was a hectic day. A morning of disappointment, with most things going wrong – the radar equipment had arrived days late and damaged so we had an ongoing headache getting it repaired, checked, cleaned and painted. Major-General Archibald of the CRA[16] arrived for a brief visit and I showed him over the equipment. I believe I persuaded him of the benefits of the LW[17] but at any rate he certainly was interested in the whole set up. Then there was a rush to change only to find my laundry had not returned. With 80,000 additional people in the town of 50,000 I can't imagine how the laundries managed at all. Even so I had no clean clothes and had to pick out my cleanest clothes and wear them yet again.

In the afternoon the whole Battery attended a ship launching. After being convoyed to Wilmington we marched into the shipyard with everything timed to the split second. We were settled on the platform which had been erected at the bow of the ship for the troops and the launching party. When everyone was in position a photographer was hoisted manoeuvring dangerously in a bucket by a crane to get the best angle for a publicity photograph.

Despite the fact that 350 British Tommies had invaded the place, work seemed to continue unabated. Six ships in various stages of manufacture were being hammered, welded, riveted, painted and generally attended to by thousands of 'ants' crawling over everywhere. The one we were helping to launch was the 118th ship to go down off these stocks after Pearl Harbor[18] in a shipyard that was the third fastest in America from keel to delivery and was not even here three years ago.

The launching, which was carried out by the wife of one of the directors, was in no way different from our own launchings. The ship[19] went slowly into the water without incident and was soon taken in tow heading for the next stage of its completion. We left but not before the publicity men had recorded the impressions of about three of our men who

15 A mimeograph or stencil duplicator is a low-cost printing press which works by forcing ink through a stencil onto paper. They have been superseded by photocopiers.
16 To gunners, CRA usually means Commander Royal Artillery, although major general is more typically an American rank. It is therefore unclear whether Archibald is an American officer; Cole may therefore have been using an American acronym.
17 Light Warning Set. Transportable early warning and/or locating radar used to direct artillery.
18 On 7 December 1941, and without a formal declaration of war, the Japanese navy attacked the US fleet in Pearl Harbor, Hawaii. As a result America entered the Second World War.
19 The *Thomas W Owen* was a typical Liberty Ship serving during the war probably as a cargo ship or possibly a troop carrier. She was eventually scrapped at Kearny, New Jersey in 1964.

had had shipyard experience at home, and interviewed an American shipyard worker and his opposite number from overseas.

After the launching, Major Metcalf and myself went to the Cape Fear club where I had arranged to meet Captain Richards in the US army and my host for this weekend. He whisked us round to some friends who live in the biggest house in Wilmington, a huge mansion with the traditional white pillars and portico at the front of the house; later I found that these were known as 'antebellum' houses[20]. The friend turned out to be Alastair Martin a rich second lieutenant in the US army. On his arrival in the nearby camp he had only been married about six months and wanted a house for his wife in the town, so bought the house just vacated by his commanding general. Ostensibly we had been invited for cocktails, but the cocktails actually consisted of French '28 champagne which was served in pint glasses and seemed to flow like water to a crowd of assembled guests.

Major Metcalf and I were soon under a barrage of the sort of questions we were by now getting quite used to. I was just beginning to get to know people when Richards dragged me away to yet another house, this time on Wrightsville beach, the coastal playground for Wilmington and about fifteen miles away. I was introduced to Mrs Houston, a Texan lady, and her two daughters, and it then transpired that we were taking them all to the Surf Club to dinner. Things moved so fast that I just accepted them as they came. They were such charming

Brigadier General Milburn and the Mayor of Wilmington welcome the British troops to the town. The Mayor is shaking hands with Lieutenant Dix

people I was sorry when the evening ended at 0230 hours and I found myself in a bachelor flat in a camp bed with about three other strange officers also in camp beds. That's what I would call a hectic day.

The really nice thing about these weekends was the advantage of being able to please yourself on the Sunday morning. With the beach less than fifty yards away, and hot sun up, who could resist a bathe as a prelude to breakfast? I couldn't and didn't. Breakfast of bacon and eggs was the next treat. Being a bachelor house for use at weekends, I was not too amazed when I looked in the larder to find something approaching chaos. But I must confess to a twinge of conscience as my eyes roved over the most amazing selection of food I'd seen for many years. What a long way I felt from home and from the front in Sicily where breakfast consisted of a tin of bully beef in a mess tin being warmed over a wood fire.

My host took me visiting after we had washed up. We called in to so many houses and met so many people that I felt like Exhibit A. I couldn't possibly remember all these people, but would never forget how hospitable they were. In fact we had so many invitations it became embarrassing to refuse them all. At around nine o'clock in the evening we ended up a house where we helped to deal with a catch of shrimps caught that day. A link with reality occurred here after quite a long session away from it. We heard the news that Mussolini had fallen[21]. This caused quite an amount of discussion among the members of the household, but I was surprised how they reacted. They were much too jubilant and, I thought, far too much of the opinion that the war was nearly won. I felt it was a dangerous mood and tried very tactfully to point out that it was nothing more than a dent in the shell of the fortress that was Europe.

The following day was our first of official demonstration. We had all our equipment lined up on the ramp outside, searchlights on the left, light AA guns in the centre, heavy AA on the right. To start with we just let people have a good run around and let the boys explain things. Then the LW [light warning] boys dismantled and re-erected their complete equipment in 10½ minutes as a bit of a show, which was quite good as that was the first time they had done so for six weeks. Major Willis, the Camp Davis AAATC expert on guns, spent the day on the equipment and stumped me that

---

20 The Latin for 'before the war', antebellum houses include features which were introduced to the American South by Anglo-Americans at the beginning of the nineteenth century.
21 25 July 1943, the day Cole was writing. On the previous day Italy's Grand Council of Fascism has asked King Victor Emmanuel III to resume his constitutional powers. Mussolini was replaced by Marshal Pietro Badoglio who sought peace with Britain and the US.

evening by going all technical on the PF [path/position finding]. I had to swot up on it to be sure that I could answer questions in future.

The phones etc., for the LW-PF combination had been messed up by the plugs and sockets nor arriving in time, but temporary fittings made the whole outfit ready to go next day. The foundations were laid and roped off at the firing point and all that needed to be done was for the LW-PF, Geny [generator], and MPR [medium power radar] to be set up. The County Fair was not the success I thought it might have been but it did enable me to get all the details tied up. The surprisingly few radar people who visited the equipment seemed impressed. Or maybe it seemed surprisingly few because of the size of the ramp and the fact that the fair spread over two days. There were lots of parties of visitors for the AW [automatic weapon][22], the guns and the searchlights, and both sections of the heavies managed to fire so we at last presented a complete picture.

During the next few weeks work was heavy. I tried out the PF-LW combination with limited success as the LW was giving a lot of trouble. Almost every day something went wrong with it and the spares position was acute. REME worked hard to make a show of it, and spent at least one whole day repairing and fine tuning but it remained unsatisfactory. I felt that the whole show reflected badly on me as we had not had a chance to prove our worth as operators. One trial shoot went badly when we were using PF as a visual because, although the PF transmission system was not malfunctioning as everyone claimed, the Sperry Predictor[23] had never been properly tested before. I gathered all the information I could and eventually worked out a fix.

We were using little radio-controlled PQ planes, which were controlled from a master plane (L1) in the air[24]. The PF followed the PQ plane quite well and we managed to check dials and line up before No 1 Section fired ten rounds and knocked the PQ out of control. Finally a great amount of training and organising was completed and we all felt confident that we could put over a good show, which was after all the main reason we were in America.

By way of relaxation I spent one evening in Wilmington with John Lane, a master sergeant from Post HQ. An exceptionally nice fellow, he had a love of England born of three years' study at the Royal Academy of Dramatic Art (RADA). He took me to dinner to the Governor Dudley, a fine old house then being used as a restaurant. Paintings of the 'Lords Proprietors' were prominently displayed on the walls. It appeared that when the British first landed in North Carolina, the portion of land around Wilmington was not a crown colony ruled by a member of the British government, but was a separate plot of land vested to a governing lord. Lord Clarendon was the first lord proprietor and, by virtue of his title, he was allowed to draw tithes from the land. Latterly, after a succession of lords had inherited the area, it was declared open land for a period of fifty years and no land development or progress of any kind was allowed. In

Planning a mobile scheme; leaning on the jeep's bonnet left to right is Colonel Metcalf, Captain Dunlop and Captain Keys.
Facing them is Lieutenant Dix

22 Probably the 40mm Bofors anti-aircraft gun.
23 Originally designed to plot the course of fast targets at sea, it was modified to work with AA, and modified again to work with radar rather than visual targets.
24 PQ-14B planes were designed and made by Culver and used as radio-controlled target drones. Radio pilots could control the planes either from the ground or from another aircraft up to five miles away. Tough and easy to manoeuvre they provided excellent targets for AA training and demonstration.

consequence it fell into a desperate state of swampy disrepair and has never fully recovered, even to this day. The house we went to was one of the lord proprietor's residences.

After dinner we picked up Ray Dix and went to Wrightsville Beach to the home of the MacMillans. Mrs MacMillan was the widow of 'MacMillan's Oil' and was reputed to be the smartest business woman in these parts. She was also the sole woman of the four governors on the board of the Episcopal Church. She had two daughters, Jane and Helen, both very nice girls. Helen was an artist by profession, as was her brother who was rather a famous name in art in America[25]. Helen painted portraits in preference to landscapes and always worked in oils. With the help of a letter I had received from my father we discovered that our families were very distantly related; it's a small world.

We sat and listened to arias from Italian opera and songs by Marian Anderson[26]. A visitor was Mrs Shaw, herself a famous singer, so we had a very pleasant and instructive evening – a delightful change. It was during moments like these that I realised that the American I knew in England, or read about in the papers or saw pictorially represented in cartoons, was so unrepresentative of the people I was beginning to meet and learning to like.

Lieutenant Robert Cross

One of my most pleasant evenings occurred as the result of an invitation to address the junior chamber of commerce in Wilmington. Together with Lieutenant Rhys Evans, another officer of the Battery, I was met by a member of the chamber in Wilmington and escorted to the meeting place. It was a small eating house which they leased every Wednesday. The room contained about twenty men, aged from about twenty eight to forty. They apologised for the smallness of the room, explained they were businessmen who contrived to get together once per week to iron out problems, and always tried to have someone interesting to talk to them each week. They'd never had a British army officer before!

We started off with a Scotch, served in a car outside as the premises had no drink for sale, followed by a really first class meal of southern fried chicken. We were then formally introduced, and I was left to talk to them on 'anything British'.

I always felt that it was better on these occasions to say who you were, why you were there and then let them ask questions. They always seemed to find something interesting to ask, and if they didn't then I felt it was a waste of time talking to a disinterested audience. I took about ten minutes to describe the Battery's visit and its purpose and then threw the party open for questions.

I got them all right. I was on my feet for an hour and a half while they fired every type of question at me, Evans filling in with replies where I could not supply an answer.. The mere fact that they had so many queries pointed to a genuine desire to know more of British customs and habits. They wanted to know about such things as:

'What the British thought of the Americans.'

'What the British thought of the Russians and the French.'

'What our personal views were on internal politics – theirs and ours.'

'What was the constitution of the British Parliament.'

'What was the real story behind the Hess/Dieppe supposed German landings[27].'

It was obvious from the start that I couldn't answer all their questions. I explained to them that I did not represent the government with any of the replies I made and in consequence they had better not ask me political questions or questions on matters of higher policy.

They still asked me for a personal opinion.

The big moment came when someone asked me what I personally wanted most out of the post-war world. When I replied that I hoped to see a firmly established friendship between America and England, they stood up and cheered.

Back to demonstration practices and a trial of the mobile scheme was planned for the last day of July. We met up at report centre (Battery) at 0745 hours and all troop commanders received their orders. It all turned out to be a bit of a shambles – particularly the SL [searchlight] Troop who didn't seem to know the drill for mobile deployment – but we did learn a lot of valuable lessons. The officers were mainly at fault as they were NOT mobile minded. They couldn't be really, having defended static positions in many cases for so long and you couldn't make a mobile battery from a

---

25 Henry Jay MacMillan was born in Wilmington, North Carolina in 1908 and, after extensive travel, died in 1991 in Wilmington in the house his grandfather had built in 1889.

26 An African American contralto who became prominent in overcoming racial prejudice.

27 The Dieppe raid was one of the first to rely extensively on landing craft, and also the first in which American troops engaged with the German forces on the ground. The raid was carried out on the 18 August 1942 and was a disaster. Out of nine targets only the Hess Battery was destroyed, many allied men were killed, wounded or taken prisoner and almost all equipment lost. Valuable lessons were learned and put into practice on D Day, 6 June 1944, but speaking almost a year earlier, in July 1943, Cole could not yet know that.

static battery in five minutes. However, now we knew where the weaknesses were, we thought we shouldn't put up too bad a show on the day[28].

It was about this time that I had lunch with one of my weekend hosts. Johnny Richards seemed to be a little troubled about a domestic matter in his Battery of Cadets. One of the cadets had 'borrowed' someone else's laundry, for which he was court martialled. The results were then awaited. My host said he would get six months in jail and dismissed the service, which seemed fairly severe to me. With us he would probably have got seven days CB [confined to barracks].

A formal dance was given that night in our honour at the officers' club so we all dressed up to the nines in Sam Brownes[29], etc. We were received by General and Mrs Townsend and General and Mrs Milburn, the commanding general and post commandant and their wives. The band, all paid army musicians and one of four in the camp, was absolutely first class.

The next day was a Sunday and I managed to have a quiet day studying magazines and newspapers. Comparison between British and American wartime Sunday papers and magazines was something incredible. The Sunday paper I tried to read, had 140 pages[30] in five sections. Section 1, news; 2, society; 3, funnies; 4, pictures; 5, sport. I was assured that it took all of Sunday to read the paper and that, in fact, was what a lot of people did.

I had heard so much talked about standards of living in America before I ever arrived here but had not heard that 90% of the houses in the States were of wooden construction. It wasn't until I saw how comfortable these frame houses could be, and at the same time how modern and labour-saving, that I realised so forcibly the unreasonableness of our own houses – the jerry-built type anyway – and at our conservatism in house construction and detail. Admittedly electricity was cheap in the US, and that went a long way towards paying the extras that helped to build up the comfort and the labour-saving appliances.

Take the house I had just entered, that of Doctor Duncan McCathern, a brother of the hostess. It had its own heating system, cooling system and refrigeration. It had a kitchen that would make the average British housewife gasp in delight and amazement, all fitted out in white enamel, including the range, refrigerator, cupboards, etc. It looked so clean and so easy to keep clean, that it must have been in fact housewife's

Left to right: General Armstrong, Colonel Metcalf, General Townsend and two unknowns. Colonel Metcalf is demonstrating the BC Scope, which acts similarly to a binocular theodolite and is used to locate the position of targets

dream[31]. The initial outlay for such a kitchen as this would probably have been heavy, but as it was nearly all done on hire purchase, it was easy to obtain – probably not so easy to retain, but that was another question.

Although Dunc was a very busy man he still found time for his hobby – guns. He had a gun room filled with guns of every type and design, each in its own sheepskin case designed to absorb the oil and prevent the gun from rusting. He had a beautiful automatic 12 and 20 bore Remington and Browning and also a pearl-handled Smith & Wesson revolver,

28 The Battery's problems with mobile deployment was not only due to unfamiliar routine. Mobile radar was in its infancy and the sets issued to Cole – probably the AA No3 Mk 2, Cole is never explicit because of wartime censorship – were only just off the drawing board and already showing design difficulties and delays in production. The 40mm Bofors gun could accept targeting information direct from the radar, was mounted on a four-wheeled carriage, could be fired without being dismounted, and had been intended to play a major part in showing off the mobility of the Battery and the accuracy of the radar. Continuing problems with the radar meant that the Battery had to resume the practice of the gun commander 'spotting' for the target.
29 Named after the British Indian officer who invented them, Sam Browne belts are a combination of belt and shoulder strap which is fitted to the belt at waist level on the left side and reaches diagonally across the chest and over the right shoulder. They were designed to help support the weight originally of a sword and currently of a heavy firearm and to ensure that it stays attached to the belt without slipping round the body. They are now often worn only on formal occasions.
30 The paper shortage in Britain meant that broadsheet newspapers were often only four pages; tabloids only eight, depending on how much paper was available.
31 Although not up to American standard, 'Prefabs', the prefabricated bungalows erected to assuage the post-war housing shortage in Britain, were often fitted out to a much higher standard than that to which most ordinary people were accustomed, and included such equipment as fridges which were rare in many domestic houses at the time.

September 16, 1943

My dear Colonel Muirhead:

I want to tell you how much I enjoyed my visit to Camp Edwards and how glad I was to hear such unanimous reports of the success of the British visitors' trip. As far as I could see there was a very admirable spirit prevailing between the gunners of the two countries who had thus come in contact with each other. I heard nothing from our men but praise of your men and the good feeling was manifest.

I myself greatly enjoyed meeting Colonel Metcalfe. Will you convey to him my appreciation of the fine work of his team and above all else the fine spirit which they have shown throughout their visit. It was very evident to me that our own American antiaircraft gunnery has greatly improved since I saw it last winter and I attribute a large part of the increased smartness and interest to the visit of the British team.

Faithfully yours,

Henry L. Stimson

Colonel J. S. Muirhead
Grafton Hotel
Connecticut Avenue
Washington, D. C.

Under-Secretary of State for War, Mr Patterson (left) discusses the Battery firing with Colonel Muirhead. The Secretary of State for War, Mr Stimson also visited the Battery (see page 65)

similar to the type issued to us, in a beautiful leather case. It seemed a habit over here to own a revolver in much the same way that every child in England had a bicycle[32].

We were having more and more visits by generals and senior officers of American units, including a civilian ministry of supply man and, on 3 August, the Battery had a visit from the American Under-Secretary of State for War, Mr Robert P. Patterson. We were part of a huge demonstration of anti-aircraft artillery methods put on for his benefit by the camp. The Americans put on a display of equipment and personnel, etc.; we did crash action[33] and a march past. It was gratifying to receive a letter addressed to the Battery shortly afterwards, in which Mr Patterson expressed admiration for our work.

The fresh air diet was keeping the men in excellent shape and, although mosquitoes bothered us a great deal at first, after a few weeks we didn't worry about them. At first our men looked almost ill beside American gunners but everyone got more and more sunburnt. Our tropical shorts caused great consternation when we first wore them in camp. There was a distinct feeling prevalent amongst the Americans that they were next door to being indecent. Later they admitted they were sensible and, as time wore on, seemed to develop a sneaking regard for them. Their slacks certainly seemed somewhat hot and clammy on those humid days and we used to bathe on each and every possible occasion. I remember with delight, one evening at Wrightsville Beach, where the highlight of the evening was eating watermelon on the end of the pier and then having a dip about midnight.

News arrived on 7 August that Major Metcalf, the Battery commander, had been promoted to Lieutenant Colonel. It was a thoroughly deserved promotion and we all congratulated him. The following day, a hot Sunday morning, I experienced my first American broadcast. About twenty officers and men were taking part in an extremely popular mid-Sunday broadcast, *The Army Hour*[34]. We were guest artists and at 1030 hours were handed scripts. We were to portray, with real background fire from our heavy guns, a mock 'Battle of Britain' for the benefit of American listeners. The script, written by the American press officers attached to the Battery was frankly the greatest piece of bilge I'd read for some time and anything but descriptive of the real Battle of Britain. However it no doubt sounded very good to the American public who were not used to hearing guns fire.

John Lane did announcer in typical American style and was really taken aback when none of the people he spoke to afterwards had recognised his voice on the wireless. I, for my sins, described water tanks[35] and got my leg well and truly pulled. We hung around all morning and afternoon doing rehearsals of timings until we'd got the thing OK. The Big Show duly arrived and was over in ten minutes, during which time we were supposed to have an audience of 55 million people, which didn't perturb the gunners one jot; they were almost impervious to nerves by then, as we had been on show for nearly five weeks. The broadcast and presentation were first class, and I was later told that the show was rated a great success. I hoped they liked it anyway, because I can't say I did.

I was becoming short of clothes by this time. The constant changing had been putting heavy strain on my resources,

32 Cole unconsciously indicates that he is from a relatively affluent background; working class families would often not have been able to afford a bicycle for their children.
33 Military slang for an emergency technique which puts artillery into action quickly by bypassing the regular procedures.
34 Founded in April 1942, *The Army Hour* was the brainchild of Lieutenant Colonel Edward M. Kirby and was aired by NCB in collaboration with the US army. The army provided the personnel and military sound effects, NCB wrote it and paid the costs. US audiences loved it as it gave them some idea of how their army worked.
35 Large water tanks were stationed in the London streets as an auxiliary water supply for those fighting the fires caused by incendiary bombs.

so I had to buy and adapt American uniforms. Our clothes were a constant problem as we had been very badly directed in England as to what we should and should not bring with us. Pips were put through epaulettes that had not been made for this purpose, and they had to serve as I couldn't get any bush shirts anywhere. I didn't care for the style of shoes. They were cheaper and didn't require coupons, but I thought of the leg pulling I should get at home if I appeared with some of the styles prevalent over here, so refrained from buying. I had to send to Canada through the British Army Staff Washington[36] for two dozen extra pips as I was losing them for souvenirs at an alarming rate.

My last weekend in and around Camp Davis was spent in two distinctly different moods. The first was the result of a tour of a housing estate that I made in the company of Roger Keys. I had been invited to stay the weekend with a very charming couple, Major and Mrs Eugene Edwards at 1508 Princess Street. Major Edwards had to work during the Saturday afternoon, so his wife took me out in the car to show me the surrounding district. The shipbuilding activities had caused a very great housing shortage and we eventually found ourselves in the heart of a new housing estate which had been developed in little over a year. All were pleasant small bungalow-type buildings, fitted with refrigerators and showers – two almost indispensable things in this climate. The estate was so large it was really a series of separate estates, each for a different group of people, such as black workers, white shipyard workers, army NCOs and their wives, girl workers etc. Most of the houses were built so that they could be dismantled after the war for movement onto farms. This was supposed to be the prelude for a 'back to the land' drive, which was being planned for after hostilities had ceased

We returned to find that Gene Edwards had returned home and had started to prepare a meal as he and I needed to leave promptly for a twenty-four hour tour of duty on coastal patrol [see above] spotting for mines and subs out at sea. We were joined by two other volunteers and went direct to the local coastguard station where a 32-foot cruiser powered by an eight cylinder marine engine was moored ready for use. It was almost the ideal cruiser, developing a maximum speed of about twelve knots, and was something similar to the craft I'd always said that I would own someday.

We cast off at about 2130 hours under a most magnificent sky and moon that made the night seem almost as bright as day. We set a course on the inland waterway, which was a curious river-like strip of water, running parallel with the sea, and never more than five miles from it, for hundreds of miles. An ideal cruising ground it was wide enough, but not too wide; deep

Captain Cole broadcasting on The Army Hour

enough for safety and having a clearly defined channel, its banks decoratively covered in fir trees. Suddenly in a clearing on the bank, there would come into view a large house, white with pillared portico, standing back in its own grounds looking absolutely majestic from our river view. The tide was not sufficient to worry about, having a small rise and fall and with a slow-moving current.

We covered fifteen miles and then moored for the night against the jetty just near the inlet, where the inland waterway joined the sea. Coastal patrol cruisers worked in pairs and a similar cruiser was also doing coastal patrol and also moored there. We had a very disturbed night due to mosquitoes and chiggers (a little insect which burrows under the skin) but rose at seven o'clock feeling fit and surprisingly fresh.

Breakfast of bacon and eggs cooked by a volunteer cook went down exceptionally well. I could not get used to the idea of frying bacon strips and then laying them on blotting paper to take all the grease away, but that didn't detract from

---

36 BASW provided links between the British and US government departments concerned with the war effort. It also had the function of organising British purchasing and supplies within the US.

the excellence of the meal. After breakfast we put out to sea on our mine spotting duties and also took the opportunity to fish. The sea was choppy in the area we were patrolling, but the boat rode well.

After about three hours at sea, we returned, pooled our catch with the other boat and gutted and cleaned the fish; to the delight of a multitude of crabs, which came and disposed of the insides, heads, tails, etc.. We caught quite a number of the crabs, but no one was interested in taking them home. I took the helm on the return journey and enjoyed myself so much that I almost felt like a two-year-old again. Back to Wilmington and then to Major Edward's father's house just in time for a sumptuous dinner.

On my final Monday at Camp Davis, 16 August, the Battery had the honour of doing a series of demonstrations before a three-star general, Lieutenant-General McNair, commanding US army ground forces. He was accompanied by three other generals and two colonels. We presented our set demonstration, and it seemed to be warmly appreciated by all the senior officers.

Colonel Metcalf, commanding the British Battery and holding a 3.7" shell, describes its firing to Lieutenant General McNair

That evening I visited the officers' club at Camp Lejeune, a Marine Base with two distinct parts, about fifteen miles from each other. The club made Oddenino's in Piccadilly[37] look like coffee stall, both in appearance and in the quantity of drinks sold. I met the lieutenant colonel in command of the club who had only recently returned from Guadalcanal[38] for a well-deserved rest. He showed me some of his souvenirs; a map printed in Japanese showing proposed developments to the Henderson Field; a really interesting piece of secret blueprint; a flag which was found inside the helmet of a Jap and was supposed to have been ready for hoisting on any other territory that could be annexed.

I had been chosen as the Battery's representative for the first advance party of the tour – Camp Davis to New York – and, along with other members of the advance party, I went eight days in advance of the main body. I had received my train tickets and a proposed schedule for our visit to New York, and John Lane, on being told that I was going advance, insisted that I leave all the arrangements for my accommodation to him. Reluctantly, because I felt that it was rather overdoing this hospitality business, I was more or less forced to say yes. Before I left the British officers had a chance of repaying some small part of the hospitality we had received in the Wilmington area. We gave a dance and party to which all our friends were invited. I was exceptionally glad that we had been able to show some form of appreciation for all the efforts that had been made to make us welcome.

The first phase of my stay in America ended when I left Camp Davis for New York. I was by then used to their money, their speech, their methods of hygiene, their manner of living. I was all set for a good coast to coast tour, much of which I would spend as a detachment commander.

---

37 Oddenino's Restaurant was one of the most exclusive in London and was one of the regular venues of Lew Stone the dance band leader. A former manager of Oddenino's became manager of the first-class restaurant on board the Titanic.
38 Between August 1942 and February 1943 allied forces took Guadalcanal, one of the Soloman Islands, invaded by the Japanese in May 1942; the island was strategically important for the protection of convoy routes between the US, Australia and New Zealand. Henderson Field was the allied name given to an airfield being built by the Japanese on the island and which they made several attempts to recapture.

CHAPTER 4

NEW YORK

Saturday 21 August 1943 was the morning I was due to leave Camp Davis for New York via Washington. I was up at 0700 hours and had to get information about the West Point nominal roll and visit Major Willis about 584[1] operation. Then I had to pay my mess bills, etc., and get my luggage off to the train. I did everything at the double and then rode into Wilmington to meet Second Lieutenant Van Noy and his wife, Technical Sergeant Dermady of public relations, and Sergeant McKeown representing the escort attachment, who was also escorting his mother. The train left shortly after 1900 hours and, after a drink or two I went off to my bunk where I slept like a child.

I woke in Richmond, which was a pleasant way of passing what might have been a tedious night journey. Richmond, the capital city of Virginia, was also one of the greatest of all tobacco markets in the world and we could almost smell it from the train.

I had breakfast on the train and excellent it was too but with the usual tea made with a tea ball. Tea, when you could get it, was either made on the Russian principle[2], or by using a little bag of tea dipped in tepid water. I really don't know why I continued to ask for it, especially as the coffee was always excellent. The meal cost $1.15 (5/9d) including tips, and my Pullman reservation cost me $3.30 and that only took me up to Washington.

The arrangement of travel in the States I found different from the travel at home. In America you paid for the journey, or more correctly, you paid for the engine pulling you. You could travel in two or three different ways, and of course with the long distances you sometimes had to have somewhere to sleep. So the railway company, or as it was called, the railroad company, provided the rails, the engine and the basic seating. Another company, such as the Pullman Company, provided sleeping and eating accommodation and charged you according to the type of accommodation you chose and booked in advance. Lower berths cost more than upper berths, which in turn cost more than armchairs. You could have a drawing room which slept two for much the same cost as two lower berths. The two sergeants were in a drawing room. All this was equivalent to first-class travel. I didn't get the second-class travelling tied up but presumed it was much the same difference to first class as ours. Third-class travel did not entail any additional cost above the rail fare. The coaches were much the same as ours in Britain but with more comfortable seats, being gangway coaches with two seats on either side of the gangway[3].

The British Battery with its equipment en route to New York

The berthing arrangements were amazing. When not in use the upper berth let into the roof and contained blankets, pillows and mattresses for both top and bottom berths. The bottom berth became two normal seats and could be converted into a very comfortable bed. There was a constant flow of air being swept around by air blowers. In the mornings you went around the corner into a really pleasant 'bathroom' with about three handbasins, a drinking fountain and shaving facilities, plugs for electric razors, mirrors, hot and cold running water, WCs and every modern convenience in fact. I felt it was a pity I'd packed all my shaving gear. A good idea at meals was that the waiter supplied us with an order pad in duplicate so that we could study the menu and write out our own order. It prevented mistakes and the duplicate copy acted as our receipt.

---

1   Possibly the SCR-584 microwave radar, operational since May 1943, but still very new. A US development, it was extremely successful when used in conjunction with AA gun laying.
2   Making a single pot of very strong tea which is kept hot, drawing off a small amount and then adding boiling water to taste.
3   In Britain during the war, most coaches either had a corridor separated from the seating by a partition which ran along one side of the train, or a series of compartments which lacked either corridor or gangway, had a door direct to the platform and could not be accessed while the train was in motion.

Train journeys in the US seemed to be most unreliable however. Trains were not nearly as efficiently run and staff didn't seem to worry unduly about whether a train ran late or not[4]. Our train was two hours late arriving in Richmond and left after a half-hour's wait for no apparent purpose. I also didn't like the US method of handling luggage. You put the luggage on the train at the commencement of the journey and didn't see it again until you got to the other end, where you picked it up from the left luggage office, some two hours, perhaps, after you arrived.

One of the finest laid-out cities in the world and by far the best I'd ever seen was Washington DC. The train was two hours late into Washington Union Station so our stay in the city was restricted to four hours, but even so I couldn't let the opportunity pass. We arrived an hour before midday, checked our main luggage into the cloakroom and put our hand luggage in a safety locker. Then we bundled into a taxi to see what we could of the capital city of America.

It was ludicrous to think we could see much of such a large, widely-spread city, but the friendly negro taxi-driver suggested how best we could utilise the time available, although he did say that it was a pity that we weren't in Washington for blossom time as it was a sight people travelled thousands of miles to see. I was content with what I could see as it all seemed magnificent. It was George Washington, I was told, who in 1790 had chosen this site as the place where the nation should erect a home for its government. Viewing it I could only wonder at what a marvellous choice he'd made.

Lieutenant Colonel Howard W Hunter (Bill), Combined Arms Center Fort Leavenworth and officer in charge of the American Escort Attachment

The driver took us to Lincoln's Memorial, which was an impressive sculpture of Lincoln surrounded on three sides with stone cut inscriptions of his more famous speeches. The Gettysburg Address[5] where he uttered his famous 'government of the people, by the people, for the people' was there, as was his speech on his second inauguration as President when he said 'with malice toward none, with charity for all'. They were probably some of the most famous and widely known speeches of all time – until Churchill came along.

As we strolled along beside the Reflecting Pond, where incidentally two men were employed doing nothing else but sail boats for the kiddies' amusement, Steve Dermady commented: 'this is widely regarded by Americans as the lover's lane of the States. More marriages are supposed to have been arranged while walking at the side of the pond than anywhere else in the country'.

We went as far as the other end of the lake where, appropriately enough, stands the Obelisk, memorial to George Washington. We had to wait for about half an hour in a queue before we could go inside and take the lift – elevator of course in America – up the centre of the Obelisk to the top. It was rather like a massive Cleopatra's needle[6] and, during the ride, a recording, timed to fit into the run and synchronised with the elevator's position, described the monument: it's height – 550 feet; weight – 81,000 tons; number of steps – 859; and the various states' inscriptions let into the walls.

The view from the top was truly magnificent. The city appeared to be divided into two; one half occupied by the various offices of government set amid parks and memorials; the other residential with houses. The offices' half was the beautiful part, with huge blocks divided by green grass, edged with rows of beautiful young trees. To see the pattern from the top of the memorial, carefully arranged to fit in with the natural pattern of the Potomac River and the Tidal Basin was a sight well worth seeing. In the distance was the Senate, House of Representatives and the Capitol; near at hand the White House, which perhaps best symbolised America, but which looked so small beside the other buildings. It didn't strike me until later that the two halves of Washington were also reflected in the choice of building materials. The governmental part of the city was all white stone, while the residential part was mainly red brick or concrete high-rise flats. The necessity for transport was never more brought home to me than here, where the distances between blocks was so big.

We went from there to see some of America's culture in the Smithsonian Institution, which was equivalent to

---

4   Cole was being a little disingenuous here considering what wartime travelling conditions were like in Britain at the time!
5   Made by President Lincoln during the American Civil War at the dedication of the Soldiers' National Cemetery in Gettysburg, Pennsylvania.
6   A 3,500-year-old Egyptian obelisk erected on the Thames Embankment, London, to commemorate the British victory over Napoleon. Despite its popular name it has no connexion with Cleopatra.

our National Museum in layout. The rather amazing thing about it was that this almost holy of holies became a big advertising medium for modern companies. Goodrich, for example, contributed almost all the Rubber Section, and told the world so in as many words.

I discovered, to my surprise, that Smithson was British and had never visited America but gave his entire fortune for the seeking out and passing on of knowledge. I was left with the impression of relative newness compared with the London museums I had visited, where antiquity was the norm. At least 70% of the Smithsonian dealt with things less than 100 years old – which of course was only right because it was dealing mainly with American history.

We went back after cramming quite a lot into our four hours and had a sandwich on the station – we had a terrific selection to choose from. I had a bacon and egg sandwich costing 2/- which would easily have made a breakfast in itself. I loved the intimacy which was suggested in cafes by calling the head waitress a hostess. I also telegraphed to Charles McCauley at the Ritz advising him of the approximate time of my arrival. A telegram cost about the same as in England – 2/- (40c) for fifteen words.

Then we were back on the train again. I thought it a good idea to arm myself with a guidebook to New York at the very start. I had never realised before what a varied career New York has had. How it started out as a part of New Netherland in 1626 and was called New Amsterdam; how the British captured it in 1664 and had its name changed to New York, after the Duke of York. It was then recaptured by the Dutch who, not to be outdone, renamed it New Orange after the Prince of Orange. It appeared that this name was to be short lived, however, as the town was ceded to the British one year later, in 1665, who again introduced the name New York.

It became a part of the United States at the Declaration of Independence in 1776, but the Americans did not change the hundred-year-old name; some two months later, the British had captured and held it until 1783. There were to be no more name changes after it was recaptured by the Americans, but in 1898, New York became so large that it had to be divided into five boroughs. They were named Manhattan, Brooklyn, Bronx, Queens and Richmond. And that's how it stayed to this day. I must confess to a misguided belief that New York was nothing else but a city of skyscrapers. It would be much more correct to say that Manhattan was a borough of skyscrapers, and that the rest of New York was a city comparable to other capitals of the world.

The British Battery en route to the parade in New York, having crossed the George Washington Bridge

By cab to the Ritz Tower Hotel, which was a grand and I'm told exclusive hotel[7]. There I met Charlie McCauley, the manager, who promptly turned over his flat (or part of it) to me, and did everything he could to make me feel welcome. His 'house' was beautiful, with modern lighting and handsome furniture in the modern style. A gin and tonic was brought by a bell hop and, after washing off some of the grime of the journey, I was invited to meet some of his friends.

On the following day, Monday 23 August, I had arranged to meet Colonel Hunter of the escort attachment at the Hotel Taft[8] where the rest of my party was staying. I arrived at 0800 hours and found Colonel Scott (the public relations officer), the two sergeants and Van Noy having or just about to have breakfast. I managed to persuade the head waiter to let me have a copy of the day's menus; in themselves they're a book and speak volumes at this stage of the war.

Shortly after Colonel Hunter's arrival a staff car followed with Major Reiman of the 38th Brigade HQ staff who had come to pick us up. We then departed for Fort Totten[9] leaving the two sergeants and Van Noy behind.

Totten was a splendid camp. Set on the water's edge amidst pines and many other beautiful subtropical trees which abounded around those parts, it was a permanent camp in peacetime with married quarters which were positively luxurious. It was also the headquarters of Eastern Defense Command (EDC)[10]. We went in to see Major General Jarman, GOC EDC who gave a small speech of welcome. After providing a clear and concise outline of the proposed plans for the Battery's stay in the New York area, including those areas – which he indicated on a map – where the various demonstrations and parades were to take place, he handed us over to a Colonel O'Connell for a conference on the fine details.

We adjourned into the map room which showed the world layout. Here we met Major Griffin (publication relations officer or PRO) and two or three junior officers. It was clear that EDC had made elaborate plans to cover every aspect of the Battery's stay and little remained for the advance party to do except carry out a dummy run over the routes of the parades and at the firing ranges.

We had lunch at Totten in the most beautiful officers' mess[11] I've seen over here so far. Colonel Hunter took me for a walk around the post and then we went with Colonel O'Connell to Teaneck Armory in New Jersey, where the men were to stay. This necessitated a ride of about fifteen miles through Manhattan and over the George Washington Bridge – a most marvellous suspension bridge, very much larger than Clifton over the Avon[12]. From the bridge we saw the battleship *Richelieu*[13] in the Hudson and, looking desperately pathetic, the burnt-out hulk of the liner *Normandie*[14] on its side.

Teaneck Armory turned out to be one huge building, originally built as a state police drill hall, and since taken over by the army. It had a massive basement with a drive direct in from the street. All the men were to sleep on one floor, and dine on the floor below. We went over the whole length of the proposed parade from Teaneck to

The Battery parading through New York in trucks with their arms

7   When Cole was writing it was possibly the best hotel in New York. The Ritz Tower Hotel was in built in 1925 on the corner of 57th Street and Park Avenue and managed by the Ritz-Carlton Hotel Co. in conjunction with Brown, Wheelock, Harris, Vought and Co. It was the world's first residential hotel built as such to avoid the regulations then in place restricting the height of houses. It contained public rooms and restaurants on the lower floors, and apartments for long and short term residents consisting of living rooms, bedrooms and bathrooms but no kitchens; food was sent up from the kitchens by dumb waiters. Still a sought-after address, the Ritz Tower is now a Designated Landmark site in New York.
8   Built during the same year as the RitzTower, the hotel was the largest hotel in Times Square with 2,250 rooms. Opened originally as the Manger it was sold in 1931 and renamed the Taft.
9   Although still used by the US Army Reserve, Fort Totten is now mostly a park and recreation area. When Cole was writing it was the headquarters of both the 66th Anti-Aircraft Missile Battalion, Battery D, and the 41st AAA Gun Battalion.
10 So Cole claimed, but official records indicate that EDC HQ was at Fort Jay, Governors Island, New York Harbour.
11 The officers' club, known as 'The Castle' is now home to the Bayside Historical Society.
12 Opened in 1931 to provide a route from New Jersey to New York across the Hudson river, the GW Bridge had one deck carrying six lanes of traffic when Cole crossed it; it now carries fourteen, eight on the upper deck and six on the lower. Clifton Suspension Bridge, begun by Isambard Kingdom Brunel, was completed in 1864 after his death. It carries two lanes of traffic across the Avon Gorge near Bristol.
13 The Richelieu class battleships were the last and largest battleships in the French navy. Four were planned but only two built, the *Richelieu* and the *Jean Bart*.
14 Entering service in 1935 as the largest and fastest passenger ship afloat, the *Normandie* was seized by the US authorities to be converted as a troop carrier. Renamed the *Lafayette*, in 1942 she was being converted at Pier 88 when she caught fire and capsized. Salvage was deemed to be too great an expense during wartime so she was left where she was until after the war.

the Battery. At Battery Place, which was at the lower end of Manhattan, we were to form up, and then move up Broadway in trucks, sitting on equipment at attention. Then we were to disembark at the side of City Hall and march to the City Hall steps to listen to Mayor LaGuardia's speech of welcome.

We were discussing the disposition of troops and bands on City Hall steps when Inspector Thompson of the New York City Police came out and surprised us. He had the responsibility for placing his men where they could best cover the parade and prevent incidents – almost a routine matter for him it seemed. He invited us in to meet the city's chief of police, a very pleasant man. It appeared that the matter had been well discussed before we arrived and was tied up. Incidentally, they meant exactly the opposite of what we do when they said 'tied up' – in America it means all arranged, in Britain impossible to arrange!

We left the offices and I went back to the Ritz Tower, where I met a crowd of people, mostly Charlie's friends and, on this occasion, mostly connected with the theatre. It was a small talk evening with excellent food served in the apartment and then on to a nightclub, 'Spivey's', Spivey being a singer[15]. It was rather empty, so went on to the Blue Angel, which was also fairly empty, so on to another club about two o'clock. I landed home at 4.30 after a first experience of New York's night clubs. The ones I saw did not thrill me.

The following day I was out at West 18th Street by 0830 hours. During the morning Colonel Hunter and I went to see the inspector in charge of motorcycle (m/c) escorts, Inspector Sheehy, an obvious Irish descent American. He called in his captain in charge of m/c escort and laid on a thirty-six police escort for the British Battery from Battery Place to City Hall, just as easily as ordering a packet of cigarettes. Sheehy spent most of his time eulogising, which I found interesting. The police service was strange to me, with a casualness about it which was exactly opposite to the police at home. The executive officers wore civilian clothes and sat in offices with telephones hanging all over the place. Part of the problem was that every state had its own jurisdiction in addition to the federal laws which covered all the states. There were strict dividing lines, e.g. the New York police had no jurisdiction in the next area where they had their own Bergen County[16] police. In addition, state police had a certain jurisdiction in the local towns in Bergen County, such as Teaneck. As Chief Sheehy said: 'in England, the law is the law. Over here, there are a million laws and no one knows much about them'. He told us some very interesting things about air raid precautions and astounded us by saying that 17,000 trucks roll into New York each and every day bringing stores and supplies (excluding freight trains). He was concerned with arranging detours in the event of bombing and the practice, which apparently they had had, showed a lack of liaison between state and city police, and local and city police.

We had a little time before lunch so took the opportunity to do two things I'd particularly wanted to do; take a ride in the subway and see the famous Woolworth building, once the tallest building in the world[17]. I was impressed with the latter and disappointed with the former, which was disgustingly dirty and in no way to be compared with the London Underground back home.

On to lunch with Sir Godfrey Haggard, the British consul general, the vice consul Mr Horwell, General Sewell head of the British information service (BIS) in New York, Hewitt Mervyn and Major Griffin, PRO EDC, Colonel Hunter representing the escort attachment and myself representing the Battery. Lunch was at the Metropolitan Club, which was an exclusive, English-type gentleman's club. Talk was fascinating and covered every aspect of the Battery's impact on the American scene, many of which I had been unaware of until then. Matters were discussed such as who had originated the idea of the tour, how it had been nurtured and come to fruition, the proposed coverage of the tour and the way it had been planned and developed. I heard details about the part the British Army Staff in Washington had played in the more detailed planning, all of which had taken place long before the Battery had even been formed in England.

15 It is possible that Cole was referring to Victoria Regina Spivey, an African American blues singer and songwriter who performed at nightclubs in New York during the 1930s and 1940s.
16 Across the Hudson River from New York State, New Jersey is divided into 21 counties; the most north westerly is Bergen, which lies south and west of New York.
17 Completed in 1913 the Woolworth building was, until 1930, the tallest building in the world. Woolworth paid the construction cost of $13.5 million in cash. Before the war Cole had been the manager of the Woolworth's store on Holderness Road, Hull.

General Sewell[18] talked typical armchair strategy, with which I mostly disagreed, but didn't say so, not wanting to provoke discussion. He was supposed to be an authority, and was writing for New York papers. Sir Godfrey, being British consular general, held a certain amount of sway, but he seemed a pretty doddering sort of man to me, being definitely neurotic[19]. He had quite the wrong slant on the Battery, and an almost worse knowledge of British methods than the Americans.

From there Major Griffin took Colonel Hunter and I to Radio City where the PRO people had arranged a tour of the National Broadcasting Company (NBC) studios. Being in British uniform and wearing a colourful artillery forage cap I attracted a lot of attention. The man conducting the tour, asked me to do a television stunt, which was quite intriguing. He asked a series of questions and I answered them in front of a microphone while at the same time being televised. In the next room were four television receivers and the scene was reproduced and the questions and answers come over the radio. It was my first introduction to early commercial television.

Captain Roger Keys

Next morning I spent in dashing around police stations.

I went to Hackensack [the county seat of Bergen County] to see the Bergen County Police and met Captain Donahue, who was in charge there. He arranged police escort for the convoy and was a most obliging sort of person, who offered to do anything we wanted doing. He remarked that there was a lack of liaison between the police and the military, mainly because the police contained members of German and Italian descent. Major Reiman, however, discounted this by saying that the liaison in parts of the USA was first-class especially in New York. It was quite understandable that, due to the cosmopolitan nature of all administrative services, security was far more difficult in America than in England.

Captain Donahue also spoke very interestingly about the coloured problem which was uppermost in all police minds at the time. They were obviously dreading the position after the war when the negro population would have become used to big money. In addition, there had been a big influx of negro workers into such towns as Englewood, where the negro population almost exceeded the white population. Mrs Roosevelt[20] appeared to be mainly responsible for creating uplift societies and the difficulty appeared to be on the one side the almost ceaseless clamour from such societies for equal recognition of the negro throughout the USA, while on the other were the people who charged excessive prices to negro workers to relieve them of some of the money they were making. In the riots in Harlem and Detroit[21] those shops were always the ones to be looted.

The undercurrent in the USA reminded me exactly of the reported undercurrent in India[22], and yet of course wasn't published in the papers. In fact, strenuous efforts were made to keep all negro discussions secret. For example, there was a big conference of all state police chiefs after the Harlem riots, which was held behind closed doors. One chief was reported as saying 'a n***r should be treated like a n***r'. He came from the South and the description of him standing up and saying that when asked his authoritative opinion was supposed to have been applauded by the assembled chiefs. I felt sure that after the war there would be almost war between the negro population and the whites, unless someone made some very difficult decisions. Our boys were warned to stay out of all negro quarters.

From Bergen we went to Teaneck police station. Teaneck itself was a most beautifully set up small town with green parks, houses widely spaced with beautiful gardens in between, only first-class houses built, each house looking clean and tidy and with no ugly signs. The key to the whole thing however was transport. If 'gas' were cut out in America, production and life would almost cease for six months until the people pulled themselves together and used their ingenuity. On from Teaneck to Englewood, where the chief of police was typical of the movie American chief; fat, heavy jowled, sitting back in his chair as though he owned the whole world and passing armchair judgment on all and sundry.

---

18 A resident of Jamaica, Brigadier General Horace Somerville Sewell commanded the 1st Cavalry Brigade from April 1918 until the end of the First World War. He died in 1953.

19 Sir Godfrey's son, the actor Stephen Haggard, was a Captain in the British intelligence corps in the Middle East and had committed suicide in February; Sir Godfrey was not informed until some months later and the shock may still have been new to him. As the circumstances were kept secret, Cole, writing in August, almost certainly did not know this.

20 Eleanor Roosevelt, wife of President Franklin D Roosevelt, was a vocal and highly respected supporter of civil rights, including those of African Americans, women and the poor.

21 During 1943 the needs of wartime production and the shortage of housing inflamed racial tension and helped provoke rioting in US cities including Los Angeles, California; Mobile, Alabama; and Beaumont, Texas. On 20 June 1943 in Belle Isle, Detroit riots broke out between black and white migrant workers which lasted for three days. On 2 August 1943 similar riots broke out in Harlem, New York, although they were restricted largely to the African American community. Cole was stationed in Camp Davis during the August riots and, despite censorship, was probably aware of them.

22 The British Indian Army was probably the largest volunteer force of the Second World War and fought valiantly for the British. Nevertheless there was a growing wish in India, supported by organised lobbying, that the country should free itself from British rule. It achieved independence in 1947.

The Battery's arrival at Teaneck

I had to be back by 2240 hours to pick up Sergeant Steve Dermady at the Taft and set off for a tour of Greenwich Village. Steve described it as New York's Chelsea, both being bohemian centres for artists. We went to about ten different nightclubs, ostensibly to promote news and coverage for the Battery. Eddie of the world-famous Leon and Eddie's night club said he would have been delighted to help but had heard that Billy Rose of the Diamond Horseshoe had laid on a special evening to include Mayor LaGuardia and wouldn't play. Other proprietors said they would be more than happy to entertain the British men when off duty and promised free drinks to all British troops in uniform. We didn't land home until 0430 hours and I really felt very tired, but still very sober.

After several days of socialising and public relations I got back to more direct Battery work on Thursday 26 August when we had to inspect the firing points which the Battery was to use during its stay in the area. I was up at 0730 hours and at the 38th Battery by 0830 from which Major Reiman and I set off for Northville on Long Island[23]. Driving on the Grand Central Parkway we made good time and did the 100-mile journey in under three hours.

We arrived at North Northville to find it was a delightful little firing point with accommodation for only about one or two Batteries. Most of the firing there was by automatic weapon, although the 90mm could fire if necessary. We went out with the Captain from EDC, who was in charge of the firing points, and he literally swelled his chest when we told him how fine we thought they were – and they were. They worked a different system to us and the administration details were under a second lieutenant. Consequently his biggest difficulty was getting Regimental and Battery commanders to agree to do what he wanted. He really was nothing more than 'keeper of the keys'.

After having lunch in a very small mess we watched .50 calibre being fired. The firing was awful, but the directing of practice was well done from a central stand which had on it:
- radio to the plane
- Tannoy/or public address system (PA as they called it)
- radio to the next point
- telephone to all offices, etc.

Altogether, I liked the point and felt that the heavy troop should be able to put up a good show there. We were to fire in competition with an American 90mm unit, two guns against two guns, but nothing was to leak out to the press about the competition, for fear of adverse propaganda.

On to Mattituck to the other firing point the battery was to use. Again, a delightful spot somewhat nearer the point of Long Island. There was keen rivalry between the two second lieutenants running these firing points which had the effect of producing two very good camps. We came back to the city by a different route, which passed through more towns. The strange contrast between the city and the town was brought home to me here. A town straggled around a main highway, but nearly always consisted of single storey buildings. You thus had skyscrapers in one and flatness in the other. Our towns at home were always two to three storeys high and the cities not more than eight. The comparison was 1:100 against 3:8 in height. I liked the whiteness of the towns and they seemed reasonably clean, but the striking feature was the frequent lack of coordination in the property owners' associations. On one block you had a wonderfully modern and attractive shop or house, and next door to it a wasteland with a railway-wagon-cum-tea-shop usually called Al's Place or Joe's Place. There seemed to be so much space that no one really cared where they set up.

Back to the city, and again there was that amazing transition to New York, where you drove as far as you could see (about 100 blocks) in between huge stone edifices down awe-inspiring avenues. Finding your way round New York was surprisingly easy, as Colonel Hunter explained. The avenues ran north to south and were numbered from the east 1 to

23 Long Island is a large island separated from mainland USA by the Long Island Sound and linked to it by several road and rail crossings at the island's western end, which forms part of New York. Northville is a tiny hamlet towards the island's eastern end.

12, with four named avenues in Lexington, Madison, Broadway, Park (Madison, the shopping; Broadway, the tourist; Park, the select; Lexington, ?). Streets ran east to west and were numbered from the south 1 to 100-and-something. Even numbers were one way west to east. Odd numbers one way east to west. Avenues you could drive either way[24].

Next day was a morning of paperwork. It had been raining heavily during the night – the first steady rain I had seen in the States, or for that matter since leaving England – and the rain had cooled the air so, for the first time in weeks, I wore service dress instead of the light tropical uniform I had been wearing. I had suggested to Colonel Hunter that we had a morning off; I wanted to write up my notes and so was at the office by 1000 hours. I'd just had word that one of the soldiers had been pronounced mental. They made arrangements to ship him back to England, but I wondered what the trip was doing to our chaps. One suicide, one mental, one broken leg, one appendix and the usual gossip and intrigue. I tried hard to get some peace to write up what I'd done during the week, but there were so many people around, including Colonel Hunter, that I never really got down to it. The offices belonged to the Bell Telephone Company[25] and there were a great many girls around. They certainly made themselves attractive, but I believe that's the secret – they *make* themselves. Compared with English girls, they had more time, money and facilities as well as the natural inclination. We had lunch on the premises and when I arrived at the restaurant the girls all eyed me up and down as though I were a strange animal. I had scallops for lunch which were much more popular than in England and just appeared on the menus as cabbage or sole or plaice would at home.

Colonel Hunter, Major Reiman and I set out to visit searchlight sites, so I called at the hotel to pick up my coat. It was 1330 hours and Charlie was still in bed. His average time had been about three in the afternoon for getting up. He was a most amazing personality a showman to the core with his famous cocktail parties and his delightfully frank conversation. He called his sister 'that old bag' and strangely enough he hardly created a stir with it. Just fascinated people.

From the hotel we went to Teaneck to review the place to see whether they were all set for the Battery moving in. They had certainly cleaned the place out and it was fitted with bunks, bedding, office furniture and all the requirements for housing and supporting the Battery when it arrived. They'd even polished the floors. We then left to revisit some searchlight sites. It was as well that we checked as the

Bofors gun during mobile demonstration

first site we went to was unsuitable for a searchlight. They had suggested putting the searchlight into a hollow, with trees on all sides, but hadn't appreciated that such an arrangement would prevent the small radar being fully operational when there was only about a 100 degree arc for the light above 20-30 degrees in elevation. However it was possible to relocate within a short distance and not too far away from existing accommodation which was excellent.

The hutting arrangements inside were spotless, a real lesson to our chaps. A refrigerator and a coca cola machine was installed on each site as well as a radio, and the men had visits from the USO[26] about twice per week. My heart went out to those fellows, who must have been bored stiff, with little possibility of enemy action. Still, they had their spotter on duty when we arrived. Why, I can't imagine, unless he was supposed to be doing guard as well as spotting but then surely wouldn't have had telephones on his head.

We went on to four more sites and by that time we were wet. I had lent Major Reiman my mac and was resplendent in

24 Although the arrangement of one-way streets differs since Cole's time, his assessment of the preoccupations of the avenues is still largely correct. Today it might read: Madison, advertising; Broadway, entertainment; Park, expensive real estate; Lexington, commercial/offices.
25 As well as running a telephone service the Bell Telephone Company was also working on gun directors and improvements in radar. Its headquarters at this time was 195 Broadway. Cole does not say so, but could be working in that building.
26 When America entered the Second World War several organisations, including the Salvation Army, Young Men's/Women's Christian Association, National Jewish Welfare Board, etc., were supporting US troops. President Franklin D. Roosevelt merged their efforts into the United Services Organizations (USO).

my British Warm[27]. It was real fun to wear it just to get the reactions from the Americans; they had every admiration for a good cloth. I found it strange that their socks for example were desperately poor quality and their uniform cloth much inferior to ours.

We discussed the searchlight problem for the remainder of the return trip, and then I picked up Sergeant Dermady and went over to the British Information Services (BIS) and fixed up a broadcast for the Stage Door Canteen[28] with Roy Lockwood, the BBC's representative in New York. From there we went into the Associated Press offices [50 Rockefeller Plaza] and made our way to the news desks to see about various press releases. It was an exceptionally interesting visit; the place was only one of the minor Associated Press places but it certainly seemed busy. We got hot news of Lord Louis

Four Tommies outside the library at West Point. The building was demolished in 1960

Mountbatten's appointment as GOC including South Asia[29]. I was particularly interested as my brother Bill [see chapter 6] had served with Lord Louis and had a high regard for him.

The following day I was up at 0730 hours to go to West Point, and realised that it had already been a week since I left Camp Davis. Colonel Hunter picked me up at 0900 and we moved out onto Route 303. The four-lane concrete road was set in completely wooded land until it ran beside the Tapen Zee[30]. Bear Mountain Suspension Bridge, looking very similar to the George Washington Bridge but a little older[31], crossed the Hudson to the north of the Tapen Zee. It was around this point that the English and American armies stood and glowered at each other for a time. The British sent naval raiding parties and the Americans built forts in the sloping, hilly banks of the river to stop them. Many monumental stones, etc. commemorating those days were dotted along the roadway.

We passed a state park and playground, and then we arrived at West Point. I had heard West Point described as the most beautiful camp and also as the most beautiful spot in the USA. It lived up to both of these statements. My major impression while at West Point was that everyone was fighting hard to do two things:
- to add to and uphold the tradition of the American army vested in West Point, which was established in 1802;
- to make the cadet as knowledgeable a person as time and the man's brain itself will permit.

Colonel Hayden, in command of the AA gunners used for demonstrations to cadets, was our host and responsible for the arrangements during our stay. He was a taciturn sort of man, who reminded me of some of the old regulars in the British Army and was himself a regular, being thirteen years at West Point. He took me round the proposed accommodation for the detachment and I found a few details to tie up, especially the place for the demonstrations, but they were soon fixed. We were to take over the famous Riding Hall[32] for two days and I thought it would make a wonderful demonstration point.

We left West Point at 1515 hours and arrived back in town after dropping Colonel Hunter at Teaneck. I had to go to Teaneck Armory to live that night, so went back to the Ritz Tower to pack my things. It was a rather hurried exit and a bit of a surprise for Charlie, who had company as usual. I had to have a drink with them of course. Then I asked Charlie

27 The British Warm was an optional short overcoat worn only by officers and which had to be purchased by them, i.e. was not issued. The coat was made from very heavy, fawn, tightly-woven Melton cloth. It fell to just above the knee was hard wearing, extremely warm and virtually waterproof.
28 The Stage Door Canteen was a recreation centre in which servicemen on leave could socialise with and be entertained by theatrical celebrities. No liquor was served but food and drink was free and the atmosphere was egalitarian.
29 Mountbatten was appointed Supreme Allied Commander South East Asia Command (SEAC). Officially Winston Churchill made the appointment in October 1943; as Cole was writing in August he either had extremely advanced notice of the fact or was telescoping two separate events.
30 A natural widening of the Hudson river north of New York forming a deep water lake. The name comes from the Dutch name for the local Native American people, plus the Dutch word for sea or lake.
31 Cole's comment is very astute; construction methods pioneered in the Bear Mountain Bridge directly influenced the construction of the George Washington and Golden Gate bridges. The three bridges were opened in 1924, 1931 and 1937 respectively.
32 Completed in 1911, the Riding Hall was then the largest indoor arena in the world. Horsemanship was discontinued at West Point in 1947 and reintroduced twenty years later. In 1956 the Riding Hall was converted for academic use. It is now called Thayer Hall.

how much my bill was and to my astonishment, I found that I had lived for seven days in this really exclusive hotel in New York FREE. That was the sort of thing that was so astonishing about America. A casual introduction to a sergeant resulted in a week in New York with all its amenities and introductions to so many people completely free of charge. To show my appreciation as well as I could, I went to the florists in the foyer and sent the most expensive bouquet of flowers I could find to Charlie's sister Sadie.

Arriving at Teaneck I got myself settled in. Teaneck Armory was the equivalent of the territorial drill hall, but on American principles. It was so large that it would house almost a regiment, sleeping, eating and garaging. It was a very modern building [completed in 1936], and so beautifully clean it made a good billet. I often thought the Americans spent a colossal amount of time and man hours on 'bulling' [cleaning] for British troops in order that relations should be as cordial as possible. That was a good thing in every way, but I hoped the American boys didn't get the wrong ideas about us being pampered.

I got to bed early – it was very much needed as I had not been blessed with much sleep during my residence in New York – but was up the following morning to meet the Battery. I was also delighted to find a letter from my father waiting for me with the Battery office. For just a short while I was able to return, metaphorically, to the bosom of my family:

Dear Clifford

Your mother and I were pleased to receive your letter and to read all about your wonderful tour. It brings a little sunshine into what is here a very austere existence. Not that we're complaining, we need so little out of life now – only to know that our children are all well and safe. Thank God everyone seems well, even if we sometimes have to wait a little for news. William is still finding it very tough in the Western Approaches. James is on the Isle of Barra, off North West Scotland, with an RAF unit. Frank has just taken over a huge NAAFI warehouse in the North. Marion, Sophia and Ernest are still at home, while Marion's Frank is with an RAF station defence unit somewhere in the country – I'm not sure where. So you see we're all still alive if not exactly kicking[33].

You'll be very sorry to hear, I'm sure, that your store suffered a direct hit during the Blitz on Hull [see footnote 17]. I went there yesterday to find out the extent of the damage. It seems that the rear stairway, rear wall and parts of the store and stockroom near the stairs were completely demolished. Fortunately no-one was in the store at the time, so there were no casualties, but the front windows were blown out and have since been boarded up. Temporary repairs have been made and the store is now operating again.

I felt a little sick at the news. I was jolted that the parts mainly damaged were where I and the window dresser used to meet.

I spoke to the manageress. She told me that your friend Bill Charles had finally volunteered and had been commissioned into the RASC [Royal Army Service Corps]. She didn't know where he was but understood he'd been promoted to captain.

Good old Bill, I thought. He comes in late and moves on fast…

I also met your friend Stan's father, a few days ago. He gave us news of your other friends. Stan has been promoted captain and is with his Ack Ack unit somewhere in the Mediterranean. Ken is a major in a supply unit – he didn't know which or where he was. Eric is down in Christchurch working on some Top Secret radio work.

That seemed familiar to me. There was only one such place in Christchurch that I could remember. It was in my old parish when I'd been with the Brigade. I remembered being taken round it once to see some of the original radar experiments. Air Defence Radio Development Centre it was called; Eric must have been one of the boffins there. Good for him; it was an ideal place for a man who had no other interest in life but radio and electronics.

Well, I've no more news. Your mother and I are both well although beginning to feel our age. She sends her love, as I do,
Affectionately, Father.

That Monday – 30 August – was a day of preparation. The guns were cleaned, the area of demonstration marked out, final adjustment to equipment made. The biggest snag was the officers' laundry, which I had failed to get fixed up properly; eventually I found a two-hour laundry. The other snag was transport. The American escort department got flummoxed and, due to the fact that Lieutenant Hicks and Captain Kalfelz were out reconnoitring routes to West Point and Northville, the allocating of positions to heavy, light, searchlight and REME transport was not done and, as was most natural, the boys got into the most suitable position for themselves, but with no regard to subsequent operations.

---

33 William is Cole's eldest brother (see chapter 6) and was in the Royal Naval Reserve; James the second brother was in the RAF, Frank the third brother was manager of a NAAFI warehouse. Marion and Sophia were Cole's sisters and Ernest the husband of Sophia.

Major Peter Croker

One difficulty we experienced here for the first time was the enormous amount of children in the neighbourhood. The road on the western side was a public road and no railings or barrier of any description were there to prevent the public from straying. To mount a guard sufficient to keep off children would have prevented us demonstrating.

We held a demonstration rehearsal and parade rehearsal in the afternoon and then at 1830 hours, after an address by Colonel Metcalf to the complete Battery, we moved into the city. I went with the Colonel and Major Peter Croker and we also picked up Pete's wife, an exceptionally pretty, gracefully charming girl, who expressed horror at the lack of civility in the North, especially the city stores. Earlier I'd phoned Marion Rousseau, the daughter of Major Rousseau who also had a son, Vincent, who was a sergeant in the army. Marion was just the most magnificent looking girl I knew. She was a model, under the name of Leslie Redgay and worked for O'Conner who was second only to Power the famous agent for models.

I took them to the Ritz Towers where we met Charlie and enjoyed a relaxing evening. Pete was on top of his form and kept the party moving, but Charlie didn't know what to make of Tom Metcalf, although he didn't say so. We finally got home at about 0130 hours, having picked up a couple of stray boys who had missed the convoy. The convoy arrangement into town proved excellent. The trucks were waiting to pick the men up at 1815 hours, and had an m/c police escort all the way. It was fascinating just to ring up and get a dozen policemen to ride you in. The convoy then returned by the traditional 2359 hours. Most of the men behaved remarkably well. One or two stayed out all night and came in tired out but paid for it by being confined to barracks for the rest of their stay in New York.

Next day, Tuesday 31 August, was The Big Day. It is not everyone who can say that they have had the honour of parading down Broadway and being received by the Mayor of New York, and the men were looking forward to the occasion. Everything went well as regards weather. The sun shone and we arose early. Frantic rushing about to dress in the best way we have yet been asked to dress meant clean everything. I discovered that I been unwise enough to leave my steel helmet behind in Davis, so had to dash up to the quartermaster to borrow one, only to discover that it was new, without flash and without sand[34]. I borrowed a sick gunner's. The men assembled in troops on the Armory square and

Motorcycle escort along Broadway

---

34 The MkII helmet, manufactured from 1938, would probably have been what Cole was intending to wear. It was usual to add sand to the paint finish to avoid mirror-like reflections. Often divisional flashes were stencilled on the side.

were placed in parade formation by the BSM under the keen eyes of the troop commanders. Officers fell in, the colonel took over the parade and the Battery was inspected.

The band and escort duly arrived, looking and feeling very important, and I believe somewhat honoured that they were to escort us. The police arrived and without much more ado we set off with all the equipment shining as well as about one hour's maintenance after a thirty-hour train journey would allow. As we drove down Riverside Avenue, surprised spectators appeared to be saying to themselves 'what on earth is all this?' 'Have we had an invasion?' And that's really what they had had. The Battle of Broadway was about to begin.

A wait of half an hour at Battery Place and then on to Broadway with its streets lined with a police-estimated 100,000 people (they couldn't have got many more on anyway) and strips of paper and tickertape floating down on us from the windows. Looking very much British and feeling very proud, the convoy of British Tommies in their bush shirts and shorts, puttees and boots, and with the traditional British steel helmet, worn at a slightly cocky angle, moved into Broadway.

I was in the last jeep and got an excellent view of the snakelike procession as it wormed its way along at a professed 10 miles per hour which was nearer to 15 or 20. We passed the City Hall steps where was the reviewing party consisting of Mayor LaGuardia, Field Marshal Sir John Dill, Colonel Muirhead, General Jarman, General Grunert, etc etc. Everyone was sitting smartly and very much at attention and there was no cheering; it was a serious parade and a high point in New York's life to see British troops, fresh from the front line, complete with their weapons of war. Around the back of the City Hall we went where we tumbled out of the trucks and ran to join up in the column of troops for the march past the mayor. The band of the New York city police struck up, playing the Royal Artillery Quick March [The British Grenadiers] at 120 paces to the minute, and the Battery commander, Lieutenant Colonel Tom Metcalf shouted as I never heard him shout before, clear and strong: 'Battery! Battery… 'Shun. Move to the right in columns of troops. Right turn. By the right; quick march.' And away we went around to the City Hall steps, where we moved into position with a calmness and precision bred of by now long practice in the public eye. The three troops formed a close formation to enable the mayor to speak, and – consternation! – all our worries about timing and the short space of time allotted had caused us to speed up until we were then actually a quarter of an hour early.

Can you imagine the Mayor getting up to welcome us, yet visibly saying to himself, where the devil's the radio

The reviewing stand in front of New York City Hall. Cole is standing in the front rank of officers, third from the right

Left: Lieutenant Colonel Thomas Metcalf speaking outside New York City Hall. Seated behind him, in a suit, is Mayor Fiorella LaGuardia
Below: Field Marshall Sir John Dill

man? We were early for a broadcast; it was timed for 12.45 and was then 12.30. However, he started to speak. And he had all the oratory that one expected of a fiery, wiry little spitfire like the famous, publicity-hounded Mayor of New York. He was followed by General Grunert who was an anti-climax, but introduced General Jarman, Commander-in-Chief Eastern Defense Command, who spoke eloquently and well and didn't forget to quote Shakespeare as a clever tribute to the British. He was followed by Sir John Dill, replying for the British army as a whole, but who proved to be a very poor speaker; maybe he's a fine field marshal. And so to the British Consul General, Sir Godfrey Haggard, who had been at such pains to pump me for material for his speech. I had told him to forget thanking individuals, to keep his speech down to three minutes and to make it general. What a pity he didn't! However, he eventually sat down to listen to Tom Metcalf who spoke on behalf the Battery. Tom showed his greatness by speaking for precisely two minutes and saying everything that was wanted in a clear, calm and studied voice which must have been heard distinctly by the crowd which had now swelled to a considerable size, and were applauding all Anglo-American references.

Pinpoint flashes came to me as I was standing in the front rank just immediately before the reviewing stand. I thought how intensely hot it was, and whether the perspiration would soon cease rolling into my eyes. I saw how the photographers concentrated on Dill and LaGuardia and almost totally ignored the Battery, in direct contrast to provincial cities. I noticed the Colours guarded by police, and the different uniforms on the reviewing stand. I was impressed by the newsreels and Gunner Newman, our photographer, who was always on hand and collected an amazing pictorial record. I heard the two bands playing during the intervals and saw the cordon of police all facing outwards. I felt the calmness of the crowd. Finally and with mortification I experienced the shambles when the Colonel ordered 'fall out the officers'; a thing we've never done correctly yet.

Back to Teaneck Armory to change. I spent the whole afternoon getting out plans for the morrow's visits to Northville [Suffolk County, New York] and West Point, and the programme for the remainder of the week. In the evening we went into town again, to that famous tourist house Billy Rose's Diamond Horseshoe, for a party given by generous citizens and sponsored by the Mayor. The party cost an estimated $5,000. I was not surprised. It was one of the highlights of the tour so far. Due to a late start (a slipup by the escort transport officer) the Battery arrived little late. However, when it did arrive, shepherded again by what seemed the entire police force of New York City, they filed in and took their places in the club, filling it to capacity. A generals' table, with Mayor LaGuardia and other dignitaries (like his very famous secretary who has resigned or been dismissed three times a day since he's been aide and secretary to the mayor[35]), occupied the place of honour and after that it was good mixture. Again there were photographers including one who took a large shot of the whole club (with his agents afterwards coming round and charging one dollar for a ten cent photograph). It was a very carefree evening. The food was excellent and we had beer and a bottle of whisky to each table, plus of course the entertainment.

---

35 Possibly James M. Kieran who became LaGuardia's press secretary in 1934. Both men were notoriously volatile.

First five glamour girls danced with five British boys for publicity. Then came the floorshow, which was the finest I'd ever seen. All the turns would have been top line in any theatre in England. Three young girls did incredible things with their bodies in a contortionist act; one man and a girl did outrageous things to musical instruments, including a harp that had the figure of a girl for the main strut and which moved. Then there was a man who composed his own songs and sang one about me, much to my surprise (Steve Dermady the PR man had briefed him of course) and so it went on. Hats and streamers and good clean (surprisingly clean) fun.

It culminated in an invasion of the floor by the British. We had literally to force people out after autograph hunting with the mayor and generals, after flirting with the girls, after singing traditional English songs with the traditionally raucous English Tommy's voice. And so back to Teaneck completely exhausted.

Wednesday 1 September was our first demonstration day in New York, and my first attempt at arranging programmes, etc. We were all lined up and ready to go by 1000 hours. There was a crowd of probably 200 people, mostly enlisted men, who were so scared at seeing General Jarman among the first of the spectators that they promptly fell

THE OFFICIAL WELCOME
August 31, 1943
City Hall, New York

"In Order of Appearance...."

"It was not the man-made deadly weapons, it was not th cannons or ships, it was the God-given courage of the peopl of Great Britain that saved the world."

FIORELLA H. LaGUARDI
Mayor, City of New York

"Your visit is a splendid example of the kind of co operation between friendly and allied nations which must in evitably result in that early victory for which we all so earnestly strive. With the common interest and common purpos we can -- we will -- achieve victory."

MAJOR GENERAL GEORGE GRUNER
Deputy Commander,
Eastern Defense Command, U.S.A.

"We are glad that you have come to visit us. We are look ing forward to the demonstrations you will give to the America antiaircraft artillery while here. We are especially glad t meet you personally. We have known you as fighting men an now we will get to know you personally as friends."

MAJOR GENERAL SANDERFORD JARMA
Commanding General,
Antiaircraft Artillery Command, E. D. C.

"I congratulate the Battery on their turnout and bearin and I will say to all ranks that if they receive during thei visit a tithe of the kindness which I have received since came to the United States they will return to England as grea Ambassadors in the cause of Angle-American relations."

FIELD MARSHALL SIR JOHN DIL

"These are the officers and these are the men who fough in the battle of Britain, one of the decisive battles of th world, perhaps. They are the self-same men and the self-sam guns that helped to smash the invasion. Good men and good guns They must be! And they have kept up the same average else where, in Malta, in Tunisia and in Sicily."

SIR GODFREY HAGGARD
British Consul-General, New Yor

"We have been in America only a very few weeks, but durin that short time we have learned to respect the American as soldier and as a comrade, and we have learned to love th American people as friends and as cousins."

LT. COL. THOS. C. METCALF, R.A
Commanding Officer, British AA Btr

in and waited to be marched around. The result was that spectators delayed us more than somewhat. The demonstration was conducted by Colonel Metcalf who proved himself a very able compere.

The press had been on tour during the afternoon and had taken complete command of the situation. They swarmed over all the equipment, photographed it from all angles, worried and browbeat gunners for answers to all the most usual and yet of course unusual questions that the press ask. Naturally, to get any sort of press coverage, one had really to go out of the way to make the facilities for the press as good as they could possibly be. Steve Dermady, of course, came into his own whenever the press appeared. Hence in the afternoon we tried hard to feed the press and tried hard to carry on a demonstration for the army at one and the same time. Even so it was considered a great success and the resultant press coverage surprised everyone.

Mayor LaGuardia signing autographs

I kept popping backwards and forwards as there was a certain amount of office work to do. Invitations kept coming in from all sources and some of them, i.e. a cricket match on the Saturday afternoon, and a dance on the night of the party, could not possibly have been kept. Prior to leaving England it had been felt there would be a definite demand, say once per fortnight, for some 'British entertainment'. Opinion was expressed that too much American hospitality would cause a distinct desire for a little bit of home. Consequently the nucleus of a concert party was formed [see chapter 1]. Time was the enemy and it never really started to function before the Battery left England. Hopes were nevertheless entertained that we should soon be able to get some practice on arrival. All hopes of this were dashed to the ground. The mass of entertainment the men received, the variety, the first-class bands, top shows, etc., had left a decided inferiority complex among the members of the concert party on the one hand, and no time for rehearsals on the other. Yet one of the men, Sergeant Austin was a fine baritone and had been in great demand singing mostly to the Americans rather than to the British as originally planned.

The BBC finally approved the draft of the Stage Door Canteen programme. It had originally been intended to broadcast it live on the Ack Ack Beer Beer programme [see chapter 1], but the powers that be finally decided to record the broadcast so that it could be put over the air when timing was a little less critical. The Battery's Sergeant Austin, was starred as the Meistersinger. Dixie [Lieutenant Dix] compered and so we finally got a potted version of the thing that I had been wanting for so long. But it was amazing that in America one's conception of entertainment underwent such a radical change. New York was a city of entertainers. Woe betide a small timer from England, thinking he or she had

something good, going over there. Their disappointment at seeing or hearing the talent on even the smallest stage or floorshow must have been most depressing.

After the afternoon's demonstrations I had arranged with the PRO EDC to censor some pictures and check some text; the Battery had to do its own censorship according to guidelines laid down. I went into New York at 1800 hours and spent from six until nine waiting on newsmen. They were a hard race. I listened to some very interesting stories by three majors (PROs), all of them ex-newspapermen from the *Herald Tribune, Boston Times,* and *New York Sun.* They said, in answer to my question, that they didn't much care for the English style of newspaper. They couldn't say why, but I believed it was because their papers screamed of sensationalism. The habit of doubling banner headlines had led to many humorous and some not so humorous experiences where one headline was not compatible with the second one.

I telephoned Marion and was invited to pick her up, which I eventually did one hour late. We went to a little old place called the Jumble Shop[36], in Greenwich Village [see above] which was typical of Chelsea restaurant clubs; I might have been at home. Paintings by local artists were hung around the room, all priced and most of them good. I should have liked to have bought two

The Battery had its own photographer, Gunner Newman, who had been a press photographer before joining the army. Here he prepares to photograph Brigadier General Armstrong, 109th Coast Artillery Group (see chapter 13)

pencil sketches done by local artists at $10 each, but of course had nowhere to store them to get them home.

When we sat down Marion trotted out a book called *Somerset Maugham's Memories,* and asked me to read 'An airman's letter to his mother' which was so much publicised in England two years or so ago [see page 50]. She said she wanted to hear an English voice recite it as it should have been recited. I obliged of course and did justice to it I think – at least I did my best. I also showed her photographs of my people at home. We chatted for a long time and it was a peaceful and happy evening.

A booklet was published to commemorate our stay in New York, which was lavishly decorated with excellent pictures of some of our doings. This was what it said:

'A storm of tickertape descended from Broadway's towering buildings at noon, August 31, 1943, when 350 veteran British anti-aircraft soldiers made their official bow to New York – America's gateway.

'These were the soldiers of the Number One Composite British Anti-Aircraft Battery, who came to the United States

36 Designed to resemble a European cafe the Jumble Shop was run by Winifred Tucker and Frances Russell.

to exchange ideas on ack ack, with American AA troops.

'The parade on August 31, was the Battery's first public appearance in New York. It was only the beginning – the beginning of an eight-day stay that saw the Tommies take New York by storm. They were cheering guests of the city at the famous Diamond Horseshoe, one of the city's nightclubs. They colourfully demonstrated their guns and searchlights to units of the Antiaircraft Artillery Command EDC.

'They had free tickets to theatres, dances, movies, concerts. They watched America's favourite sport, baseball, at Yankee Stadium, when New York played Washington. They were guests at the Stage Door Canteen and at the New York Victory Centre.

'The Tommies had themselves a wonderful time.

'The Tommies showed, too, that they know their ack ack.

'The Tommies are best described by the words of a certain American soldier. "They're good guys and good soldiers".'

AN AIRMAN'S LETTER TO HIS MOTHER

The letter was written by Flying Officer Vivian Rosewarne, co-pilot of a Wellington bomber stationed at RAF Marham, Norfolk. He was one of a six-man crew shot down and killed while providing ground support for troops retreating from the beaches of Dunkirk. He was 23. The letter was found in his belongings and, with his mother's permission, was published anonymously in The Times on 18 June 1940:

Dearest Mother,

Though I feel no premonition at all, events are moving rapidly and I have instructed that this letter be forwarded to you should I fail to return from one of the raids that we shall shortly be called upon to undertake. You must hope on for a month, but at the end of that time you must accept the fact that I have handed my task over to the extremely capable hands of my comrades of the Royal Air Force, as so many splendid fellows have already done.

First, it will comfort you to know that my role in this war has been of the greatest importance. Our patrols far out over the North Sea have helped to keep the trade routes clear for our convoys and supply ships, and on one occasion our information was instrumental in saving the lives of the men in a crippled lighthouse relief ship. Though it will be difficult for you, you will disappoint me if you do not at least try to accept the facts dispassionately, for I shall have done my duty to the utmost of my ability. No man can do more, and no one calling himself a man could do less.

I have always admired your amazing courage in the face of continual setbacks; in the way you have given me as good an education and background as anyone in the country: and always kept up appearances without ever losing faith in the future. My death would not mean that your struggle has been in vain. Far from it. It means that your sacrifice is as great as mine. Those who serve England must expect nothing from her; we debase ourselves if we regard our country as merely a place in which to eat and sleep.

History resounds with illustrious names who have given all; yet their sacrifice has resulted in the British Empire where there is a measure of peace, justice and freedom for all, and where a higher standard of civilization has evolved, and is still evolving, than anywhere else. But this is not only concerning our own land. Today we are faced with the greatest organized challenge to Christianity and civilization that the world has ever seen, and I count myself lucky and honoured to be the right age and fully trained to throw my full weight into the scale. For this I have to thank you. Yet there is more work for you to do. The home front will still have to stand united for years after the war is won. For all that can be said against it, I still maintain that this war is a very good thing: every individual is having the chance to give and dare all for his principle like the martyrs of old. However long the time may be, one thing can never be altered – I shall have lived and died an Englishman. Nothing else matters one jot nor can anything ever change it.

You must not grieve for me, for if you really believe in religion and all that it entails that would be hypocrisy. I have no fear of death; only a queer elation ... I would have it no other way. The universe is so vast and so ageless that the life of one man can only be justified by the measure of his sacrifice. We are sent to this world to acquire a personality and a character to take with us that can never be taken from us. Those who just eat and sleep, prosper and procreate, are no better than animals if all their lives they are at peace.

I firmly believe that evil things are sent into the world to try us; they are sent deliberately by our Creator to test our mettle because He knows what is good for us. The Bible is full of cases where the easy way out has been discarded for moral principles.

I count myself fortunate in that I have seen the whole country and known men of every calling. But with the final test of war I consider my character fully developed. Thus at my early age my earthly mission is already fulfilled and I am prepared to die with just one regret: that I could not devote myself to making your declining years more happy by being with you; but you will live in peace and freedom and I shall have directly contributed to that, so here again my life will not have been in vain.

Your loving son

CHAPTER 5

THERE'S ONLY ONE WEST POINT

I had known since 27 July that I was to have the honour of taking command of the section moving to West Point[1], but I and the detachment actually left New York en route there on 2 September. The rest of the Battery remained in New York to carry out firing and searchlight demonstrations.

I got packed up and sorted out my papers, which were accumulating so fast that I hadn't room to keep everything and had to buy a case for souvenirs. Once my packing was done and my briefcase filled with all the necessary documents, I left Teaneck at midday in the sedan with Colonel James Hunter. For Colonel Hunter it was like going home, but for me it was moving further into pastures new. The heavier vehicles had already left at 1030 hours and the remainder were not leaving until 1330 hours. We caught up with the convoy vehicles about one mile short of Bear Mountain Bridge, arranged a rendezvous for the detachment and then went on to Bear Mountain Park Inn[2] for lunch. Evidently several hundred other people had had the same idea, despite the fact that the place was so many miles from anywhere. How did they get the gas to get there, the food to eat there, the girls to serve? When you saw things like that you couldn't help wondering about the war question. However, I didn't let it worry me, because I was only too glad of some food.

The meals at the inn were expensive, but then the place was unusual to say the least. Old teak and pine had been carved into birds and animals, and grottoes of wood were everywhere turning the inn into an extraordinary wonderland. The stairs, the balustrades, floors, chairs and tables had that warm patina which looks so lovely when the wood is polished by age and handling.

After lunch we entered West Point, managing to get in before the MPs caught up with us; Colonel Hayden was surprised and a little embarrassed to find we had got into the camp without being escorted by military guards. Colonel Hunter pointed out the sights along what was to him very familiar ground.

The Superintendent, Major General Wilby[3] was in conference, so we decided to investigate the quarters and found them ready, and preparations made as requested. Post headquarters had even provided me with a little office (the pen being mightier than the QF 3.7 inch heavy AA gun), and the mess hall for the men was just adjacent. MPs had been dispatched to escort the convoy in and meanwhile I made arrangements to get them into position in the Riding Hall.

The British contingent lived under canvas during their stay at West Point

1   The United States Military Academy at West Point, often known as USMA, The Academy or simply West Point is the oldest US service academy. It was established in 1802 on an earlier military garrison fifty miles north of New York.
2   Bear Mountain State Park was formed to encourage recreation and conservation and opened in 1910. Bear Mountain Inn was built using material found in the park and opened five years later.
3   Major General Francis Bowditch Wilby graduated from West Point in 1905 and became its 39th Superintendent from 1942 to 1945.

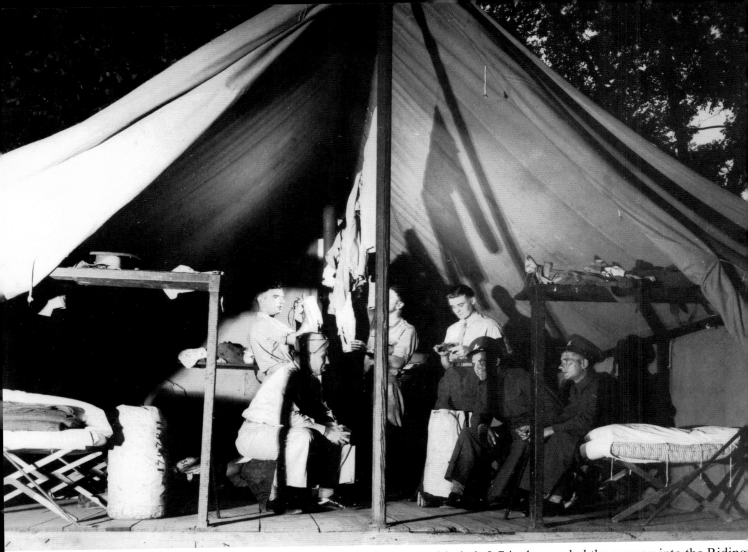

It was a proud moment in my career when the British troops with their 3.7 inch guns led the convoy into the Riding Hall, swung into position, and settled the equipment. They were the first British troops ever to bring their weapons of war into the most famous military academy in the USA. I called all the men together and told them the purpose of their visit, the duration, the proposed schedule, and warned them of the points of etiquette that had to be observed, such as not smoking when watching a review or formation of cadets and not going onto the famous Flirtation Walk. I also asked them to make sure that they upheld the traditions of which the British Army is justly proud. After being dismissed they marched to their quarters in time to wash, change and have a meal.

During the afternoon the detachment was able to see something of the camp. Guides had been provided by the coast artillery section of the post, and they were available to show the men either round the camp or wherever they wanted to go. Some went to Highland Falls, the nearby community with the traditional bright lights; most, after their tottering time in New York, just went to bed and slept. Three of the British officers, Lieutenants Cross, Colborn and Mollett were being accommodated in guest quarters in Cullum Hall[4], while John Hale and I were to stay in Colonel Hayden's home. All the officers were invited to dinner at Colonel Hayden's house that evening to meet the officers with whom they would be mainly in contact during their stay.

Colonel Hayden put a very beautiful room at our disposal with its own bathroom. There certainly was a bigger percentage of bathrooms per house in America than we had at home, but then they needed them so much more, due to the heat. The room contained mostly photographs of his cadet son; the son who was following in the footsteps of his father and grandfather[5]. Naturally, the father was very proud, but from conversations I had heard, they were a bit worried as to whether the son could make the grade or not; of course the son made it, but the father almost winced at every 'demerit' (as they called black marks) that the son got.

Mrs Hayden put on an excellent buffet supper for us, preceded by a visit to Hayden's bar. This bar deserved special mention, because it was so little expected. It was in the cellars of the house and contained souvenirs of the colonel's travels which seemed to me to have been all round the world. I found a menu from Scott's in Piccadilly with lobster thermidor as the speciality, also menus from most of the famous London hotels, souvenir bar pieces from the world over (a predominance of English) and an abundance of liquor. Signs going down the stairs, over doorways, all had little jokes to tell. After dinner we had a cosy chat on the porch, which was just beautifully cool but, mindful of late nights in New

4   Named after Brigadier General George Washington Cullum and financed by monies left in his Will. Cullum was a military commander during the American Civil War, a military engineer, graduate of West Point in 1833, instructor of engineering there 1848-55, and superintendent 1864-6.
5   Colonel Hayden's grandfather graduated from West Point in 1862, his father in 1888 and he himself in 1917. His son James 'Buster' Hayden went on to graduate in 1945 and had a distinguished army career, ending, like his father, as a colonel.

York, the party broke up at around ten.

After a really good night's sleep we were called by the colonel in the morning, breakfasted and then went out. The men marched with conscious precision down to the Riding Hall. It was their first march in West Point, and it attracted a lot of attention. It had to be in working clothes of course which was unfortunate, but couldn't be helped. In deference to the atmosphere of the academy, the officers had given clear instructions that the men were always to march in a body, with an NCO in charge, and were to be properly dressed at all times, even when moving to and from the wash house.

The first part of the morning was occupied with cleaning and polishing the equipment and I left the officers to work out the demonstration after telling them that I wanted it redesigned to fit the size of the Riding Hall. I told them I would arrive at 1030 hours to watch a complete rehearsal. I found this was so much better – to let them have their heads and watch for the answer – and in this case they worked it very well. A rehearsal indicated that we should have no difficulty, and by 1145 hours we were all set. Lunch, and the afternoon was fixed for a tour personally conducted by Colonel Hayden who gave each man a beautifully printed guidebook of the sort usually issued to visitors, plus a mimeographed copy of the tour so that they could follow where they were going. Several times during my visit to West Point, I felt that there was something historic about the visit, and here was one occasion. Tommies being shown the inner secrets of the academy by one of its oldest members.

We started off the tour by marching to Cullum Hall. On the ground floor were hallways containing plaques and memorials and also guest quarters, where male guests of officer instructors may stay, and where the three British lieutenants – Cross, Colborn and Mollett – were housed. The hall was a memorial hall, and contained the finest single floor room I'd ever seen. It was lined above the handrail with half cannon on either side of plaques. Each plaque was the memorial to some West Point cadet who had distinguished himself in some way. Above these were paintings of generals, all famous in West Point and American history. One of the most famous was General Eisenhower, whose son John was a cadet at the academy at the time of the detachment's visit[6]. The room was not only a museum piece, however, but was put to practical use in that they held cadet dances there, the adjoining part of the ground floor being used as a cadet guest reception room.

Gunner and cadet exchanging hats in the cadet show room

As the cadets were not allowed to marry when they were cadets, the veranda on the river side of the hall with magnificent river views of the Hudson was used by them to hold the hands of their favourite girl. More engagements, including that of Colonel James Hunter when he was a cadet, had been made on Flirtation Walk, as the veranda was called, than on any other comparably-sized piece of ground in the USA. Engagements in West Point, marriages in Washington I thought [see chapter 4]. Even without going any further on our tour, we realised the tradition of this place.

From Cullum Hall we went to the cadet library [see page 41]. Housed in a fine, stone, ivy-covered building, the library was in all senses of the word a library. It contained more than books. It contained the usual selection of librarians, many of them retired West Pointers, and also contained relics of history of the military academy, and some relics that are not in the history of the academy. Among the important documents and paintings held there I saw an original letter written by General Grant[7] and orders to the various battalions given in orders books, including one opened at a page which gave a historical description of the length of hair on the head and the frown that could be brought to the adjutant's face if anyone permitted hair to grow on the face (i.e. beards were out). Paintings of generals and superintendents of the academy, of Grant, Lee[8], and traditional members of the early American armed forces hung on the walls, painted by the only American artist ever to become president of the Royal Academy; Mr Sully[9]. A Japanese machine gun occupied a prominent place, and a collection of badges of US army units, corps, regiments, etc., was suitably displayed.

6   John Eisenhower graduated on D Day, 6 June 1944. He served in the US Army during the Second World War but was kept out of the main fields of battle in case his capture or death was used to influence his father Dwight D Eisenhower who was Supreme Allied Commander Europe.
7   Ulysses S. Grant was a military commander during the American Civil War and later the eighteenth President of the United States.
8   Robert E. Lee was a commanding general of the confederate army during the American Civil War and a combat engineer.
9   Born in 1783 at Horncastle in Lincolnshire, Thomas Sully's family emigrated to America when he was nine. Apart from occasional visits to England, he remained in the US until his death in 1872.

Left: The Catholic chapel and Father Murdoch
Below: Inside the cadet chapel. The organist's head can just be seen above the pew at the front right

From the library, the detachment moved on to one of the cadet rooms to see how a cadet was expected to keep his kit and room. To such an extent had the tourist trade grown, that it had been found necessary to set up a room purely to show. Thus lockers had glass fronts and everything was laid out like a museum piece. It proved to be almost too much for some of the British Tommies as they inspected the unbelievable ultra-neatness which cadets accepted as part of their training. I was assured, however, by a West Pointer, that the rooms really were laid out like this by the cadets themselves, and woe betide anyone who failed to set his room up correctly.

A cadet must at all times be available, or must leave information about exactly where he can be found. So they had worked out an absence card which could be so arranged to show exactly where the cadet was at any time of the day or night; if any instructor found that the cadet was not in the place he had said he would be, he would punish him by making him 'walk the area', which is a kind of fatigue and debaser rolled into one[10]. The 'honor system' was a great part of the academy.

On to the gymnasium, which was the finest I had ever encountered. It contained everything on its six floors that the human mind could devise for making the cadet fit. With the rigorous check that was kept on the cadet's moods and how he mixed with the outside public, there had to be an outlet somewhere, and his high jinks came out in the gym and on the playing field.

We met Marty Maher, a white-haired old man with a total of about 33 years West Point service; he was for thirty years the enlisted man responsible for swimming instruction to the cadets. He was beloved by all present and past cadets and, after a short period of retirement, had been called back to look after the services in the gym[11].

The Detachment was taken by truck to the Catholic chapel which was modelled on the lines of an English Catholic church and was the home and work of the Catholic chaplain, Murdoch[12], who was only too eager to welcome the men and explain the little church's position in this vast academy. There were three main places of worship. The Catholic chapel, the old chapel and the cadet chapel. The cadet chapel, modelled again on old English architecture, contained the finest organ in the USA, so they claimed at West Point. It certainly sounded a fine organ, as the Tommies, strangely silent and picking their way with an unusual care, walked down the aisle to watch the assistant organist playing one of his own compositions. The cadet chapel held the most commanding view of the camp, overlooking the Hudson and the surrounding districts. Was it typical that the cadets had their own prayer?

The visit to the chapel was followed by a tour round the perimeter of the camp. Later in my US tour Colonel Potts, a West Point man with a long career in the army and the commandant of Camp Davis, told me of the strategic value of West Point. It was situated at the bend of the river, so that sailing men-o'-war coming down the river had to change

---

10 Officially known as 'punishment tours', cadets must walk a specified number of hours based on the severity of their infraction of the rules. During their freetime, cadets walk their hours backwards and forwards in uniform and under arms in a part of the cadet barracks courtyard known as 'the area', hence 'walking the area'.
11 Martin Maher Jr was born in Ireland in 1876, emigrated to America, was employed as a waiter at West Point from 1896 before joining the US Army in 1898. He served as swimming instructor at West Point from 1899 to 1928 when he retired from the army but remained at West Point as a civilian employee before finally retiring in 1946. He died in January 1961.
12 Monsignor George G Murdoch extended the Chapel of the Most Holy Trinity, West Point by adding on the rectory in 1934.

course, lost wind, and were in consequence at that crucial moment in the hands of the shore batteries which were West Point.

The detachment then went on to the Michie Stadium[13] built into the hillside and containing all the modern conveniences that a first-class football stadium should have. Polo fields, reservoirs, ice houses completed the tour, the latter being something new to the British as they had never before seen ice cut from a frozen river – the ice at West Point came from the Hudson – in the winter and stored for use during the summer.

Finally we arrived at Washington Hall where the cadets ate and which was a triumph of modern messing. It was built so that it was possible to feed 2,500 men at the same time and was in the form of a half hexagon with the mess kitchens in the centre, enabling all three sides to be fed simultaneously without interfering with each other. The cooks in the mess kitchens were naturally overwhelmed to find 500 men, mostly British Tommies, suddenly invade their domain asking for free samples. The layout of the tables, each holding ten men, formed a standard geometric pattern, while the high ceiling and the mural walls created a vast effect of space that it was difficult to forget.

Leaving our transport, we marched to watch a football practice; our first introduction to American football. Rigorous practice, the first of the season, was going on and the main thing that could be heard, apart from the purely visual effect of dozens of husky, shoulder-padded men charging at dummies, was a continued series of hoarsely shouted ejaculations that sounded like 'let's go, let's go'.

By this time the British troops had to move into position to witness a Cadet Brigade Parade. Whilst marching along one could hear whispers from officers and men of the academy admiring and expressing surprise at the precision and arm swing of the Tommies. Our men were obviously taking a delight in showing off their drill before they were finally overshadowed by the spectacle of 2,400 men on parade.

I'd been invited to sit with Colonels Hunter and Hayden on the reviewing stand. My own impression of the parade was a number of moving squares and rectangles of blue and white, blue at the top and white at the bottom, which finally merged into one long string of rectangles winding its way past the reviewing stand. It was impossible to pick out an individual, which no doubt accounted for the despair of a proud mother sitting next to me who thought she saw her son in the third file in the third rectangle and then in the second of the fifth, or was it the third of the sixth… Sizing was exceptional and inexplicable. Did they only pick men of the same size for the Corps of Cadets? The band finished up by playing the British contingent a pretty compliment, striking up with the march of the British

Trophy Point looking over the Hudson River valley. The four British soldiers are standing by one of the memorial globes surrounding Battle Monument

---

13 Pronounced 'mike-y' the stadium is named after Dennis Michie who, in 1890, was captain of the first football team at West Point.

Corps of Cadets. The statue in front of the large window is the Thayer Memorial which now stands opposite the commandant's quarters. The building behind the statue is possibly the West Academic Building, now the Pershing Barracks

Grenadiers [see chapter 4]. We all felt a little awed, a little proud and very tired with our terrific tour, and not a little pleased at the attention that had been paid to us.

The next day was a Saturday. The detachment paraded at 0800 hours and marched down to the Riding Hall. Demonstrations to enlisted men took place from 0900 to 1130 hours with about 600 men watching. We put on a really good demonstration, bringing a searchlight, a Bofors gun and the heavy gun section into action in quick time. We had luncheon and then further demonstrations, this time with 2,400 cadets coming through in groups of 600 as our spectators. It was a fine sight to see 600 cadets in white trousers and blue coats lined up in seats on the balcony and to hear their almost tumultuous clapping at the end of the show.

The first demonstration was the best I'd seen since we formed as a Battery. It was a strange psychological effect, the men showing off in front of cadets and doing extremely well. Some record times were put up, including putting a 3.7 inch gun into action in three minutes twenty seconds from halt to action. The demonstrations played havoc with the men, however; bringing a heavy gun into action six times in a day is extremely heavy work. They were rewarded in the evening by a good meal, followed by a get together with the men of the coast artillery battalion in their clubroom.

The officers had to do a quick dash after the demonstrations were over as we had to be present at a cocktail party given by General Wilby who this time was at ease and made us feel the same. After changing into service dress, Colonel and Mrs Hayden took us along to the superintendent's quarters[14]. These quarters had belonged to successive superintendents since shortly after West Point was built. The general himself took pride in the fact that the buildings and gardens had not cost Uncle Sam one cent. It seemed that the cadets paid for its upkeep by subscription and seemed to vie with each other in continuing the unique tradition. Consequently it had become one of the showpieces of West Point.

We were entranced with the layout of the house, the banks of flowers, the cut glass on polished tables, candlesticks and candelabra, paintings of previous superintendents and the general flowery air that prevailed in the loggia and hallways. Out in the gardens cocktails were served in a flower arbour where we were to eat our evening meal. Drinks were excellent. I should imagine, after conversation with one of the majors, that the superintendent had one of the best cellars in the States. Certainly the Manhattans and dry martinis were as good as any I had. I had to have both to try them, much to the astonishment of Colonel Hayden, who thought I ought to drop flat after that.

Mrs Wilby was an ideal wife for the general. She had pep, personality and a pleasing disposition. She was an ideal hostess, always dashing around to see that everyone was happy, eating and/or drinking, and yet she seemed to be able to stay long enough to chat on some personal detail. She told me about a copper beech tree which had been imported from England and now occupied a regal position in the middle of the gardens. The garden gate had a plate affixed to it telling of the original donors of the money and the landscape artist who created the gardens. They were certainly fine gardens

14 Built in 1820, the superintendent's quarters are the oldest building remaining at West Point.

with tumbling water and little ponds; Mrs Wilby asked the company if anyone could explain why the goldfish were more prolific in the lower pool than the higher pool. We didn't know – or perhaps didn't dare to make any suggestions – but her question broke the ice.

It was a delightful dinner with white-coated servants moving silently around with food, after already having done a really good job work with prawns and a hundred and one other tasty things served with the cocktails. What a pity that just at the moment when I was feeling most happy the thought crossed my mind that there was a war on. For three days we had been at peace. For three days we had been able to forget that a war existed. I looked around the assembled company and realised that, while wars may be won and wars may be lost, institutions like West Point Military Academy had to continue and their pride and their purpose had to be maintained if they were to provide a continual and effective contribution to any future defence of their country.

I believed that it was absolutely necessary for institutions such as West Point to retain their individuality and not be dragged into the commonplace by the bond of people at war. The difficulty was making the men realise this point of view. Take the case of a single remark, which really made me think. Leaving the old chapel after our inspection tour, I overheard one Tommy say to another: 'well, say what you like, but I can't forget our boys in the hell of Sicily'. For some time I had been able to enjoy and appreciate the peace of West Point, the glamour, the showmanship, the resultant craftsmanship in the creation of a newly commissioned officer. I realised that that officer knew nothing of war, and everything about a peacetime army and its pomp and ceremony, but then West Point was a school more than a military academy. It should not have been necessary to teach the 14- to 18-year-olds the horrors of battle at this stage; better to teach them the history behind wars. In any case, the last year saw the cadets move out under canvas and their battle training was done away from the camp itself where they were better able to undergo such a course.

We had to go. We had to be back in Teaneck by Saturday night, as the following day we had another advance party. I never did catch up with my private affairs; work and pleasure or, as it was fast becoming, work and work was taking up twenty-five hours in a day.

The parting from the general and his wife made me feel that we had not only been welcome and successful, but that the British troops had excelled themselves and given all with whom they had come into contact much food for thought. I felt quite proud of the officers and men and told them all so.

The ride back was beautiful. Lights in the towns en route, made me think I was back in the days when our greatest worry was which way to dim headlights and how fast one could get from town to town. So we said goodbye to West Point, the best detachment I ever had, the nicest, the matiest, and the most successful.

West Point cadets watch the Battery demonstration in the Riding Hall. The building now contains four interior floors and has been renamed Thayer Hall

CHAPTER 6

THAT OTHER ENGLAND

Many people, to whom I have mentioned that the Boston area was included in our tour, have pointed out to me its historic connection with the old country. Consequently, and perhaps surprisingly, I continued on the tour with mixed feelings for I had begun to appreciate the contrast and to look forward to seeing further evidence of the differences between the two countries. Yet, naturally, I appreciated the opportunity of seeing for myself the area in which the English pioneers of years gone by tried to settle.

The camp we were going to, Camp Edwards[1], was about sixty miles from Boston and a number of miles from any other town of appreciable size, so the possibility of mixing with people was not great. This camp was similar to Camp Davis; huge with all the barracks built the same as those at Davis. The camp was commanded by a colonel, yet contained an anti-aircraft artillery training centre (AAATC), and an engineer's amphibian command each commanded by a general.

Colonel Hunter, representing the escort detachment, and I made up the advance party and left West Point and New York on Sunday 5 September. We had a day coach on the train which had single lines of armchairs on a swivel arrangement on each side of the coach, so that you could turn to look out of the windows or inwards to stretch your legs. They were very comfortable cars, but seemed to me to be a great waste of space in those days of difficult travel. Views of the coastline showing the inlets, fishing smacks, little towns and villages kept us interested during our meal. Suddenly we came across the beginning of the long line of big factories, which I'm told studded the coast of New England.

We arrived at Providence[2] and had no time to view it except as a series of lighted streets and a railway station as we had to move on to Camp Edwards by car. A two-hour run, but it was dark and I couldn't see much, so I thought the wisest policy was to sleep.

The following day I was up early and at work by 0720 hours having had breakfast with a number of colonels. I dislike the mess system which puts all colonels at one table, all majors at another, etc., etc. I was also taken round to meet Brigadier General Handwerk, the commanding general of the AAATC. From then it was procedural checking of the proposed programme, the firing location, quarters, equipment park and the arrangements for the Battery's arrival next day. I arranged for two stenographers to type for me and kept them working hard for a long period, but by the time they'd finished, they had produced a monumental advance party pamphlet designed to save everyone time and thought.

I went around all the quarters, suggested altering the proposed parade area as it was too small, and then in the afternoon I went out to the firing point at Scorton

Neck[3]. Sand and scrub invaded by a few barracks, and with cleared and flattened patches of sand into which the guns could be run for firing was all we could see. The officer in charge, a captain, was exceedingly pleasant and obliging and things were fixed up in double quick time. We were able to see a very big stretch of the peninsula of Cape Cod from the firing point and one of the officers likened it to a moustache curling up from a man's face.

We returned back to Edwards through Sandwich Village, an unusual name as such small collections of houses were not normally called villages or hamlets. It was supposed to be one of the most typically English villages in America. Just before entering the village I saw two things that interested me. First a mosquito project, where land had been reclaimed and the mosquitoes quelled by continuous spraying over a period of time with insecticide carried on a man's back and used similarly to a flamethrower. Then there were irrigated cranberry fields, which looked like clover fields with drains in them. Men in large conical, Chinese-type hats were culling the harvest of cranberries.

---

1   Among other units, the Second Battalion 64th Coastal Artillery Regiment (Anti Aircraft) was based at Camp Edwards from 1942 to 1944. It formed the core of the anti-aircraft artillery training centre (AAATC).
2   The capital of Rhode Island (the smallest US state by area) and one of the first cities established in North America.
3   Almost the nearest stretch of beach to Camp Edwards, the quarter-mile long firing point was situated seawards of what is now Carleton Drive. The guns fired north into the sea.

Saltbox House[4] in Sandwich Village was supposed to be the oldest house in the USA, although there was another house in St Augustine, Florida which made the same claim. In the village, they still carried on the traditional village occupation of glassblowing, but old Sandwich glass was considered to be a museum piece[5]. The whole village was overgrown with ivy and reminiscent of some of our English villages. Descendants of the same tribe of Indian [the Cotochese] who inhabited the area some hundreds of years ago still lived in the area.

After supper it was back to work for me, while the others went to a show. I managed to do a really good spot of work and felt quite tired but quite pleased. My first impression of the camp had not been a good one, but after a whole day I was a lot more impressed and felt that the Battery would enjoy being there. My only remaining doubt was that I didn't like General Handwerk very much; the first one I'd met that I didn't get on with excellently.

The afternoon of following day, Tuesday 7 September, was when the Battery was to arrive. That morning I spent mostly interviewing people and writing. Captain Scorer surprised us by arriving about 1400 hours with Colonel Metcalf and Major Peter Crocker arriving a short while after. Derek was dressed in battledress for the first time since we arrived over here and looked unfamiliar. They had moved ahead of the Battery convoy, which was travelling the 350 miles from Teaneck, New Jersey by road.

They had all been up since 0200 hours and on the move since 0400, and were hungry and tired. The meals en route had been a farce. Imagine our horror then, when the Battery rolled in at 1900 hours, considerably ahead of time, and urgently needing a meal which should have been taken en route. The convoy had been planned to arrive in two parts with the heavy equipment expected to get here some three hours after the main body. 350 miles by road in twelve to sixteen hours was very tiring and I was extremely sorry that I had not insisted on a hot meal awaiting them. The catering staff had gone off duty and the only thing we had been able to lay on (and then as a favour) was hot coffee and doughnuts, which simply went like nobody's business.

Just as the Battery arrived I got a message that I'd received a phone call from a Lieutenant Cole and worked out that it must have been my brother. He had gone over to America by bomber to take command of a newly completed frigate, built in a shipyard somewhere in Falls River. I believed he might get his brass hat out of it[6]. I received confirmatory news from BAS [see chapter 3] that he was over, and they said he was coming to see me. I hoped he could make it but didn't really see how.

Next day started with a ragged conference. Most of the heat and frayed tempers caused by the problems of the convoy had however left the members of the Battery. Because of the size of the demonstration area, we worked out a new type of demonstration that morning. It was almost like being an actor and having to suit our entrances to the size of the stage, but I believed we were becoming really accomplished in getting such details settled. We put on our first show at Camp Edwards the following day, so we spent most of that day getting the equipment maintained and polished.

A rumour went around during lunch that Italy had packed

Analysis of firing; note that most of the those watching are American personnel

4   Saltbox houses are called such because they are said to be the same shape as the wooden box with a lid in which salt was once kept. Built around 1637, Hoxie House, probably the saltbox house to which Cole refers. It is considered to be the oldest house in the Cape Cod area, although several houses in the US pre-date it.
5   According to the Sandwich Glass Museum, glass manufacture ceased in the town in the 1920s.
6   A senior officer. The term derives from the cocked hats worn by Napoleon and his officers; indoors they carried their hats under their arm or *chapeaux a bras*. 'Bras' became brass in English, hence 'brass hats'. Major Cole is commenting that his brother might be made up to a senior officer as a result of his new posting. Later notes show that, at this time, William Cole was Lieutenant Commander, Royal Navy Reserve (RNR).

up[7]. After lunch, we discovered it was true. <u>ITALY HAD QUIT</u>; it was a great piece of news. All the boys felt justly proud of the work of their brothers in arms, the Eighth Army. The officers of the Battery felt proud of the men who were in the Eighth before coming out here. The Colonel gathered all the men together at 1620 hours – the armistice was being signed at 1630 hours. He addressed all ranks and outlined the entry of Italy into the war and subsequent events. At precisely 1630 hours he called for three cheers for the troops of the Eighth Army, and for their brothers in arms in the British and American forces. With a movement as of one man, the men rose to their feet in the three most convincing cheers I've ever heard in my life.

The news of course called for a celebration so it was timely that the GOC American Ack Ack Troops in Camp Edwards, General Handwerk, had invited all the officers to a cocktail party. This was our formal introduction, and in celebration we waded into the cocktails in no uncertain manner. It's a pity they were so strong!

Demonstration Firing, following the usual pattern, started the next morning and went fairly well. For me it was a day for doing a thousand and one trifling details all connected with the smooth working of future parties and the smooth working of present arrangements.

We had been invited to a dance that evening given in our honour by the girls of Taunton, a town some forty miles away. We duly arrived and were introduced to the hostess of the club and the president of the Girls of Taunton Social Club. I had supper with the president, a lady of about sixty five and a widow. Her daughter was a leading member and vice president of the society. Between them, they appeared to have a dictatorship of girls in Taunton. They personally interviewed any girl who wanted to join the club and decided on her morals or otherwise. If in doubt, they demanded a reference from the local preacher. When they had a dance or social these girls were notified, and all went by bus paying their own bus fare. They were shepherded into the dance hall and, when the dance finished, they were shepherded back into the buses. No man was allowed to leave the hall until the girls were away; MPs were always patrolling outside the building. It was the first time that I'd ever seen such a security system work.

The following day, 10 September, was a big one for the Battery; it was the day of the Boston parade. A joint parade of American AA troops and men of the British Battery together with representatives of all the other services and

sprinkled with sixteen stars of stage and screen. We had to arrange for a 'smart looking soldier' to be an escort to one of the film stars so got one of the British gunners all 'poshed up' and sent him off in advance. John Hale went in early to find out arrangements for the British contingent. The Battery had to provide a hundred men, two 3.7 inch (heavy) guns, two 40 mm (Bofors) guns and two searchlights. The parade seemed likely to become almost as big as in New York. I had spent hours yesterday working out the detail with the AAA contingents; getting the various elements into formation at the right time. The vehicles were to move into Boston in one convoy,

Selling war bonds with the stars at the Boston parade

the men on trucks in another. Lieutenant Colonel Tom Metcalf was to go on the group commander's staff as the British representative while Colonel Muirhead from BAS, was on the marshal of the parade's staff. The three of us went into Boston separately with an American Colonel Phillips, who was in overall charge of arrangements. The Battery contingent, under the command of the officer in charge of the heavy troop, Captain Rupert Ledger, moved off at 1000 hours to join the main body, four battalions of American AA troops under the command of Colonel Duncan 38th AAA Group.

Sandwiches were eaten en route, but the men didn't like them, they were dry, skimpy and unpalatable. That's one thing the American escort detachment didn't seem able to understand; the British Tommy needed a substantial meal if he was going to work hard, and parades were hard work not just a grand piece of fun.

The assembly area for the army troops was fixed near the start of the parade because they were to move out immediately after the marshal, an American band and two film stars in jeeps. The film stars, including five starlets, were lunching

---

7   The signing ceremony took place at 2.00pm on board *HMS Nelson* on 3 September, but was not publicised until 8 September. Although Italy had formally surrendered, much of the country was in the hands of the Germans so allied troops still had to land invading forces. The British Eighth Army landed at Calabria on 3 September, while the US Fifth Army landed at Salerno one week later, i.e. the day after Cole is writing. Cole therefore appears to be mistaken either about the time the armistice was signed or the day on which they heard about it, particularly bearing in mind that Italy was several hours ahead of American Eastern Standard Time.

at the Hotel Statler, outside which a huge crowd had assembled waiting for a glimpse of their idols. The drivers of the twelve jeeps, each with the name of the film star on a pennant fixed to a pole, were standing by outside the hotel; the film stars were to be interspersed throughout the parade. As the British were following the jeep containing Betty Hutton, we had the benefit of seeing how much these people are tied to publicity. Betty Hutton had to throw herself about in the most amazing fashion, throwing kisses continuously and generally trying to look glamorous all to please the crowd. Men shouted out the most amazing things to her and generally everybody seemed to go mad. Betty Hutton had a mounted policeman escorting her, while in the jeep was the glamour-boy-soldier escort, a press relations man and the driver. At certain periods and for the benefit of the crowd, she would kiss her escort and give him a huge hug, which never failed to bring applause, cheering and laughter from the crowd.

The crowds were tremendous; it was estimated that 500,000 people watched the parade. Photographers were everywhere, but the thing that struck me most was that, with that huge parade of navy, army, air force, WACS, WAVES, SPARS[8], bands and civilian services, etc., the only things that attracted any attention at all were the film stars and the shorts of the British Tommies.

The result of the parade and the day's drive was that $200 million in war bonds were sold. Yet how much would it have been without the film stars? Their movements were government-sponsored and it would be almost true to say that the film stars were raising more money for the war effort than any other type of publicity. As one of the gunners was overheard to say: 'What a strange war!'

After we fell out of the parade, I had a quick change into service dress in a nearby 'Gents' [lavatory] and then Colonels Phillips and Muirhead were ready to go. We went by car to the Harvard Club, probably the most exclusive club in Boston, for cocktails with the Governor of Massachusetts, Governor Sawtanstall. Strangely enough, having been given the opportunity of having tea or cocktails, I chose tea. Who could possibly go to Boston and not have tea, after the Boston Tea Party so many years ago. The tea was good, as good as I'd had over there; I had four cups! The Consul General, C.G. Long, was there as well as two more generals and a rear admiral and we were all introduced. We couldn't stay long unfortunately. I had to go with Colonel Phillips to pick up the escort and the colours, to eat and then to be back in the Boston Gardens for the film star show. We went round the corner to a drugstore for our tea, attracting a lot of attention as we ate ham and eggs.

The Boston Gardens was a stadium built over the main railway station. It was a huge building capable of housing 15,000 people in tiers. Spotlights, loudspeakers, scoreboards, boxing rings were all hung from the ceiling and on this occasion the ground floor was covered with chairs leading up to a massive stage set up for the band and artists. We had about an hour's wait before the men arrived during which we had a beer. A Chief Petty Officer of the British Navy told me he was a cousin of Glynis Johns and thought it amazing that I should know her so well. I had met her at Brigade HQ in Middle Wallop [see chapter 1]. We toasted each other in beer and then I got him into the show.

---

8   WACS were members of the Women's Army Corps; WAVES were Women Accepted for Volunteer Emergency Service, a division of the US Navy made up entirely of women; SPARS were the women's reserve of the US Coast Guard – the name came from the initials of the Coast Guard's Latin motto and English translation: *Semper Paratus*; Always Ready.

Colonel Phillips, Colonel Metcalf and I had seats reserved in General Handwerk's party. The first people to arrive were Mrs Flannigan and her children, the family of the mayor's executive officer, who were closely followed by the general and his wife, his aide and his daughter. The general's daughter was a vivacious girl of twenty who had just left college. The girls in America seemed to go into education much more seriously than we did. It was considered ordinary for middle-class people's children to go to college, as they called it (which in nine cases out of ten resembled our high schools), until they were nineteen or twenty. They were so proud of their schools too, wore college rings and were really proud to wear them and show them; I couldn't for the life of me think why because they were flashy, large and ornate. The men in the college wore them too. In our eyes for a man to wear a ring that size was pure snobbery, but it was the American idea of the old school tie.

By this time the show was starting. There were no programmes, which was a pity as it was a pure celebrity show and lasted for two hours and twenty minutes. Kay Kyser[9] and his band – they really were famous in the US – opened the show and they were *good*. Kay Kyser was a slapstick type of comedian bandleader but could wield a baton and acted as compere to most of the show. Jimmy Cagney did a couple of short turns – Yankee Doodle Dandy being one. Fred Astaire danced in his own inimitable style. Harpo Marx, complete with harp, wig and silence 'took a ride' out of a girl partner (he cut off most of her dress while she was singing opera). Julie Garland sang her lollipop song 'Over the Rainbow', out of the film *The Wizard of Oz* and was very sweet and natural doing it. Betty Hutton almost broke the mike into small pieces by her dynamite show, 'It's moider it is'[10], and she threw herself and the mike about so much that she was out of breath ninety-five per cent of the time. Greer Garson, that most beautiful English girl[11], made a fervent appeal to the people to buy War Bonds and announced the 200 million figure. Her appeal dripped with sentiment, but was beautifully spoken nevertheless. Five starlets were given a

At the Boston Star Show. Above, left to right: James Cagney, Gunner Newman the Battery's photographer, Fred Astaire. Right: Betty Hutton and Mickey Rooney

9   Famous band leader and considered to be the first celebrity to perform in military camps for the troops.
10 Probably the song 'Murder He Says', from the film *Happy Go Lucky* starring Betty Hutton, Dick Powell and Mary Martin.
11 Born in Manor Park, Essex (now Greater London) and educated at King's College London, Greer Garson won an Oscar for the title role in the rousingly patriotic 1942 film *Mrs Miniver*. Churchill claimed that the film had done more for the Allied cause than a flotilla of battleships.

further chance of getting used to applause, bright lights, huge crowds and the type of publicity that only a film star can get.

The real hit of the evening was Mickey Rooney, who came on, did impersonations, played the drums in the band, and proved what a versatile, amusing, youthful artist he was. Lucille Ball had a two minute spot, came on and did nothing, despite the tales of our photographer Newman, who said she had thrown a fit backstage because she hadn't a dressing room to herself and had had to dress with the starlets. A girl whose name I didn't get sang a song from Rigoletto, and what a superb voice she had. Kay Kyser announced her as the girl with the triple threat; she's got beauty, she's got youth and she's got a grand voice, and she certainly had all three[12]. Without question we should hear and see a lot more of her.

After the show we went to pick up the colours party which had been brought in as a 'Land of Hope and Glory' finale. En route back to camp we stopped at a coffee stall and ate hot dogs, the real thing with mustard and mixed sweet pickle – my first in the States; it took me a while to get used to them. Arrived back in camp at 0300 hours.

The Battery was to move that day, Saturday 11 September, so we rose early. Imagine my surprise to wake up and find my brother, William, in naval uniform, standing by my bed. He had a pinched face and was rather lean but looked extremely fit. He'd landed in Newport, travelled to New York where he stayed (at the Brabazon Plaza, the navy's HQ in New York[13]). Then he found out from BASW where I was stationed, got some leave and travelled to Buzzards Bay by rail, and then by coach to Camp Edwards. He had arrived the evening before only to find that I was in Boston, but two of the subalterns, Ray Dix and Roger Key, who were not involved in the Boston Parade, had gone out of their way to entertain him and fix him up with a bed. They certainly took him around according to all reports. Well, I dressed and we went over to breakfast together talking incessantly about our experiences. Time unfortunately being short and my programme being full I knew that I couldn't give Bill as good a time as I would have liked. Still, we got together and, as the Battery was to move at 0900 hours to the firing point at Scorton Neck fifteen miles away, I took Bill with me in advance.

After going the wrong way on Route 6, we eventually landed at Scorton Neck, most of the travelling time being taken up by talking of home and each other's doings. I

Clifford and William Cole meeting 3,000 miles from home

was kept busy for the next two hours, so I had to leave him to be entertained by other members of the Battery, including Colonel Metcalf. He seemed to get on all right, he always did.

That afternoon I had to take a detachment of fifty men to the Firestone rubber plant in Fall River, so I arranged for him to come with me. John Hale and Bob Dunlop took a contingent of fifty to a Hanover ammunition factory at the same time, while twenty men went to homes of the British-American war veterans (where I hear they had a marvellous time). Bill and I set off in an open car following the fifty men in two large trucks. As the journey was fifty-eight miles there and the same back everyone got a little dusty. However the ride was pleasant and we talked New York, etc., eating chocolates, peanuts and popcorn on the way. We passed through several towns, the most interesting being New Bedford and Fall River[14], and Bill thought the ship he was in America to take over might have been built at Fall River[15], but of course didn't know. I was struck by the fact that, although we'd been born into the same background we now led such totally different lives.

We had no difficulty in getting into the works[16], even though we all had to have permits and labels to enter, and each had to sign our name in the visitors' book. The managing director and most of his staff were there and they were

12 Possibly Georgia Carroll who joined the band as a vocalist early in 1943 and married Kay Kyser early in 1944.
13 The Brabazon Plaza Hotel was known as *HMS Saker* and was the main Royal Navy administrative centre in the US; both Royal and Merchant Navy personnel stayed there and it was the nerve centre for British maritime interests in the US.
14 During the nineteenth century New Bedford was an important whaling town in Bristol County, Massachusetts, when Fall River was a leading textile manufacturing centre. Today Fall River houses a large collection of Second World War naval vessels.
15 Rather than Fall River, it is possible that Lieutenant Cole's ship was built at Fore River near Quincy just south of Boston. The Fore River Shipyard built many warships and liberty ships during the Second World War.
16 The Firestone Tire & Rubber Company took over the huge waterfront premises of the American Printing Company, Fall River in 1937. During the Second World War the company made artillery shells, helmet linings, aluminium barrels for transporting food, and military products requiring rubber.

Members of the British Batteery touring American factories. They are looking at the manufacture of aeroplane tanks

exceptionally decent to us. We had a photograph taken before entering the works, and many photographs inside the works where the tour was given a lot of publicity. They took a really good photograph of Bill and I as we were brothers having met again so far from home. We were in the directors' office and they promised to mail a copy over to mother and father in England; a very nice gesture. In due course our parents received the photograph, which greatly thrilled both of them.

Security was tight in the factory, but it was somewhat spoilt by the fact that everyone was given a mimeographed sheet which told us exactly what was being made, the different processes and their locations. And we were allowed to take these sheets away with us! Even so it was interesting seeing the range of products, from pressed splinter-proof helmets to bullet-proof waistcoats and a huge range of moulded tyres for military vehicles.

Fire precautions were extremely strict as they had had one fire which gutted the works[17] and didn't want another. Result; no one was allowed to smoke on the premises. Instead we were offered gum to chew. One of the directors personally escorted Bill and myself round and gave as a running commentary as we progressed. Women were the majority personnel in the factory and seemed to like it reasonably well, although mass production such as this could be a most monotonous job. The fun and banter they exchanged with the Tommies as the party moved around must have made one of the few interesting moments in the day.

After the tour, which we had to rush for time, we were given bottles of soft drinks to slake the dust of the journey. I had root beer for the first time and it tasted for all the world like mouthwash – I didn't like it at all! A speech by the managing director and a reply by me completed the afternoon and away we went.

We had a fast journey back, spoiled only by the fact that the braking system on one of the lorries went wrong. We had to leave the lorry by the roadside after telephoning its location to Camp Edwards. We arrived back in Scorton Neck cold and hungry, only to find that there was no food, and nothing to drink. I was very annoyed; in fact I lost my

Two directors of the Firestone Tire & Rubber Company show their products to Clifford and William Cole. Appropriately for someone serving in the navy, William is wearing the life jacket

17 In October 1941. 30,000 lbs of raw rubber was lost. Although the US didn't join the war until December of that year, the loss of so much raw material adversely affected the war effort.

temper, probably for the first time in America. However, I managed to get the men something. I then discovered that all the transport had left for Camp Edwards, leaving nothing to transport the fifty men into camp for a dance which had been supposed to be in their honour. A night of real chaos.

The following day was a Sunday and I had been given permission by Colonel Metcalf to have the morning off after parade to take my brother into Providence on his way back to New York. We managed to borrow a sedan car and so went into Providence in style. I felt sad that I should have to leave Bill without really having had an opportunity to entertain him in traditional style. However, we were happy to have been able to get together at all.

We arrived in Providence with a few minutes to catch the train. I really felt as though I was losing a part of me when Bill said goodbye. The next moment he was gone and I really didn't know whether I would see him alive again. As it turned out I was to see him in England within the year, but of course I didn't know that when I was left standing on Providence station.

I arrived back at Scorton Neck to find that I was just in time to go to a show arranged for the troops by Gertrude Lawrence[18]. She had a grand set of people, mostly soldiers, with her and they put on a really first-class show. After the show, which was held on a specially-erected stage with a specially-erected grandstand on the sand by the seashore, we were invited to a reception in the day room.

We had a good programme arranged for the following day, commencing at 0930 hours with Heavy Ack Ack. The firing was good; the Vickers as usual firing better than the Sperry[19]. It had been noticeable throughout the tour that a succession of small things had thrown the Heavy results off, but the 40s [the 40mm Bofors anti-aircraft gun] were consistently reliable. The searchlights had been independent, but seemed to have been able to achieve quite a good measure of success. The searchlight teams had nothing much to do at Scorton Neck, but had been practising for a guard of honour which was to be mounted for the visit of the Secretary of War.

However, just to complicate matters, the American newsreel people came on the following afternoon and asked for a special show for that night. We laid on a night firing exercise with five searchlights, two 3.7s and two 40s. The searchlights put up a cone and the two light guns and two heavies fired into the centre of the cone; most impressive, so I was told.

I found I had another job to do. I had to go to Camp Edwards and censor a broadcast which was to be made on a programme called *Vox Pop*[20]. It was sponsored by Bromo-Seltzer, a commercial preparation to relieve indigestion and hangovers; the programme had been going for eleven years and was still popular. The general idea was that they interviewed people in every sphere of life and asked them questions, and then gave them presents such as

Secretary of State for War, Mr Stimson, accompanied by Lieutenant Colonel Metcalf, inspect the British Guard of Honour (see letter on page 32)

watches, ladies dresses, material, layettes for babies, etc. as a reward. The presents were very handsome and must have been worth I should say about $100 for each recipient. Before the broadcast they had a warm up in which they asked members of the audience to come on the stage and do prescribed silly little things for money, thus causing a great laugh in the audience and warming up for the real applause on the broadcast.

That evening, five British Tommies were to describe their experiences and the show was really given up to the British AA Battery. About 2,000 people were in the audience, all in very good mood. Before the show I met Parks Johnson and Warren Hull, both of whom had been with the show for some time[21] and were very popular, and I also went over

---

18 An experienced theatre actress, Lawrence's husband, Richard Aldrich, was a lieutenant in the US Navy.
19 Vickers and Sperry both produced analogue predictors for use with anti-aircraft guns. British troops knew them as Predictor AA No 1 and Predictor AA No 2 respectively.
20 A popular radio programme which included human interest features, interviews and quizzes.
21 Parks Johnson had presented the radio program *Vox Pop* since its launch in 1932, but Warren Hull had only recently replaced Neil O'Malley.

the whole script, or at least the questions that were to be asked, just to see that they weren't likely to create any bad feeling or anti-American/British propaganda. Gunner Newman, our photographer, was there as usual taking pictures.

Just as a relief for the British boys, they had the original Popeye and his wife 'Betty Boop'[22] on the show. They were both young looking, despite the fact that they had been in films and on the air for many years. It was extremely interesting seeing this soldier (he'd been in the Army CA (AAA) for six weeks) doing such a low voice act with no apparent effort.

Tuesday 14 September was the day of the Secretary of War's visit. A clear blue sky heralded well for the big day. A guard of honour under Lieutenant Cross was early afoot looking immaculate, and the bush telegram was working overtime to give a time for the visit of Mr Stimson. The firing point was all set up with the heavies to fire first, followed by the Bofors. Mr Stimson duly arrived at the firing point after having been welcomed by an American guard of honour at Camp Edwards. He was accompanied by Lieutenant General McNair commanding home forces, Major General Green, commanding AAA Command and their aides. The British guard of honour at the firing point – twenty-four men strong – give the general salute (very smartly) and Mr Stimson inspected them. Lieutenant Colonel Tom Metcalf then escorted him to the 3.7 inch position and firing commenced. It was an exceptionally good show and one with which Mr Stimson appeared to be duly impressed.

All the officers had lunch with Mr Stimson and his entourage which included six generals, and I got all their autographs for the Battery book. About fifty sat down to lunch of soup, fish and the most beautiful steaks I've seen for four years. There was no speechmaking, just eating. The Secretary then disappeared and the Battery was given cease firing, which enabled the equipment to be got ready for the next move. In one and a half hours we were on the way to Camp Edwards, saying goodbye to Scorton Neck and thanking them for the good firing facilities and for the help given to us in doing our job.

There was feverish activity by everyone as a convoy had been arranged for 1630 hours to take the Battery into Boston. Before we left, the Colonel gave a talk to the Battery pointing out the difficulties which might likely be experienced in Boston with the so-called Irish element. It was a fact that there was more pro-American (one can hardly justifiably call it anti-British) feeling in Boston than anywhere else so far encountered, although I had been told that Chicago and the Middle West had similar elements. Editorials in the papers had spent a week criticising Mr Churchill's Harvard speech in which he hinted at a union after the war[23]. Their main idea was that America was fighting to be free and they didn't consider being a member of a union that admitted all the colony troubles that the British were supposed to have, being free. Therefore they quoted the lines of 'Old Glory' and said America for the Americans[24].

At around this time I went with Colonel Metcalf to an evening boy scouts meeting in Falmouth, to talk to them about their brother movement in England. We took Gunner Heys with us, who was an assistant scout master in England, and Colonel Hunter acted as guide. Going first to the house of Colonel Carswell, we met his wife and his son who was a patrol leader in the scouts 43rd Falmouth Company[25]. Having an hour to spare, we wandered down the main street, a street in a town of about 25,000 inhabitants, something like my own home town [Goole]. Frame houses were a feature of the residential district, each one separated from the next by a nice lawn and lots of trees. The main street, a symphony of neon lights telling us of Ed's Place, the stores, the theatre, was fairly quiet at seven o'clock at night, but the main attraction was still the novelty shop. An English-type church was a very attractive feature of the town, again set in plenty of green space.

By that time we were ready for the boy scouts. Colonel Metcalf and I had taken this hour's opportunity to analyse things. We thought very much along the same lines, I was pleased to say (because I admired his calm and his judgement). After watching the ceremonies attendant upon the opening of the scout meeting; saluting the colours, obedience to the scout law, etc., the colonel delivered a wonderful little speech to the assembled boys, whose ages ranged from eleven to

---

22 Cole is being unintentionally confusing here. Popeye's girlfriend was Olive Oyl, while Betty Boop was a character from a different cartoon. However, Popeye was voiced by Jack Mercer and, at this time, both Betty Boop and Olive Oyl were voiced by Mercer's then wife Margie Hines. Incidentally according to his biography, Mercer, like Popeye, joined the US Navy, not the army, during the Second World War.

23 On 6 September 1943 Winston Churchill received an honorary degree from Harvard University and during his speech said in reference to the British and United States combined chiefs of staff committee 'it would be a most foolish and improvident act on the part of our two governments, or either of them, to break up this smooth-running and immensely powerful machinery the moment the war is over.'

24 'Old Glory' is one of the nicknames given to the American Flag. Cole is probably referring to the American national anthem, the *Star Spangled Banner*, another of the flag's nicknames, each verse of which ends with 'the land of the free and the home of the brave.'

25 Falmouth is a town in Barnstable County Massachusetts and the terminal for ferries to the island Martha's Vineyard.

Above: Bofors night firing. The illumination is provided by searchlights

Right: the six generals who accompanied Secretary Stimson on his visit to the British Battery. Left to right Generals Kirk, Wells, Campbell, Spiller, Green and Smith. They are standing in front of an aeroplane, but what sort is almost impossible to tell

Gen Spiller   Gen. Green

Kirk

Gen. Wells

Gen. Campbell

Gen. Smith

seventeen. He then handed over to Gunner Heys, who delivered a three-quarter of an hour's talk in a masterful way and demonstrated his intimate knowledge of scouting. It was however very interesting to note how a flair for dramatisation and publicity had crept in, even among the gunners, after the overdose to which we were being subjected.

We felt hungry en route back to camp and called in at the USO [see chapter 4] where the manager welcomed us and told us his usual story of the history of the USOs. It certainly was a very nice place and it seemed to me that by pooling the resources of the YMCA, the NAAFI, Church Army, WVS, etc., they had really achieved a more viable composite organisation of real strength and merit instead of our many smaller units.

Once again it was time to move as on Wednesday [15 September] the Battery was to split into three contingents each going their separate ways. I took command of the detachment to go to the staff college at Fort Leavenworth [Kansas]; Captain Scorer, the administration captain, took command of the party going to Camp Irwin [California]; and Captain Keys, the light troop commander, took command of the party going to Fort Knox [Kentucky]. Lieutenant Colonel Metcalf had to divide his time between Camp Irwin and Fort Knox and then join up with the third detachment at San Francisco, while Colonel Muirhead, the Senior Artillery Officer BASW, was to join the detachment at Leavenworth. We were all to meet again on 7 October in Camp Haan, California.

The forming up of the correct vehicles to load onto the correct trains took time, especially as the weather was

the worst so far experienced in the States, blowing half a gale and pouring with rain. We finally got all the equipment loaded and I checked the train and arranged for a guard to be mounted. That evening we enjoyed one of the few quiet evenings we had had since landing. I spent it writing and watching some Technicolor photographs projected by Derek Scorer of scenes he had encountered in the States. I finally went to bed at 2230 hours ready for what might be a very hectic period of detachment.

The following day was very busy with parades, kit loading, packing, checking to see that all blankets were handed back, false alarms about train positions, lack of transport to the point where we boarded the train as all our own transport was on the train, more cooks spoiling more broth, order, counter order and disorder before the eventual sorting out of all the odd points and finally a check by me to see that everything was OK.

I was especially happy because I sat in my office and brought my diary up-to-date. I wanted to be able to sit in my compartment on the train and describe the journey. It's something I had always wanted to do; have a three- to four-day journey on a train to discount or prove all the stories I'd heard about one of these journeys.

We left our barracks and went the mile to the train. No Pullmans were on yet, but the men were all there waiting. After an hour and a half's wait the carriages duly arrived and we got the men settled to a prearranged plan, only to find that we had to alter it to enable the officers to get any accommodation. We had failed to take into account the innumerable number of train attendants, Pullman conductors, etc., who had naturally got themselves settled in the compartments and, equally naturally, refused to move, although not in so many words. However we did a little reshuffling and got all the ninety-five British, thirty-two American other ranks, six officers and one warrant officer on board, and they immediately settled into their various occupations – what they were I had yet to see but felt certain that the main one was going to be sleeping.

And so we left New England. I looked forward with keenness to the next phase of our tour; a cross-country jaunt of eight day's travel in two stages, the first to Fort Leavenworth in Kansas, almost half-way across America.

CHAPTER 7

A LONG JOURNEY

It is no secret that the average Englishman has no idea of the vastness of the great North American continent. I must confess to abysmal ignorance myself in that matter. I was curious, therefore, to know what my reactions would be to a train journey which would take three and a half days. Having settled myself down I realised how much more attraction there was in the first hour in the train itself rather than the scenery; I'd glanced out once only since we set off. In front of me, in the section of the train I called my own – my bed, my office and my workshop – I had neatly placed my deed box (annexed for the trip from the quartermaster at Camp Davis) and my souvenir box, both of which I intended during this trip to sort out.

The train, with four Pullmans, a diner, a baggage car, twelve vehicle trucks carrying two heavy guns, one 40 mm gun, one searchlight and, bringing up the rear, a 'caboose' or, as we know it, guard's van, was a streamlined diesel electric. The engine, as far as I could see, was two trains in one, so making it possible to pull either way with equal speed. The escort attachment commanded by Captain Grewe, had the first Pullman and we had the last three.

We certainly had a cross-section in our officers. Rhys Evans: Welsh, generally even tempered, but when roused developing that childish fury that knows no bounds and would not be appeased except by segregation. Ray Dix: often bombastic, very clever, sometimes ruthless, always disliking anyone ordering him to do anything, a one man's man, could be a bitter enemy, disliked by some for his Jewish faith, self-opinionated, but more often than not cleverly right, excellent public speaker or compere, generally a very difficult man to lead, but with plenty of initiative. Philip Mollett: a typical Englishman in the eyes of the Yanks, pipe smoking, young, old school tie, always liked privacy for his dressing and undressing, a child at heart, but a good friend if you knew how to treat him, always open to have his leg pulled and half the time didn't realise it was being pulled, capricious, a fine looking young man, but one who had not discovered how to use his brain to the best advantage and had to be led rather than being a leader. Len Vyse: quiet generally, easy-going, rugged and clever in his stoic sort of way, mean when he was roused, often lazy, but worked hard when the occasion demanded, independent, but occasionally came out of his skin and went to town. Eugene Grewe (American): hard-working, stern, petite, methodical, little sense of humour, but then so unapproachable that there had never been an opportunity to test his sense of humour. Altogether, it was going to have to be a very strange sort of joke at which we all laughed, an amazing party we all enjoyed and a good place that pleased all of us.

The leaves were beginning to change colour with the approach of autumn, or as they seemed to call it in America

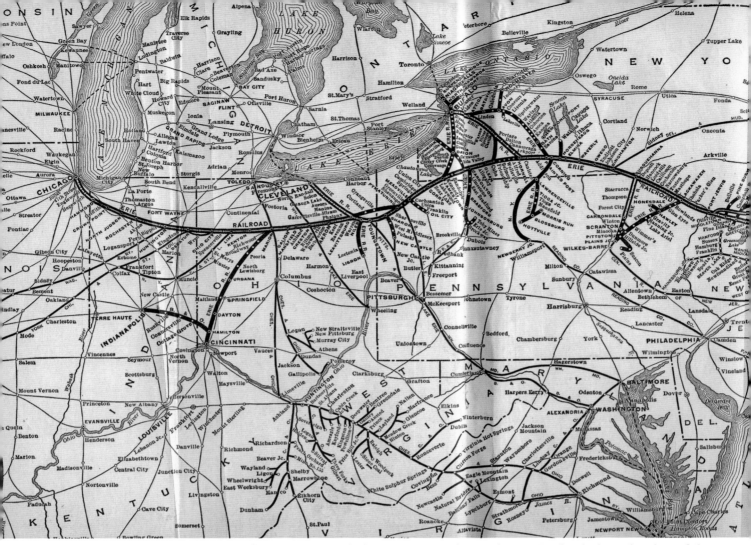

'early fall', being the equivalent of our August period. As we passed out of New England, the colouring of the trees and of the grasses began to assume a beauty that was reminiscent of the English autumn, spoiled only when in a neighbouring field you saw the long wavy spikes of corn on the cob. I regretted not being a botanist. The country that we were passing through was a paradise for anybody who wanted to see different kinds of trees and ferns. According to the *Christian Science Monitor*:

'California redwood trees, may one day be a common sight across the nation because of the hobby of a San Francisco businessman. Clarence F. Pratt has sent seedlings to practically every state, and they are thriving. He digs the seedlings himself on weekends, keeps them planted in tins in a little nursery, and takes batches of them with him to distribute on business trips. Upon request, he mails seedlings at his own expense to anyone who will plant and care for them. His only stipulation is that they be given plenty of room, because in 5,000 years each might be fifty feet or more across!'

We had already started on what were to be the interminable stops, shunting and sidetracking always associated with troop trains to get them out of the way of faster or more urgent traffic. We paused in the town of Walpole [Norfolk County, Massachusetts], whose main immediate feature seemed to be a machine foundry with little or nothing else. It was so difficult to judge from a train when the town was covered with a halo of trees. As we left, it became apparent that there was another feature of Walpole; sand quarries and brick foundries, quite a few disused.

The diners on the cars were supplied as day cars and were shunted on and off the trains; one shunted off after the evening meal and the following day we picked up a new one. After two hours on the train one lot of thirty-six men had eaten. Creamed chicken à la king. The folks at home would not have been able to imagine that on our trains. The food was by ticket to the other ranks; officers had to pay at the rate of one dollar per meal. Five shillings per meal was expensive, especially when you had three meals a day at that price. At any rate the food was good, and for the first meal we must have got half a chicken each. It was followed by the best ice cream I'd tasted yet. Negro waiters seemed almost to fill the car and the service was excellent and, much to our astonishment, the steward in charge told me that he wouldn't charge us for the meal – it would be on them. A very nice gesture and one we were quick to take advantage of.

During the meal we passed through a town, very slowly, as though we wanted to let people see that we were a troop train. The town was Mansfield [Bristol County, Massachusetts] and steel manufacture was the only thing in the way of industry I saw. On the other hand, there seemed plenty of friendly populace. Half the time, they didn't know who we were, so I felt sure that the friendly waving must be the same as any other body of troops with equipment would get.

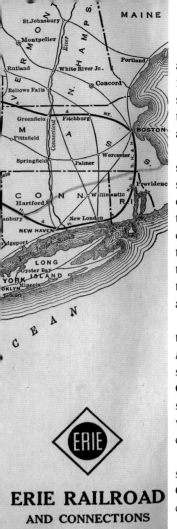

ERIE RAILROAD
AND CONNECTIONS

Beds were then made up and card parties getting well underway. The boys were accustomed by then to American money and the odd Americanism was beginning to creep into their language. All the men had been given permission to wear sand shoes and shirt sleeve order, as the carriages were quite warm, with one air-conditioned exception. I had tried to lay plans to ensure that standards didn't drop too far but I wondered how far my attempt would be looked upon as a dictatorship and stopping the natural fun.

Sitting and lounging about played havoc with the digestion and the muscles so organised stops were arranged for physical training (PT) and exercise for the men. Every time we stopped for the engine to pick up water[1] we got out for ten minutes PT. In addition the officers regularly inspected the vehicles to see how they were riding. The flat railroad trucks were each sixty feet long and took two vehicles, but had no side protection. The occasionally desperate jerking of the train was heavy on the vehicles, but we expected them to be okay as they had all been wired onto the flats and blocks fitted in front of and behind the wheels. Six guards were out on the vehicles and, from reports the following morning, they had had a freezing night, their overcoats having been packed and their only protection against the piercing wind being the cab of a motor vehicle.

It had already grown very dark by 1915 hours and the boys opened up with one of their sing-songs. It was quite a treat to hear them singing the old songs *It's a long way to Tipperary, Run, Rabbit, Run*, etc., etc., but then in usual style someone started singing smutty lyrics. Out came the comb and paper and that, combined with the noise of Captain Grewe typing letters home on his portable typewriter, made Dixie and myself appear very studious; I was catching up on some of our souvenir pasting, he was reading. Mollett, wandering about like a father waiting in the maternity home for news, didn't know what to do and didn't want to let anyone else get on with whatever they were doing.

We laid on lights out for 2230 and reveille for 0700 hours, but by nine o'clock the only sounds were the clink of coins from two groups of four fellows playing cards. Captain Grewe and I were the last to bed and I just had a wander through the train to see that everything was OK.

The following morning after shaving and washing in cold water I found we were stopped next to our other troop train (going to Irwin), and that in fact we'd only covered 132 miles in the night, being then stopped in sidings at a town called Maybrook [a major rail hub in Orange County, New York State]. For the first time in America we were beginning to see hills and hilly districts. The train had, no doubt, been routed to keep to the coastal plains. We checked over the vehicles and extra wired some parts to prevent shearing.

By that time the porter in charge of the Pullman had cleared away the beds and we were a normal train again, with people glad to sit in their seats. The porter had been continually moving from one train to another for six weeks, without ever knowing his destination until he arrived there. He had not seen his wife for that period and didn't expect to see her for another four weeks. I wondered when he received letters if ever.

Philip M. eventually settled down to reading Emily Bronte's *Wuthering Heights*; not particularly because he wanted to read a book, but because it was a book about Yorkshire, of which he was not only proud, but darned snobbish. He wanted to, and did, tell everybody that it was a book about Yorkshire if they gave him the slightest opportunity. Rhys had so far not said or done anything but sit and snooze and read. I thought at the time that his must have been an interesting book (*I am thinking of my Darling* by Vincent McHugh).

The railway track we were on was clean, without the weeds that seemed to encroach on most other tracks we'd been on. By then we were out of Massachusetts, and off the New York, New Haven and Hartford line into New York State, and on the Erie Railroad. We had been told we were going to Chicago but not on a direct route, so there was little possibility of us visiting any big cities with the exception

Exercise en route

---

1   At the beginning of the chapter Cole stated that the locomotive was a diesel-electric which would not need to pick up water regularly. It had presumably been changed for a steam engine without Cole mentioning the fact.

of Akron[2]. We were not to stop there, but just to get onto the main Chicago-Kansas City line. I was interested to note that the trains in the US had a much bigger number of freight cars than in England. It seemed nothing unusual to see fifty or sixty cars to one engine, and I did see one towing over 120 cars.

Ours was a teetotal train and drink of any kind was not allowed. I also discovered that we were going to a dry state. That was a good thing in many ways. We should save money, have less trouble and be able to converse and listen to conversations more quickwittedly. Not that it had been any other way so far, but you had to be absolutely keen to answer the thousand and one questions we got asked.

At that point in my musing, breakfast was called; it was excellent although this time we had to pay for it. The American boys seemed to be a little discontented with the food. I asked how the troops enjoyed their meals and usually got the same answer: 'oh, all right', pause, grimace, from the Americans. 'Fine, grand, OK,' from the British.

I wondered whether the American soldier in America was pampered and spoiled. In England the British boys were used to being joggled around, but as a result always appreciated the better, anything that was done for them. I was interested to see, as I toured the train that 60% of the men were asleep, 20% gazing into space, 10% playing cards, 5% reading a book and the rest doing odd things like mending or cleaning their kit.

Philip, in his usual style, confused the waiters at breakfast by changing his mind three times over the question of how he wanted his eggs, as though it was the most important thing in the world. He also enlightened us by a very vivid description of how he was seasick on a cross-channel journey and crowned the whole of his foolishness by buying my collection of eighty-two match book covers for thirty dollars, nearly all of which I had been given. Amid all the excitement of breakfast and its aftermath, the train stopped in Port Jervis [Orange County, New York]. We managed to pick up papers to find the Fifth and Eighth Armies in Italy had made contact at Salerno [see footnote; chapter 6]. Good news because the Fifth had been having a very bloody battle.

We were by then emerging into country where land was under cultivation. Shallow rivers, waterfalls, wooded hills and cultivated valleys – no towns – presented a really nice break after swamps and trees alone. The scenery was getting more beautiful and I was reminded of something I'd read, written by Louis Bannigan:

'Crossing the Iowa Prairie by train, one July day many years ago, I was enchanted by the gorgeous masses of hollyhocks that lined the right of way. A brakeman explained that a traveller had scattered the seed for 200 miles along the tracks. These glowing spires were the result. Ever since, the pockets of my coat have a handful of nuts or fruit pits and an envelope of perennial flower seeds. Most of them are gathered on walks in autumn, as casually as they are planted. Now I have patches of beach plum and pitch pine along the New England shore and sea grapes in Florida and peaches and creamy-bellied yucca almost anywhere. It's a lot of fun as anyone who tries it will learn.'

Hornell was a very friendly town as evidenced by the editorial of the local paper:

**'The Evening Tribune, September 17, 1943
THEY HIRED THE MONEY**
by S. Burton Heath, NEA [National Editorial Association] Editorial Writer

When the argument over collection of 1917-18 war debts grew hot, Calvin Coolidge settled it, so far as he and others of his view were concerned, with the rhetorical semi-question: 'They hired the money, didn't they?'

Apparently there is much of the same philosophy still current. President Roosevelt, who is internationally minded way beyond his Yankee predecessor's wildest moments, now disclaims the statement sent to Congress over his initials that 'victory and secure peace are the only coin in which we can be repaid' for our lend-lease to the anti-Axis world.

Mr Roosevelt now says that one of his ghosts prepared the letter to Congress in which that sentence appeared, and he never approved it. He would not have said just that, he discloses.

That is too bad, because we doubt if even the President, a phrasemaker of consummate skill, could have improved upon the statement he now repudiates. He could have elaborated, explained, justified. But he couldn't have made it say so much that is true with any greater clarity.

In his apology, Mr Roosevelt says that, while we may not collect coins that jingle, he expects our debtors to come through with such repayment as they possibly can.

That means nothing at all. We all expect creditors to pay, so far as they can. Our creditors expect, and probably are quite willing, to pay up so far as they can. The trouble is that for practical purposes, they cannot pay in any coin that we can accept with one possible exception. Some of them could pay with the territory. But do we want territory? Haven't we troubles enough with the limited empire, we now possess?

Probably skillions of words have been spoken and written in argument about World War I debts, and now the same words will be spoken and written about World War II debts. When it's all done, we will not have been paid, and the reason will boil down to this:

Our debtors can't pay in money, because there isn't that much money. They can't pay in goods, because we can't take that much in goods without wrecking our own economy. They could pay, partially at least, in insular territory, in which we should assume the white man's burden and, ultimately, turn it free.

Mr Roosevelt's ghost was right the first time.'

I took a ride in the cab of one of the vehicles so that I could see the country in perspective – and also to get a novel experience of riding in a lorry on a train. I rode there for about an hour. You certainly got the views of the countryside. We'd been following the Delaware river which flows to the sea at Wilmington, Delaware. We passed such towns as Port Jervis and Callicoon [Sullivan County, New York] and followed the valley the whole way up to Deposit [Delaware County, New York], where we stopped, changed our guard and then continued on our way.

---

2   The city was vital for the manufacture of rubber and home to all four major tyre producers. Goodyear's subsidiary Zeppelin, based in Akron, made airships for use during the Second World War.

We'd soon been in Massachusetts, Connecticut, New York and Pennsylvania and still had three more days to go. Prompted by the changing scenery, Mollett bet Dix that he could write more states in the US down from memory than could Dix. The time limit was set at half an hour. After much mental touring of the States each claimed to have got forty-seven states out of forty eight[3], but couldn't think of the other one. The winner was left to the American judge, Gene Grewe, to decide. First he had some crossing out to do of states that had been set up by new pioneer, Ray Dix. He invented two new states, but got two more right than Mollett, so they tied. Both got forty-three right. Both missed Vermont. Anyhow the game was instructive and we wondered how many Americans travelling in England could name the counties. To settle the bet Dix and Mollett arranged another contest. Grewe was to name towns, and D and M to write down which state they were in. Dix collected the dollar with eight out of twelve right.

With the entry of coffee and sandwiches, hawked by the Negro waiters as an addition to their salaries, came a period of discussion among the officers. Talk varied from foreign policy in Siam to the merits and demerits of J. B. Priestley. I wanted to collect my thoughts about America and Russia, America and England, America and China, America and the Theatre, America and Democracy, America and its States. All these things were the subject of great controversy in America at the time and they certainly required very careful thought before making any statement of opinion.

We stopped for thirty-five minutes in Hornell [Steuben County, New York], a town I should estimate at about 40,000 people[4]. We had once again caught up with the Irwin contingent. A crowd of people obviously attracted by the first train stayed to look us over, almost as though we were a circus or zoo passing through. They had very good intentions, because they gave us magazines, papers and a big welcome. One woman even went so far as to give Vyse her address and ask him to write to her saying that she would write back. The men did their ten minutes PT, much to the amusement of the populace, but I could not let them go across to the shops. They would have got no beneficial exercise and we should have got no boys back on the train for at least half an hour after the time we wanted to start. Not because of any ulterior motive on their part, but because people would have been too kind to them and delayed them. Instead we sent two members from each carriage to buy newspapers, oranges and anything else the men needed. That became the drill at each PT stop, although at Huntingdon [Huntingdon County, Pennsylvania] we nearly left two of the shopping men behind.

Shaking of the train made writing difficult and, in the middle of writing a letter, a heated discussion broke out in my carriage. An American corporal stopped at a place on the carriage where four Tommies were reading magazines. He pointed to an article about the RAF and in fun, presumably, pointed out that the RAF weren't everything. That started it and it developed into a kidding match, with the Fifth and Eighth Armies being banded about like matchsticks. At one time I felt the humour was going out of it because the Tommies were beginning to pull the Yank's leg to such an extent that it was developing into a series of artlessly-worded insults being thrown at each other. However, when one Tommy asked whether the Flying Fortress was an advanced trainer[5], I knew that the position was saved. It gradually settled down without the necessity of my interfering, but it showed how quickly an incident could flare. Fortunately there was only one American. If there had been more the fur might have flown or I should have had to have broken it up.

Again my attention was drawn to the changing scenery. Earlier I'd seen a glorious view of a large valley stretching at right angles to the train as far as the eye could see, with the hills blue black in the background. Then we seemed to be

---

3   Today there are fifty states in the United States. In 1943, when Cole was writing, neither Alaska nor Hawaii had joined the union. They both became members in 1959, Alaska on 3 January and Hawaii on 21 August.
4   American towns are generally less densely populated than English ones; in the mid twentieth century Hornell had a population of around 16,000.
5   The Boeing B17 Flying Fortress was probably the most successful heavy bomber of the war and undertook precision daylight bombing raids against German targets. Propaganda would ensure that the British troops knew that.

cutting across a section of valleys, mostly heavily wooded, with streams running down the centre. That gave way to the first corn (wheat) that I'd seen. The absence of potatoes, wheat, oats, barley, cabbages, etc., had been most noticeable.

We stopped at the station at Salamanca [Cattaraugus County, New York] and again people were very friendly. It was on an Indian reservation – somehow I hadn't thought they really existed, but this was a real one[6]. The Indians lived there, but as to how they lived or why they lived like that or what they lived on, I remained ignorant.

To keep the men's interest going – and to keep them out of mischief for a couple of hours – I'd arranged a small whist drive, with prizes, for the second evening. I had made arrangements to have the diner, so we could get it properly organised. Packs of cards were gathered up and scorecards made and, at half-past eight, I went to find the people for the drive. Found twenty three and discovered that five more who wanted to play were in a game of Nap[7], which was getting ridiculously high in the stakes for other ranks. $25 [several weeks' pay for most ordinary soldiers] was on the table when I arrived, but I couldn't very well butt in at that stage. All the men had drawn a month's pay and it probably made them feel rich.

While I was directing the whist, Grewe and Evans got deep into a chess game – in many ways they were very much alike and often played chess together. Rhys played a good game, always. During the journey I played a very fast and very interesting game of chess with him, which I lost, after gaining the ascendancy, through pure carelessness. As usual Mollett dithered between everything. We decided to call some of his sayings 'Mollyisms', and even invented one for him, to start the ball rolling: 'absinthe makes the heart grow warmer'. The whist drive was a complete success, ten hands being played and I'm sure everyone enjoyed it. For the third evening we'd planned a singsong.

Pay parade. This is later in the tour in the Mojave Desert near Camp Haan

We passed through the big industrial city of Akron [Summit County, Ohio] during the night, but only saw the lights. The guards were frozen and I had to pay out a dollar for the guards' hot drink during the night. It was customary in the army to have a hot drink for the guard, no matter if there are not funds or facilities. If they don't get one the men think they are being cheated out of it, especially if waiters bring round coffee as they did last night at 2215 hours. Even so they had to go without on the third night of our journey as the baggage car, which was not a corridor car, was put in between the Pullmans and the vehicles.

The night was extremely cold for everyone; we in our Pullman never got warm and lost a lot of sleep. In the morning we had the heaters turned on and sweltered, but were unable to open the windows, without getting covered in soot. Memories of being so desperately cold meant that we kept the steam heat on during the night, but roasted and again slept less than normal; the Pullman porter had to admit that he couldn't just get it quite right. Health aboard the train was generally good however and the medical corporal had nothing to do.

Day three dawned on the train but we were well on our way, being about a hundred miles south of Detroit at a place called Marion [Marion County, Ohio] on the Erie Railroad. We'd travelled about 1,400 miles so far although the route we were using was probably three to four hundred miles longer than the main route to keep us on flat country. Apparently the Erie railroad was used for all big traffic that required headroom, as there were few hills or tunnels. Consequently it was no unusual sight to see a hundred invasion barges pass by on one train. On the small-town railway crossings, I found they put an old man or woman in the road with a stop sign. What happened at night, when they couldn't be seen, I didn't know, but thought a lamp was probably used.

Breakfasts, like most mealtimes, were mostly a riot of fun with Dixie ribbing Mollett and Vyse alternately – the officers were all in excellent tempers. Grewe just sat and occasionally smiled and sometimes excelled himself by coming out

6   The Allegany Indian Territories managed by the Seneca Nation.
7   A card game, similar to whist, Nap (Napoleon) was very popular in the nineteenth and early twentieth century.

with an odd sentence in his very staccato speech, which we always had to ask him to repeat.

The waiter in charge talked to us that morning and really unbent. It seemed that he had been in service with rich people in Miami, Florida. He told us of the day about ten to twelve years previously, before the Wall Street crash[8], when rich people used to hire diners just for themselves and had five or six homes in all the best places in America and Europe. He was profuse about their antics, their wealth and the 'bad' days which had now come to pass. He labelled all present-day things as trash compared

40 mm anti-tank drill

to the good things of ten to twelve years ago but I felt he was a little biased on the subject as he admitted that the same number of years had seen an exceptionally big change in standards of living, even before war came. I suspected that he was a little sore that his day of big tips and big parties with their resultant benefits to the service people had, according to his story, gone.

According to Walter Winchell[9] we ought to have all been geniuses. He defined genius as 'the infinite capacity for taking trains'. We'd been over two days in the train and I was getting used to it. Time was nonexistent, but I still couldn't find time to read. There were so many books in this world; so many masterpieces which I knew of and which I wanted, really wanted, to read and so far had only glanced through one magazine. Yet I'd found time to write, even though I'd had to share my table with Evans' and Grewe's chess game. It rather cramped my writing style but was good for morale!! I'd also been eating Hershey's milk chocolate[10] and felt that I'd neglected those at home by not sending them some.

After one of the last meals on that particular diner, the negro waiter was quick to remind me that I should have a whip round for the tips. It appeared these waiters get $62 (£15.10.00) per month and relied for the rest on tips. Naturally, they looked after their interests, although I couldn't help thinking that they got paid more than the troops did. We had a collection and the Tommies collected $6.75, the Americans 25¢. It looked as though they didn't like things, especially as 15¢ of this was given by one sergeant.

The conductor brought me two maps which showed the whole route we were travelling. He told me that that it was just under 999 miles from New York to Chicago, that twenty-three railways met in Chicago and that Chicago was the place where East meets West. As the city was at the base of Lake Michigan, the railways ran along the sides of the lake and converged in Chicago.

First he told me we should not go into Chicago, but only as far as 50th Street, where we changed engines and the diner. Then we would move back again onto the Wabash line and the Chicago-Burlington-Quincy Railroad[11]. We had by then been through another three states; Ohio, Indiana and Illinois and had two more to go through, Missouri and Kansas, which made a total of nine states on the trip. We stayed just sufficiently long to get a glimpse of the city from the railway, which was disappointing, especially as the conductor said that there we should have seen a city at peace – no blackout or dim out. Everything was carrying on as normal with the exception of soldiers and sailors on the street and industry geared up to a higher pitch, with consequently more money to spend for all workers. And this was the city which, one heard through the press, dared criticise Britain at war[12].

---

8   The stock market crash of 1929 which signalled the beginning of a twelve-year depression. Considered to be the most severe stock market devaluation ever, share prices fell by 89%.
9   Probably the most powerful and feared gossip columnist and radio commentator in America in the 1930s and 1940s.
10 Hershey's was and is the largest chocolate company and one of the oldest in North America.
11 Both lines headed west out of Chicago taking different routes, but intersecting at various towns.
12 During the war the editor of the *Chicago Tribune* was Robert R McCormick who reported in 1938 that the British Ambassador to the US was 'stubborn, slow thinking and bellicose'. McCormick was anti-British, leaked several militarily-sensitive documents through his newspaper, opposed any US involvement in the Second World War and was convinced that Chicago was superior to everywhere else.

While on the train we tended to read local papers which gave interesting and different opinions on subjects I thought I knew well. For example I read a copy of the *Chicago Herald*, a Hearst paper[13]. Its editorial was a diatribe against the young communist parties and against Russia generally. A piece of real armchair politics, but at least I saw both sides of the question.

Chicago really started at Hammond, twenty miles away. The distance across Chicago, its suburbs and factories, was forty-two miles. Lake Michigan's shores, for forty miles, were lined with factories which stretched even on to Lake George, which was linked to Lake Michigan by a small river along whose banks Henry Ford had built a huge assembly plant. In peace time this plant was reputed to turn out 2,000 cars per day, but it was then turning out trucks, armoured cars, etc. Factory after factory normally turning out automobiles, was turned over to tanks; one factory alone was supposed to turn out twelve sixty-ton tanks per day. They were loaded onto barges and transported via Lake Michigan to Detroit for shipment all over the world. There was no doubt about the terrific productive capacity of Chicago when you saw the railways coming into and going out of it. Marshalling or, as they call them here, classification yards were there in abundance. This area was also John Dillinger's country; sixteen miles from Hammond was where he made his escape from jail with a soap pistol[14].

Moving through the outskirts of Chicago, we were in Eleanor Roosevelt's country. There she was revered because of the terrific housing project which she sponsored to house factory workers. They paid only $8.30 per month, and never failed to bless her as they paid [see chapter 4]. For the first time since leaving the New York area we were in a city of steel and concrete. We saw the gas and coke factory, granaries, steel manufactories, that covered acre upon acre and all working hard. The Pullman works which made the cars we were travelling in – and a good job they made of them too, except for the many cracks that let in the dust and soot – were about a mile from the track.

Just to provide contrast, there were a few odd fields of rhubarb. I'd never seen it growing in fields before and had always associated it with an upturned flowerpot or bucket with a bottom out.

I had an interesting discussion with an American soldier, a member of the escort detachment, about the WACs[15]. Judging from what I'd seen and heard, the WACs were in the same sort of repute in America at that time, as our ATS was before conscription started[16]. Only 'common' girls were supposed to join. I thought it a pity that we hadn't brought ATS girls over. We might have helped to correct that impression.

Just outside Chicago we and the Irwin train stopped in a siding for two hours to get our engine changed and rearrange the whole train. I took the opportunity to inspect the vehicles and found everything OK. I also inspected the insides of equipment. I couldn't imagine how everything had survived in the light of the heavy jarring and bumping that everything had had. The two trains moved away together, but Irwin moved faster and again took the lead; the two trains kept on the same route right up to Kansas City and then Irwin went on for another three days.

Dinner was a luxurious meal. Mollett was again the chief attraction. He certainly had stood up to some ribbing. That night his best Molleyism was: 'well, if I had to stay in the States, I should like to be governor of Georgia and make a real job of pulling that country together. It's the American skeleton in the cupboard'[17]. It was all the more funny when you realise that he had difficulty in organising a tea party.

By the time we had had dinner it was dark and, apart from lights, we didn't see anything of Illinois at all. We just moved out across the famed Mississippi, with its bridges brilliantly lit up, into the state of Missouri.

The next day was Sunday (19 September) and I was up at 0710 hours, and dying for a cigarette only to find I'd used my last one of the last packet. Rhys Evans came to my rescue. It was remarkable how quickly you got used to American cigarettes. Over in England, I was a 'Players Please'[18] man. I never smoked anything else and spurned free packs of Americans because they were too strong. Then I became a Chesterfield man and could hardly remember what an English cigarette tasted like.

As the day was Sunday we were thinking about holding a service of song, if we could get through our cleaning up in time. We had about 120 miles yet to go but everybody still began to pack up. We had a conference to work out details of unloading, etc., with all officers and the sergeant major present. We were determined to get things through OK without a lot of fuss and bother and everyone was briefed about disembarking. Time was on our side, so we thought we should be OK. Nothing appeared to have gone wrong with equipment so far as travelling went, although by this time quite a number of the men were affected by tummy troubles, diarrhoea, etc., which was supposed to be due to change of water.

13 William Randolph Hearst was an American newspaper magnate who, at one time, owned thirty newspapers.
14 Dillinger escaped from Crown Point Jail, Indiana before he could be tried for the murder of East Chicago police officer William O'Malley. He escaped using a fake gun made of wood and painted with shoe polish, although he quickly swapped it for one of the guards' guns. Members of the Dillinger gang, Harry Pierpont and Charley Makley, used guns carved out of soap in an attempt to escape Death Row in the Columbus, Ohio penitentiary.
15 Members of the Women's Army Corps. Starting life in 1942 as the Women's Army Auxiliary Corps, it dropped the 'Auxiliary' part of its name in 1943. It was originally modelled on the Auxiliary Territorial Service (ATS) which was the women's branch of the British Army during the Second World War.
16 Rightly or wrongly, the women's auxiliary services in Britain initially suffered from a reputation for immorality; 'officers' groundsheets' was a commonly expressed sentiment. Regardless of whether such a sentiment was true or not, the adverse publicity hampered recruitment as many girls didn't want to get the reputation of being the sort of girl whose morals fitted her for the ATS.
17 During 1943 and 1944 a commission of twenty-three members of the Georgia General Assembly were revising and simplifying the Georgian constitution.
18 A reference to the ubiquitous advertising for Players cigarettes, often featuring a bearded sailor sporting a cap with the legend *HMS Excellent* on the hat band; in earlier advertisements the hat band said *HMS Hero*.

Everyone was dressed again in battledress after three days in shirt, trousers and slippers. Strewn around the carriage was that monument of British imperial folly, the sun helmet[19] which had, as its only justification to existence on the trip, the right to appear in after-the-war fancy dress balls as the most travelled and least used hat in being. At the time it was nothing but a damn nuisance.

My first view of the skyscrapers of Kansas City was over the River Missouri. It was another big industrial city of steel and concrete and fine looking from eight miles away. We never got nearer than four miles to the city so didn't have a chance to buy its papers nor see its people. It's funny how these huge cities dotted the line, between which, as the old Negro said, 'there was miles and miles of miles and miles'.

We arrived at KC at 1300 hours and expected to be in Leavenworth by 1500 hours. By 1530 hours we were still on the train. Finally, after a lot of shunting, changing engines, and stops in sidings, etc., we eventually crossed the Missouri and arrived in Fort Leavenworth. We didn't see the very famous penitentiary[20], but finally clocked in at 1800 hours. Bob Dunlop and Jack Van Noy were there to meet us. Unloading took one hour, a piece of fast action and a credit to Motor Sergeant Howard who certainly could work when he was given independence. The rest of the men had had food and were settled in by 2000 hours.

The arrangements were excellent and left the escort detachment with nothing to do. Feeding was done on cafeteria principle by the camp. Sleeping and barrack quarters were all completed ready for occupation. Feeding was expensive for officers, approximating two dollars per day, but our quarters were a magnificently appointed house, set in its own grounds and situated in an avenue, which like all the streets and avenues round it, was lined with beech trees. The only snag when we first arrived was that the MT [military transport] accommodation was very small and it was difficult to get all our equipment in. We got over that by leaving most of it where it was. After a very welcome bath, I went to bed which, for the first time in over seventy-two hours was not banging and swaying on our long journey.

---

19 Also called the pith helmet, safari helmet or solar topee, the sun helmet was made of cork and covered with fabric, usually white but often khaki for military wear.
20 At the time, the United States Penitentiary Leavenworth was the largest maximum security federal prison in the US. It is a civilian prison but is located within the grounds of Fort Leavenworth.

CHAPTER 8

WE REACH THE MIDWEST

On our first morning at the fort, Monday 20 September, I talked to all the men on parade and outlined the programme during their stay here. I pointed out that Kansas was a long way away; the town of Leavenworth was about thirty miles from Kansas City. As we were going in on Thursday for a War Bond Drive I suggested they investigate the camp and the town of Leavenworth, but if they did go to Kansas, the last bus back as far as they were concerned was 2210 hours.

It was a day of cleaning equipment, everyone setting to with a will to get the guns, etc. up to standard. The officers had to go along to HQ to be introduced to the ADC and the general. General Karl Truesdell was not in – he'd had to go to Washington to be decorated by the Brazilian government – but his second-in-command, Colonel Shellenberger, was. He made us welcome, but we didn't take up much of his time. The general's executive officer saw us next and with Colonel Muirhead from BASW and the two attendant majors who had just arrived we spent some time talking mostly army small talk. When anti-aircraft and infantry met, it was almost like East and West; conversation was always forced. However Colonel M and he discussed the American and British method of including AA in the field army and although it didn't make a penn'oth of difference and didn't mean anything anyway, we successfully wasted half an hour of each other's time and came away having done our duty. Colonel Muirhead saw his role as looking after the senior officers in the fort and speaking on behalf of the British army when necessary so our duties didn't overlap in any way and we dovetailed nicely.

The camp was certainly a beautiful place and the countryside around it was lovely. A background of wooded slopes, huge office buildings, revelling in such names as Grant Hall, Sheridan Hall[1], etc., polo fields, football fields and, above all, civilians around us by the score. Fort Leavenworth combined a staff college and an induction centre. It

Heightfinder and crew at work

1   These two halls are part of the same building. In the late nineteenth century Sheridan Hall and Sherman Hall were two separate structures. Grant Hall was built in the early twentieth century to join them; the result formed the camp's probably most imposing building. At 159 feet the clock tower on Grant Hall is the tallest building in Fort Leavenworth.

was the first time that I'd seen the American civilian changed into a soldier, and I must say it was instructive. A huge notice told the rookie that he was not allowed to have visitors for the first three days. What a hardship! The amazing thing was that the womenfolk wept their eyes almost out when parting from their men here. This show of emotion at camps was something foreign to us, and I personally thought it a very bad system. The civilians around this camp changed its character into that of a beautifully appointed small town. The 'town' had its own theatre, movies, stores, cafeterias and was really self-contained. Not a bad start for the army rookie, and certainly a fine place for a staff college.

On show in Washington Square, Kansas City

A visit to the demonstration ground, sorting out of guards, arranging crash action demonstrations, and the disposition of equipment filled the remainder of the morning, as we were due to be part of the display at the county fair the following day. The British consul in Kansas City had asked to see me that afternoon, to talk over parade arrangements for Thursday. We were going to sell more war bonds. The talk was that our equipment was also to be on parade, but I had to see about that during my visit. Captains Grewe and Dunlop, Colonel Muirhead and myself went into Kansas City that afternoon; the rest of the officers, with the exception of an orderly officer, joined us in the evening.

During the first day I met five majors and a wing commander from various units in Britain who were at Leavenworth on the staff course, preparatory to becoming members of joint Anglo-American staffs. They certainly seemed to work the officers hard when they were there. The course was similar to the one we had in England but set in much more pleasant surroundings and with a slightly more technical bias than ours.

Driving into Kansas City was my first experience of WAC drivers. Dunlop told me of the WAC who refused to drive through KC; he had to take over. It reminded me of the three ATS drivers we had whom we nicknamed Lock, Stock and Barrel. As drivers they made excellent cooks. Fortunately, this was not my main impression of either ATS or WAC drivers. Our driver drove very well and got us into Kansas City in a little less than an hour. Our appointment with the British consul, Mr Price (who strangely enough was a cousin of Major Steel's), and his vice consul, Mr Davidson, took us to the fifteenth floor of the Commerce Building[2], one of the five skyscrapers that form the business part of Kansas City, Missouri.

Kansas City was divided into two halves; the Kansas half dry, the Missouri half wet[3]. The business section I went to shortly after I arrived was in the wet part. Along with other Englishmen I was to take part in a big parade through the city so we had to attend a conference to get full details. We were introduced to a number of representatives of the mayor, each one a very rich citizen taking an active interest in the war bond drive, as part of their war effort. I was whisked away almost immediately by one gentleman to see the route. We were to finish in Washington Square, where they had already set up a B25 Bomber, a TLC [troop landing craft], and a glider in an endeavour to sell war bonds. Very reminiscent of Trafalgar Square and war savings weeks. Kansas's figure for the drive was set at $77 million, which seemed a lot of money, but as events turned out this figure was topped.

We went back to the consulate after approving the layout and then into the conference where we accepted almost everything they suggested but kicked at any organised entertainment for the evenings. The consul wanted us to help him do his job, naturally, and would have had us going on a tour of his friends and their friends selling Britain. We would have gone for that in a big way, were it not for our many disappointments at previous camps with organised entertainment for every single night. We felt that we could do it equally well by just mixing with people.

Mr Ryan was the publicity man for the broadcasts we had been asked to do, and he turned out to be a most entertaining

---

2   Built in 1906, the Commerce Building was the tallest building in Kansas City until 1921 when the Historic Federal Reserve Bank Building was constructed.
3   Manufacture and sale of alcohol was prohibited in Kansas apart from a low alcohol beer which was defined as a cereal malt beverage or CMB. Missouri was one of the leading producers of alcohol and consequently had few laws prohibiting its sale and consumption.

man. He had arranged four fifteen-minute broadcasts on four different stations, and was anxious to get some ideas. We tried to give them to him, but also asked him to come to Leavenworth to speak to the men who were to broadcast. He wanted us to go to a dinner being given by the American War Dad's Association – the members were all fathers with boys in the war. Americans seemed to have a passion for conferences, meetings, discussions, dinners, etc. Colonel Muirhead was persuaded to go and he told me that he had an amazing evening, with songs and lots of fervour. He finally emerged the first honorary War Dad of the war, after being made to wear a special hat and swear a special oath which, it appeared, all members have to swear. A flyer from VIII Bomber Command[4] was the star guest. He had been shot down in France and, after four months, escaped through 'underground channels'. He was doing everything – press, publicity, interviews, etc., – and finding it hard going.

Mr Ryan was not only interesting but well travelled and informative. He said that the average American was really not SMUG, but SNUG and knew as little of the expanse of America, as did the average Yorkshire yokel know of England – in fact probably less. When the Englishman thought of an American, he was apt to forget that there was really no more an average American than there was an average member of the British Isles. Colonel Muirhead and I commented on the amazing job of getting such a cosmopolitan people so thoroughly Americanised in such a short space of time and Ryan thought it was mainly due to the conferences, meetings, evangelistic-type stuff that had been and still was part of the makeup of America.

Next morning we were up at 0715 hours and had a morning of 'fiddling'; parade details, parade times, with absolutely NOTHING in the way of County Fair going on. All our equipment was well set up, clean and looking really good, but the only people we got were MPs [military police], two colonels, and about half a dozen women and children. Bob Dunlop took a picture of what he called Leavenworth at war, with a couple of children crawling over a 3.7 inch gun while an anxious mother watched they didn't fall off.

The whole day was like that up to 1500 hours and then we 'ceased firing' for the crash action demonstration that was to take place before 800 officers at 1630 hours. Dixie amused everyone at 1600 hours by putting on the recording of Stage Door Canteen made by himself and the boys [see chapter 4]. I heard it half a mile away over the PA and went over to investigate. The officers duly materialised and after a brief speech by Colonel Muirhead, Dix, who was MC, took over and like a proud mother showing her children off, he shepherded the Bofors, searchlight and 3.7 inch guns through their demonstration.

The show was then thrown open to the officers for their questions. The type of question which was asked was typified by the officer who went up to Philip Mollett in charge of the searchlight and said he was very interested in searchlights. Mollett then went into a comparatively technical explanation, only to be told that the officer's only previous experience with searchlights was seeing them in the sky in Havre during the last war. It was a bit hard on a group of experts.

Lieutenant Dix had a lot of fun with the girls in the PX[5]. They all trooped over to look at the guns, so he got one of the gunners to sit on the predictor battery and then asked the girls over. He told them that it was an instrument something similar to the Nickelodeon or Juke Box, in which you had to put in a dime before it started to work. So having lifted the elevation telescope to 90° beforehand he got one of the girls to put her dime in the upturned telescope and at that precise moment the man on the battery switched on and the predictor started to work.

We had a conference of officers at 1800 hours to discuss the parade in Kansas; there was to be a practice on the following day for the march past. There appeared to be no difficulty in getting a drink in KC although it was

Top: Civilian crowds in Washington Square, Kansas City
Above: Military Payment Certificate for use in the PX

4   The 8th Air Force was established on 22 February 1944 as a redesignation of VIII Bomber Command, US Army Air Forces, based at High Wycombe. When Cole was in America, the earlier title would still have been being used.
5   PX or post exchange is the shop on a US military base. It is open to all military personnel but not to civilian employees. Wherever it is in the world it trades in US dollars which may be in the form of military payment certificates.

'dry'. I was told that the police said nothing about this direct flouting of laws, because the hotel proprietors paid sufficient money to the right people for their offence not be noticed[6]. That really was the strangest thing about America; that that sort of thing could be accepted as seemingly quite natural.

The following day, a Wednesday, we were up early and had arranged a series of netball games to keep the chaps interested. I also took the opportunity to gather all the men together and tell them all the details I knew of the parade. Then they fell out for the demonstration, which Major General Truesdell, the commanding general of the fort, came to see. It was good, despite the fact that number one gun had a slight accident when coming into action. He complimented us on the show and showed great and intelligent interest as I took him round to each piece of

BC Scope and Spotters; the BC Scope acts similarly to a binocular theodolite and is used to locate the position of targets

equipment and introduced him to the section officers. Cease firing and all equipment was moved down to the loading ramp, some for loading tomorrow, the remainder for the parade in Kansas.

That day, 22 September, was the day we heard the terrific howling, like a banshee, coming from the Leavenworth penitentiary. It signified that someone had escaped. The penitentiary was one of the most famous in the US, second only to Alcatraz, and I'd been informed that very few attempts were ever made to escape. Later we realised that the alarm had come from the army detention barracks as MPs, all armed, closed a network round the camp for about ten hours[7].

Lieutenant Dix had not been on the parade when General Truesdell viewed the demonstration. He profusely apologised afterwards but felt I would understand when he told me that he'd had an opportunity of visiting the prison and that it was so fascinating that time just ceased to exist. He said he went up to the prison gates after hearing the escape signal, and asked if a British officer could see the prison. After a consultation with the guards and a phone call to the warden, he was given permission and escorted on a tour around the prison.

He had souvenirs of trouser buttons (with US penitentiary stamped on them), warders' buttons, badges, laundry cards, bin cards for the stores, etc. He told me about the vast dining hall in which 2,000 prisoners sat at one meal. It was spotlessly clean. The tables had a metal mug, knife, fork, spoon and seats fitted with a spring, and the front two tables in each row had white linen serving gloves for the prisoners who were detailed to serve. Food was wholesome but plain and he tasted some as he went around the kitchens. Every man could be seen from the floor because of the way in which the seating and serving had been arranged (the description reminded me so much of West Point, although I wouldn't dare tell a West Pointer!). Around the walls of the dining room was a warders' gallery, where men patrolled.

His overwhelming impression was of warders, warders and more warders; doors, locks and more doors with locks; guns and yet more guns everywhere. The cells all radiated from a centre hub like a cartwheel. There were six floors of cells, exactly as shown in the picture *The Big House*[8], each with a gallery. The men were allowed radio from 0630 to 2230 hours. Each had a pair of headphones and the kit layout would have put an army barracks to shame. The cells had no walls, just bars on three sides and each had a porcelain, open-type latrine.

A count was taken immediately prior to his going in and there were 1,961 prisoners listed as so many Americans, so many Mexicans, so many Negroes, so many Indians, and one Chinese (I should imagine he felt lonely). The warders just took visitors around as though they were showing them around a pig farm, showing just as much interest in the individual as they would one hog in a thousand. The prisoners had all been convicted of serious crimes such as rape, murder, robbing banks or post offices, sodomy and kidnapping. The stores, in which everything was made by the prisoners, were tended by a civilian who had a staff of the better-type of prisoners.

Prisoners were paid for their work, some at a much higher rate than our fighting soldiers were getting – up to $40 a month – and they were allowed to spend up to $10 a month in the commissariat. It has always seemed a strange thing to me that a man who had been confined for committing the offences which these prisoners had been, could get more money than a man who was fighting to protect his life, others' lives, and his country, and could still listen to the radio and be at peace.

6   Cole is accurate in his assessment. Since 1908 'Boss Tom' Prendergast had run Kansas City as a political fiefdom and ensured that prohibition laws did not affect liquor sales in the city. In 1939 Prendergast was sent to Leavenworth prison for tax evasion and served 15 months. On his release he did not resume his political chicanery, but in 1943, when Cole was writing, Prendergast's iron rule was still too recent to be forgotten.
7   As well as a civilian penitentiary, Fort Leavenworth contains the United States Disciplinary Barracks, America's only maximum security prison for military personnel.
8   Directed by George W. Hill the film was about the brutality of prison life and released in 1930.

Colonel Muirhead discusses the display with Mayor Gage in Kansas City

That evening Gene Grewe caught the bus from Leavenworth to Kansas City. I had learned to appreciate that Grewe was a man with a definite, if somewhat latent, sense of humour. I had also learned to appreciate the soundness of Grewe's decisions, but found that he would not always *take* a decision. In this he did not differ in the least from the majority of officers in the US Army.

This was something about which I didn't want to comment because of its rather delicate nature, but which I was bound to say was one of the worst features I had noticed in the American army. There was often failure on the part of Americans in authority to give a definite decision. I had tried to analyse it and had come to the conclusion that it was purely psychological. The very nature of the American was his independence, his freedom to speak, his freedom to move and act on his own initiative. Thus when it fell to the lot of one man to decide for many he was torn between the love of independence in his men and the fact that this independence should be sacrificed to his own responsibility. Therefore his natural reaction appeared to be that he should immediately let someone else make the decision. That someone had to be a superior officer. And the worst feature was that the worst offenders were the officers of the rank of lieutenant colonel and major; just the very rank where decisiveness was most urgently required. Such dithering became immediately obvious when we were loading up to leave Leavenworth, but more of that later.

That bus journey was one of the most amusing of my trip to the States. I sat next to a man aged about sixty eight, rugged, dressed in the blue jeans outfit of bib and brace overall I was beginning to get accustomed to, lean of face and stern in appearance; altogether I was told, a typical midwestern farmer. He was slightly inebriated, which caused him no embarrassment but a little difficulty in enunciation. He was also very emphatic about all he said, and he told the whole bus when he did say anything, which was often.

My first contact with him was when I took out my cigarettes, passed one to Gene, took one myself and was just on the point of returning them into my pocket when I heard 'I'll have one of those'. I turned round to find this old man holding out his hand. I had learned by then that this was not being cheeky, just merely an American's way of being friendly; so I gave him three to tide him over the bus journey. He then took a good look at me, realised I wasn't an American soldier and immediately offered to pay. I told him it was alright, but he repeated five times that he hadn't had the opportunity of getting cigarettes, being in such a hurry to catch the bus.

He told me he was a farmer, farming a piece of land for forty-five years, but that now he was a member of a Dairy Association. Despite my earnest desire to peep behind that apparently tragic change, I dared not question him closely for fear that he would command the undivided attention of the bus. He was keen to tell me that he was an admirer of Churchill and also Roosevelt, and also that he was a member of a political group. He assured me that he would, if he had any say in the matter, want Roosevelt to leave the handling of the Germans to Churchill. He said he felt that Churchill would make a better job of it than Roosevelt as the American was naturally more tenderhearted. I asked him why he thought that either would have a chance to do the job with Stalin doing most of the German killing. However, he came back at me that Roosevelt and Churchill had been watching things closely and had fed only just enough war materials to the Russians to enable them to press Germany hard, and if they, the Russians, got tough, Roosevelt and Churchill would cut off the flow of supplies and that would cause a Russian collapse. A nice theory, for one so inebriated; but where did he get it from?

He amused us then, by going forward to the driver-conductor and whispering in his ear. The bus stopped at a petrol station, the old man got out and disappeared behind the station; meanwhile the bus waited and the man duly reappeared from behind, boarded the bus and away we went.

In the meantime, a soldier had got into conversation with Grewe and was telling him of the farming and meat packing for which Chicago, Kansas, St Joseph's and the midwest are so famous; coupled of course with the names of Armour and Swift[9]. It appeared the cattle, having been watered, fed and then weighed, were transported by railway track from Texas and the stock breeding countries. En route they were not allowed to be watered, but if they got unruly they were sprayed with water, which quietened them down, particularly in summer. They were then brought into the stockades, through there to the slaughterhouses – huge places that only the strong of stomach can see – and on from there, through varying processes until they finally came to rest in a tin.

I went with Gene into a club in Kansas City which seemed to specialise in showing old films. We saw one of Charlie Chaplin's earliest; 1919 was the year it was made[10]. Later we went into one of the nearby officers' clubs at the Hotel Phillips. An American flyer insisted on showing me the pair of RAF wings over the right pocket of his tunic. Probably because he was a little merry, but no doubt also because he was proud of having served with Royal Canadian Air Force as an instructor, he insisted on toasting the King – which of course embarrasses anyone in these circumstances[11], but he added as an afterthought, 'and the President', so we were all right. He brought his wife over; she had English relations and said she just loved to hear an Englishman talk.

Thursday 23 September was the day of the third war loan bond drive in Kansas City, so we were up and about in our shorts and bush shirts, despite the fact that it was intensely cold. The weatherman had promised a warm afternoon, so I felt I was justified in ordering shorts to be worn, especially as they were so much better both as show uniform and for the men to demonstrate in. We took two 3.7 inch guns and instruments, one 40 mm gun, one searchlight and a power plant. The men travelled in three buses, supplied by the camp and driven by WAC drivers. We were being escorted by an American detachment of two jeeps, two scout cars and a platoon of infantry. It had taken me exactly five minutes to work out the details with the officer in charge: line up at 0930, move off 0945, arrive outside Kansas City, Kansas 1115 hours. We moved off without incident, except that the drivers of the vehicles managed to get in a mud bath, spoiling the cleanliness of the guns. Arrived according to schedule to be met by rows of motorcycle police (I got one of their badges as a souvenir). I asked for latrine facilities for the men before the parade, but as they were not available we told them to break off into the bushes – much to the embarrassment of a lonely lady who had been admiring the size of the guns. The ride had been cold and my teeth were still chattering. However, we soon moved off to first halt, dismounted and got into marching order.

A march past a reviewing stand, a snappy 'eyes right', and on for two blocks. Back into the vehicles and on to our next halt. That concluded Kansas City, Kansas's chances of seeing us. There was quite a crowd and they were very kind to us, clapping and cheering as we marched. But that was only the small part of KC. We idled along to Kansas City, Missouri, dismounted and again formed up. This time the march was longer. There was another reviewing stand to march past, and like the other it contained the mayor, Colonel Muirhead, the British Consul, and other military and civilian dignitaries. Unfortunately I had no idea where the stands were and had to rely on spotting them.

It was quite a sensation marching at the head of the column. With a

Kansas City. Cole heads the column, Lieutenant Dix is almost obscured behind him

9   Armour & Co. and Swift & Co. were major meat packers based in Fort Worth.
10 Probably either *Sunnyside* or *A Day's Pleasure*.
11 Apart from the discourtesy of toasting one ruler in the country of another, only the British navy is permitted to toast the monarch sitting down; other services must stand.

Changing barrels on the Bofors gun

disciplined group of men you knew what should be going on behind you, so you didn't turn your head to see. But the temptation to see what the show was like was very strong. However, I resisted. Ahead of us, the Americans were marching, followed by their vehicles. I had specifically asked that a band should not be present as our step is longer than the Americans' and the cadence different[12]. Consequently, in order to attract attention to the parade, the m/c police were moving up and down the column and ahead of it with sirens wailing and screaming.

Combined with the clapping of the people and the attention to be given to get orders on the right foot I found my mind working twenty to the dozen. I spotted two flags on the right-hand side of the road, which I took to be the reviewing stand, but couldn't see any dignitaries. Imagine my astonishment when I suddenly heard an 'eyes left' from behind and turned to find that I was just passing the reviewing stand on the *left*-hand side. Lieutenant Dix saved the day. I gave 'eyes front', and all was well, but it was a sticky moment. As Colonel Muirhead told me afterwards, he could see my eyes glued on the two flags ahead. What an awful thing if we had marched past all those assembled people without saluting (or would it have been?).

We duly were transported to Washington Square where we were to give demonstrations to the public at 1400 hours and 1600 hours, Lieutenant Dix compering. We took five minutes to sort out the programme, and then broke off for a lunch of sandwiches and coffee, the coffee supplied free by the service canteen in the square.

The escort detachment pleased me; they were supposed to be going back right away, but expressed a desire to stay and see the show, which was really an unsolicited testimonial. A crowd of about 400 assembled by two o'clock. MPs got them in the right place for viewing and the show began. Mayor Gage[13] was present and was taken around by the colonel, being photographed all the time by representatives of the press.

It was a good show, tempered for the public, a bit of eyewash added and all topped up with Dix's superlative showmanship. After crash action and a snappy bit of drill, the public were allowed to go round and ask questions. We had probably the most wonderful crop of silly questions ever, and it was only then that I discovered that we were the first unit of any country including America to bring guns into the city. With 2½ years of the war gone by, the public had never seen an anti-aircraft gun.

Those people did not know that there was a war on. We were not the battle-scarred heroes of the Blitz, the warriors of a nation that had almost heard the death rattle in its own throat. We were a group of actors putting on our show in the open air, our stage the green sward of the square. Props might just as well have been elephants or a trapeze, or horses with gay trappings or balancing chairs. We were applauded at the end and congratulated on a good show as if we were a circus.

One dear old lady, almost in tears, asked desperately for a man from Yorkshire to talk to her. She came from Morley, near Leeds 46 years ago, and that was almost all she could say because after that she dried up and nearly wept. I spoke to her myself, and just talked about Yorkshire to her for a few minutes before handing her over to a Yorkshire gunner. She couldn't thank us enough for reviving memories of her homeland.

A public show, given by local bands and artists, was nearly stolen when the photographers got our boys on the stage and took photographs. Then Sergeant Austin, without a proper accompaniment, got up on the stage and proved how versatile we British were by singing *Trees, For You Alone*[14] and another song, all of which we have now heard hundreds of times, but which we can all hear hundreds of times again.

Another demonstration and so cease firing. And another unsolicited testimonial, which made my faith in our visit

---

12 There was and is a lot of difference between British and American marching orders, and even between the different services within the same country. In general, however, British forces tend to take a longer stride to a slower beat than their American counterparts; the British armswing, where the hand travels from level with the shoulder at the front, to waist height at the back, also tends to be longer.
13 John Bailey (Jack) Gage was mayor of Kansas City, Missouri from 1940-6. A lawyer by profession he made several welcome reforms after the chicanery of 'Boss' Tom Prendergast's political manoeuvring (see above).
14 The first is possibly *Loveliest of Trees*, based on a poem by A.E. Houseman and written by John Duke; *For You Alone* was written by Henry Geehl and is said to be the first song performed in English by the famous tenor Enrico Caruso.

something real. Two American soldiers standing by, not knowing I was behind them, were talking. One turned to the other and said 'you know, these boys have got something we haven't got; that precision, that speed, that coordination is really something'. I felt a little happier.

The vehicles went away under Sergeant Stokoe, escorted by the American troops of the 742nd [Military Police Battalion]. The men changed into service dress and the square, settled down as if 100 British people had never even been there. The officers had had a room at the Kansas City club put at their disposal and, apart from a little incident over shoes getting sent back on trucks, we changed and got ready for an evening in Kansas.

Lieutenant Mollett and three Tommies had spent the whole afternoon broadcasting on four different stations. Their script was the usual sort of propaganda assembled in American-style by the Americans for American consumption. The broadcasts had been organised by Mr Ryan [see above] and we all went for a drink with him, his very charming wife and son Bill, but left early, as Mrs Ryan had only just got out of bed after six days illness.

The others, having heard such a lot about burlesque went to a show. They told me afterwards that it was like the Windmill in London without the saving grace of anything clever being put over[15].

Captain Grewe and I spent the evening in the officers' club and I was asked at least twenty times, what rank, etc., I was. I lost both my AA command signs/flashes; one to a very charming young lady in red, who had asked Gene at the bar what and who I was. She later turned out to be worth $10 million, her father having been a brewer with large holdings in a lot of brewing and liquor firms. She introduced me to her mother who was most disconsolate when I told her that we should be gone the next day. She wanted to invite Grewe and I to spend the day with them at their mansion in the country. I was later told that it would probably have been the finest entertainment I should have experienced, as their parties were known all over the country.

I also met a Dutch second lieutenant in the club. He came up to me, and in broken English, pointed out that he had noticed my uniform and he just wanted to say that he'd had a grand time in Australia. He escaped from the Dutch East Indies, went to Australia, joined the RAAF [Royal Australian Air Force], transferred to the AAF [US Army Air Force], came to America one year ago, qualified as a pilot and was now ready to go back to fight the Japanese. I felt that what he had undergone at the age of twenty, was so much more probably than I shall ever undergo, yet people were making a fuss of me because of a little more glamorous uniform and a red artillery hat.

Next day, Friday 24 September, we left for California. Half of the equipment had already been loaded by Motor

3.7 inch in action

15 By 1943 American burlesque majored on striptease. The Windmill Theatre circumvented censorship by displaying nude tableaux on stage; as statues could be displayed in public places unclothed the management argued that live girls on stage could legally also be unclothed provided they did not move. The censors were forced to agree.

3.7 inch crew ready for action

Sergeant Howard, while we were in KC. He was a very good fellow when left on his own and certainly did the job well. The escort detachment, because they had had no messing arrangements to make, had helped us out by guarding the equipment for the previous twenty-four hours; they were on the job at 0200 hours I was very pleased to note.

We were up early to superintend the rest of the loading and embarkation, when things went haywire. A colonel, a major and a captain of the transportation office in KC decided that our trucks had always been loaded wrongly and wanted me to take all the equipment out of the lorries. It was quoted as impedimenta on the bills of lading, and as such would have had to travel as second-class freight in the lorries but third-class freight in freight cars. The difference in money would mean about five to six hundred dollars. I assured Captain Grewe that the equipment in the lorries – predictors, etc., – needed the extra protection of the lorry springs and tyres if it was to travel without breaking and that I definitely wanted the equipment left in the lorries. After waiting all morning and causing me some concern as to whether we should get away that day they eventually sorted the thing out after Grewe had given them a written statement that it was on my recommendation that they moved like that. Another example of the Americans' unwillingness to make decisions once in uniform.

With that sour note unfortunately finishing our otherwise successful stay in KC we left Leavenworth for San Francisco on a three-day train journey through scenery of indescribable beauty.

CHAPTER 9

ON TO THE WEST COAST

So once again we started on a three-day train ride going to San Francisco by the northern route. This time I had Colonel Muirhead as a companion, he and I sharing a compartment. We soon crossed the Missouri out of the town of Leavenworth – the town which made such a mockery of prohibition – and went on towards Denver, our next railway change. The conductor told us that Missouri was Indian for 'big-money'[1] and added that it had certainly meant big money to farmers, boatmen, producers of electricity and the thousands of other people who have lived on its banks. By that time we were on the Burlington Route and were fortunate enough to have a *Zephyr* diner[2]; a really up-to-date, clean, and well upholstered car it was too.

The Pullman conductor was an excellent sort of chap, most helpful and most informative. He was telling me the story of the town of St Joseph [Stearns County, Minnesota] just as we steamed into the place; how financiers, thinking they were onto a good thing, bought property in St Joseph knowing that a train terminus was to be made in this very central town; how they raised the prices of their land to an enormous figure, and how in consequence the railroad people said OK and transferred their terminus to Kansas City, in twenty years creating the enormous city of Kansas, while St Joseph hardly prospered at all. There were however still big meatpacking plants at St Joseph.

The Missouri's banks here had overflowed and great semi-marshes were prevalent, with water lilies the predominant weed. The conductor talked of the Missouri as a Londoner would talk of the Thames. He told us of the great duck and Chinese pheasant country around these parts, and how shooting was controlled and that no one gun may shoot more than four cock pheasants and three hens, and of how he discovered the secret of shooting pheasants in three days. He said that when you got used to the whirr and the rise of the bird, you wait a given time and then shoot below, as they had the habit of rising and diving again. So you caught them as they started their dive.

I mentioned to the conductor that it was somewhat difficult to see the countryside owing to the dirty windows. He soon fixed that by getting the porter to clean them and then told me the difficulties of rolling stock these days and how 1,200 new Pullmans were expected by the first of the following year. He said the army were the only service that would sleep two men in a lower birth; the navy and air force only allowing one man to a lower birth[3]. Poor old army again!

By the time we had left St Joseph the darkness was setting in and the bunks were being let down. That part of the country was famous for its steaks. Kansas steaks

A streamliner

were to the midwest, what southern fried chicken was to the south and we saw thousands of cattle roaming around. I had my last meal of the day: chicken à la king. It seemed a strange thing in cattle country that so much chicken was served on the diners. It reminded me of the American I met a short while ago, who said he ate no other meat but chicken, and proffered as the reason that it was the only way to be sure he wasn't eating horseflesh.

On we went into Nebraska – the land of the cowboy and the steer – of rolling downs and yellow meadowland, but the nature of the land was so different from the 1,600 miles east of Kansas. It seemed as though a new type of paint had been chosen by the Great Artist. Herds of cattle were certainly there, farmhouses, each with a windmill, dotted around the countryside, but no cowboys as yet. We sped along at a much faster rate than we came to Leavenworth, sitting in our air-conditioned carriage and just reading, writing, and playing bridge.

We reached Denver [Denver County, Colorado], which looked a very fine city, again a railway terminus, at 2200 hours, and changed engines and the diner. Leaving the city we were told that we were not going by the Rio Grande over the Rockies, but that we were going to go north and skirt them, then come into Salt Lake City, Utah. It was hard to appreciate on a railway map just what the Rockies were, but as you left Denver, you realised it more fully, because

---

1   Early white explorers called the river Missouri after a Native American tribe who lived on its banks and whose name meant 'the people with wooden canoes'.
2   The Zephyrs were the first American diesel-electric powered streamlined passenger trains. Introduced in 1934 they were made of stainless steel, very light, very fast and highly distinctive.
3   Railroad cars with seats were transformed into cars with beds by converting the seats into a lower berth while a shelf-like hinged platform was let down from the wall to form the upper berth. As seats were designed to sit two, obviously the army assumed that beds converted from them would sleep two.

there, looming up in the distance to a very great height, was one long range as far as the eye could see. Apparently we were going to miss probably the most beautiful country in the whole of the States. Pity, but who was I to grumble?

The American Red Cross fed us doughnuts and orangeade, and handed out free cigarettes and matches on the station at Denver. They met all trains that way, and distributed these gifts to service personnel; a service much appreciated by us all, particularly as most of us were almost broke. We'd spent much more money than we'd intended in Kansas; the food was expensive at camp and the PX was a good one. As we had to pay for meals on the train all the officers decided to eat one less meal per day. It was really quite funny; six British officers going into San Francisco with not enough money even to pay for meals. The American Red Cross also posted letters free and gave each person a postcard on which they stated, very modestly:

'Colorado is tops
'Romance; rich in the legends of yesterday and today, conquistadores, fur traders, Indians, cowboys, cattle barons.
'Adventure; trails of prospectors and pioneers, Gansey fighting mountain trout, unexcelled big game hunting.
'Beauty; mountain peaks that touch the sky, more than 52 over 1,400 feet high. Lakes, valleys, canyons, mesas. Natives' World fair!
'Living; a kingdom close to heaven, modern cities, beautiful homes, fun in a million ways.'

Who was I to contradict? All I could do was look at mile after mile of nothing but prairie, and then convince myself by looking at a map of the route that we were near such magic place names as Boulder, Colorado Springs, Royal Gorge, Idaho Springs, Rocky Mountain National Park, Estes Park, Mesa Verde National Park. And so we sped on, with that magnificent skyline of mountains on the horizon. No photo could take it, no pen describe it, it just created an emotion and a desire to stay and explore.

I managed to buy a copy of the famous *Denver Post*. It announced a fall of Smolensk to the Russians[4] – all good news, in fact. It was some hours since we left Denver and the whole way had been a very gradual, almost unnoticeable climb until we reached nearly 9,000 feet above sea level and still there appeared to be hills in front of us. It had been almost impossible to realise we had been climbing as the country was just a series of humps and hollows covered with small heaps of stones and wooden corrals. An odd ranch house here and there were the only signs of human habitation except for the neatness of the countryside. Nothing spoiled it, no ugly houses, no signs, no scrub or marsh, no trees, no nothing except grass and hay for miles and miles and hours and hours. For about half an hour I stood on one of the flat cars and watched the country unfurl. It was simply grand, as the speed was not too fast, the air not too dirty, nor the movement too jerky.

When I awakened next morning I found myself in the most glorious country. Had breakfast with Colonel Muirhead, and found that he really was one of the most well-read men I knew. He gave me a running commentary on the country here, which was astounding in its completeness and accuracy. Yet he had never been on this route before, merely read books connected with the Mormon trek.

It appeared that Joseph Smith formed the Mormon Church, and its story of persecution and movement is an important part of the history of the United States. Brigham Young followed in Smith's footsteps and it has been said of him, firstly that he was one of the cleverest statesman the United States ever reared, and secondly that he was in his day much

---

4   The second battle of Smolensk was fought in September and October 1943 when the Russians attacked the German defences and cleared the Germans from the town they had occupied since 1941.

what Stalin was in his; a clever man, always able to turn his ingenuity to better the conditions of his people, even at the expense of accepted traditions.

Young sent an army to Mexico to help fight in the American-Mexican War[5]. They nearly all came back and the United States government paid a sum of money to Brigham Young for their services, which helped to create Salt Lake City. We travelled along the trail created by the Mormons in their search for freedom from persecution. It was an amazing part of country, and it filled us with awe how anyone could lead an army of 25-30,000 people along this route and survive. We were travelling in the luxury of a train in the autumn while they were having to walk behind loaded ox carts at temperatures sometimes of thirty degrees below freezing. Over the top of the Wasatch mountains, down the Echo Canyon into the valley where the town of Ogden now stands. The Mormons turned sharp left here to found Salt Lake City fifty miles away from this point, but one of the families, or sections, the Donner people instead of turning left kept straight on. The majority of them perished in the deep snows that fill these valleys in the winter time[6].

Among the interesting sidelights was the sight of the freight trains on the parallel track. The largest engines in the world with four driving shafts, two sets of eight wheels, simply huge locomotives that drew freight car after freight car. There was an absence of animal life and the infiltration of advertising signs along a road running parallel to the rail caused a pain in the heart when you saw them against this background of majesty.

We stopped for two hours in Salt Lake City to change diners and shunt onto the Western Pacific line[7]. Colonel Muirhead went to see the Mormon Church and Tabernacle, but was very disappointed that, for reasons he never fully understood, he wasn't allowed in the church; he thought that perhaps only Mormons were allowed in. He thought the Tabernacle, where the choir sang, was fabulous, however[8]; an organist was practising while he visited and a guide took him round. Salt Lake City was a very fine city, with its capitol building standing out on a hill in the centre. Built much after the style of the Capitol at Washington, it looked even more beautiful as it stood out in relief, white against the mountainous background.

As I couldn't see the whole of the city I bought views of it and one of the views reminded Gene Grewe of a story of the Mormons. It appears that, shortly after they had settled there and got land under cultivation, a swarm of locusts started to invade the land. The ministers prayed for help and by some strange miracle, the sky was suddenly filled with seagulls which ate up the locusts and then disappeared. A monument was erected to commemorate that occasion.

We visited on a Sunday, so few people were about as the services in the Mormon Church lasted approximately two hours. I should most certainly have liked to have stayed there longer, but we had a conference on Tuesday morning and so had to be in as quickly as possible. Such was the speed with which they were pushing us through that the railway people gave us 'hot priority', which was the same as that given to troops who have to embark on a

Above and left:
Transportation and firing
in the Mojave Desert
near Camp Haan

---

5 Begun in 1846 when Texas joined the US; Mexico considered the state as part of its territory. The war ended in 1848 with the Treaty of Guadalupe Hidalgo, in which Mexico ceded to the US what is now California, Nevada, Utah, most of Arizona, New Mexico, half of Colorado, Texas, and parts of Wyoming, Kansas and Oklahoma.
6 The biggest group in the Donner party consisted of the families of George Donner and James Reed of Springfield Illinois. Most of the party were not Mormon and pre-dated Brigham Young's foundation of Salt Lake City; the following year, 1847, Young used the trail the Donner Party had blazed to reach the Great Salt Lake valley.
7 In 1909, the Western Pacific became the last railroad completed into California linking Salt Lake City and San Francisco via Winnemucca and Sacramento.
8 The Mormon Temple and Tabernacle are separate buildings but next to each other in Temple Square. The tabernacle, completed in 1867, seats 7,000 people and is nearly acoustically perfect; a pin dropped in the pulpit can be heard throughout the building.

convoy that was in port and waiting. After leaving Salt Lake City and watching the salt lake and the salt flats where the world's motor speed record was set[9], there were 500 miles of sand desert with hills on the flat ground, just as though they were jellies turned out of a mould onto a glass tabletop.

By midday the following day we had arrived in the small town of Portola [Plumas County], California, which marked the abrupt end of the desert and the changeover to hilly pine and Californian redwood forests. We hadn't seen enough houses to hold more than 5,000 people, apart from Salt Lake City, in over 1,200 miles. Delightful little streams, which must have been full of trout and other fish careered across the stones in the valleys. No big range of mountains that, just a succession of hills and valleys with a railway worming its way through the valleys. Great clearings were constantly coming into view, where the redwood was being cut up for timber. How remarkably straight the trees were and consequently what little wastage. We had been travelling through the most beautiful country that I had ever seen.

We passed through the city of Sacramento, and went on and yet on until we duly arrived at Oakland [Alameda County, California]. Shipbuilding was going on a terrific pace with everywhere floodlit. It was a magnificent night sight. As Dixie said, if this was a dim out on the West Coast, we should have liked it for Blackpool in peace time. But not so magnificent was the shunting and slow-moving little jerks which continually punctuated our manoeuvres from one position to another. By this time the train consisted of a streamlined diesel-electric locomotive hauling four Pullmans, a diner, baggage car, twelve flat cars and a caboose. We arrived at 0030 hours expecting transport to be waiting for us. Instead we got a bad-tempered railwayman whose only interest was in maintaining the train and greasing the wheels. He had the train moved back five miles for that sole purpose, but gave us no indication what was to happen to the 130 people on the train who were all dressed in their battle dress and webbing equipment ready to move.

Left to right Captain Derek Scorer, Captain Rupert Ledger, unknown, Captain Bill Winder (REME) en route from Camp Edwards to Camp Haan

As we looked as though we should be a couple of hours, I gave the order to take off equipment and bed down. Bunks could not be made so the men made the best show they could and slept anywhere they could find. We then got word via railway sources that we should be disembarking at 0730 hours the following day, going to camp and eating breakfast immediately on arrival. Major Peter Croker arrived soon after 0400 hours having spent some time finding out where the train was and getting transport to it. By that time I had had one hour's sleep if you could call it that and Dix had been on his feet for the whole night. Major Croker told us how the wires he had sent via the Western Pacific asking that the men stay on the train for the night and have their breakfast in the dining car had never materialised. He was very, very angry; in fact it was the first time we had seen Pete Croker lose his cool. Normally he was a very calm customer; efficient, pleasant and a model officer with much control and staff experience. We eventually called the men at 0630 hours and got all the kit onto lorries and away. Within two hours everyone had eaten a good breakfast. Then it was all action again as they changed into parade dress and prepared for yet another big show.

9   When Cole was writing the record was 301 mph, set by Englishman Sir Malcolm Campbell on the Bonneville Salt Flats on 3 September 1935.

CHAPTER 10

THE GOLDEN GATE AND RIVERSIDE, CALIFORNIA

The parade through San Francisco was very reminiscent of all the other parades we had carried out. We were welcomed on the City Hall steps by Mayor Angelo Rossi of San Francisco, who said nice things about us, welcomed us and offered us the keys of the city. Colonel Muirhead responded in a brief but concise speech. After that we were grateful to return to the camp to get on with the settling in process.

For the first time, there had been a slight disturbance on the edge of the crowd at the City Hall when a number of Irish Americans had unfurled banners and shouted anti-British slogans including 'Hands off Ireland'. The police quickly dealt with the matter and none of the British troops were even aware of what had happened until it appeared as headlines in the press next day – with pictures which in other circumstances would almost certainly have been rejected. We had been warned to expect something like this in Boston and New York, where most of the Irish immigrants had settled, but we had hardly expected it to happen in San Francisco where most of the immigrants were Mexican, Chinese or, before the war, Japanese; the latter were mostly in internment camps by the time of our visit.

On the evening of the parade the men were invited to a war bond show in Oakland[1] as guests of honour. Film stars, including Paulette Goddard[2] were to be there. Lieutenant Bob Dunlop had taken his band of trusty men and heavy gun to demonstrate in Oakland and said afterwards that it had been the probably the most successful demonstration he'd put on. The bond show was in the Civic Auditorium[3], a hall very reminiscent of the Boston Gardens, but not quite so large. Anyway, they sold $15 million worth of bonds in the one night. One orchid fetched $1 million.

Ray Dix went over with the men to see them settled. Going over the famous Oakland Bay Bridge[4], which was nearly four and half miles long, Dixie looked back and saw the bridge framed against San Francisco in the setting sun. Layer upon layer of gold and black seemed to rest upon the tops of the skyscrapers set so unevenly that they could almost have

---

1   About eight miles east of San Francisco, Oakland is the county seat of Alameda County.
2   A major Hollywood film star, Paulette Goddard was nominated for an Oscar for best supporting actress for her role in *So Proudly we Hail!* released in June 1943. The previous year she had divorced Charlie Chaplin; she married Burgess Meredith in 1944.
3   Now called the Henry J. Kaiser Convention Center, it was built in 1914 and seats just under 6,000 people.
4   Known locally as Bay Bridge, it carries the road between San Francisco and Oakland and opened in 1936, six months before the Golden Gate Bridge. When Cole saw it Bay Bridge carried cars on its upper deck and trucks and trains on its lower deck. Today both decks carry cars.

been the pipes of some mighty organ. For him this, not the show, had been the highlight of the evening. He also liked the trip in the jeep and said it was the most fascinating jeep ride he'd ever had. Motor Sergeant Howard was driving. He was in charge of the convoy, so he was doing escort in the jeep, buzzing around his convoy like a destroyer around a sea convoy. It was amazing because of the manoeuvrability of the jeep; he drove it as if it were part of him.

Next day, Wednesday 29 September, we started giving our demonstrations. One of the heavy guns had been unserviceable as it needed a new part in the breech mechanism, but Staff Sergeant Mason arrived with it, having flown from England and across the States to make sure that it was fitted correctly. Captain Bill Winder, REME, arrived from Irwin to supervise the gun's proving, and by that Wednesday it was working perfectly. Major Emmanuel and his wife arrived; in fact, everything but the kitchen sink was there.

Gun and searchlight detachments were being moved about in all directions. Bob Dunlop got back at lunchtime to do a press show before going to Vallejo Valley. Another detachment went to Muir Woods in the heart of the Californian Redwood Forest[5] while about 600 US service personnel watched a two-hour demonstration of gun, rifle and gas drills. Lieutenant Dix was in charge and put on one of his best shows with his special band of 60 British Tommies at a baseball triangle on the fringe of San Francisco. The generals seemed very pleased despite the fact that Dix was working under difficulties with no PA system. Then Lieutenant Philip Mollett did a very good job with his searchlight. About 200 men and officers watched his show, which was put on independently in another corner of the baseball field we were using.

At the same time a party of officers and senior NCOs including Colonel Muirhead, Captain Winder, Lieutenant Dunlop, Sergeant Major Green, Sergeant Hughes and Sergeant Stokoe was assembled in the Tapestry Room at the Palace Hotel to meet the press. Sergeant Steve Dermady came and picked me up at 1830 hours, and we went to Brigade Headquarters to check over press stories prior to release. We were having to do our own censoring so anything that was detrimental to British interests was not passed. It was interesting to note that so far I'd only had to remove one picture. Meanwhile Dixie, we learned afterwards, created a terrific impression at an engagement. He addressed the Canadian Legion and started off by saying 'who called the cook a bastard? Well, who called the bastard a cook?' That really made them sit up and he scored a terrific personal triumph, after which he was in demand for speeches.

After the census work we went to Chinatown and to one of the Chinese restaurants; from there Rhys Evans and I went on a walking tour around the city. I could not possibly recount all the chance remarks that I heard about myself, my uniform, and that of my friends, nor is it possible to recount all the encounters with the different types of people I

Above: US servicemen show a lot of interest in the Battery's display

Opposite: 3.7 inch heavy anti-aircraft demonstration in San Francisco

5   Muir Woods National Monument is a national park twelve miles north of San Francisco.

met on these excursions. We were staying at the Mark Hopkins Hotel and from a roof garden on the nineteenth floor[6] of the hotel, itself on the top of a hill in San Francisco and with a completely glass surround you could see the whole of San Francisco in panorama. At the time we were there we saw it in all its stages; in daylight, in the setting sun, at dusk, and at night with the myriads of twinkling lights forming a huge Christmas tree pattern. One oddity I noticed; there was no thirteenth floor in the hotel. It went from twelve to fourteen. I hadn't noticed before, whether that was usual in hotels[7].

The following day Major Steel, Lieutenant Dix, Colonel Muirhead and myself went along to a local battery of AA guns to inspect installations, including a 40 mm gun mounted on a tower. The men gave us a demonstration of gun drill, which I think was as good a show as I'd seen over in the States. I thought they had an exceptionally fine gun site. The accent in the first place was on camouflage; everything was made to look like the surrounding country. The guns had sliding roofs over them which could be run back in double quick time. Machine guns were in little huts that collapsed and the range section, which was some way from the guns, was also in a type of hut that swung outwards. The huts, mess-halls, etc., had all been built like shacks to match the housing project, and altogether it was a very creditable show, especially when it was considered that the whole thing was built by the men from materials scrounged from various places, mostly the navy yard nearby and mostly scrap from derelict battleships from Pearl Harbor.

After that visit, we went over to the navy yard to see a standard gun tower sited on the end of the pier in between two huge dry docks to defend them. One of the docks was empty, and the other had a submarine and a destroyer in them being repaired. Those two dry docks were simply huge[8] and held the largest units in any of the allied navies. The shipping there was intriguing, with strange craft I'd never seen before. Huge tank-landing craft like liners with a drop stern, concrete ships and troop-landing craft. We didn't realise it at the time but we were having a preview of some of the units which were to take part in the second front invasion of Europe. Tom Metcalf was to see these craft again the following year when he took part in D Day. They were then lined along the estuaries of the South Coast ports in England, or waiting on huge transports in quiet country fields a few miles behind the coastal areas near Southampton and Plymouth.

The men had a trip to Muir Woods, visiting not demonstrating this time, but most of the officers couldn't go. The British consul had worried me for some time to go to a cocktail party at his private residence. He wanted us to meet some of his secretaries and staff, who had expressed a desire to meet British officers. Len Vyse, Evans, Winder and Colonel Muirhead went along to the British consul's cocktail party, but I went out with Captain Gene Grewe who had invited me to meet his girlfriend, Nina. He said that she lived in San Francisco and had learned so much from Grewe and from the press about the British that she'd never have forgiven him if he hadn't introduced one of them to her.

6 The glass-walled cocktail lounge had been created in 1939, offered a 360-degree view of San Francisco and was known as Top of the Mark.
7 It is! To avoid problems with superstitious guests or visitors, it is standard practice in North America either to number a building's thirteenth storey as 12A or 14, or to give it a name.
8 Probably the Moore Dry Dock Company. Before the war it was mainly a repair yard, but turned to shipbuilding during the war. It closed in 1961.

We went out by taxi to Sea Cliffs, a hotel on the beach overlooking the famous Seal Rocks, which had a special lounge from which you could watch the seals as they swam[9]. The walls were covered, to my astonishment, with posters from Britain, both from this war and the last, and photograph after photograph of celebrities who had dined there. Gene added to the collection by giving the owner of the hotel a photograph of the Battery. After taking Nina home, Gene took me up Telegraph Hill, one of San Francisco's highest points, from where we could see a panorama of the Embarcadero, the city's waterfront area. But it was getting late so, after a visit to the Coit Tower, the memorial on top of the hill[10], it was time to return home.

We went via that incredible place the International Settlement[11]. Entertainment was predominant and showmen were prolific. The streets themselves added to the atmosphere in that many inclined at an angle of 30°. It seemed almost impossible for a car to climb them, yet you saw cars parked sideways along the curb in the most precarious positions. Captain Grewe told me of an experience with a searchlight and trailer on those steep streets which was both embarrassing and expensive.

From there we went through Chinatown. The houses were built so close together that they made extra-large windows at the front in order to get light. Certainly they were not like anything I had ever seen before, with palm trees in the front garden and an oriental atmosphere. San Francisco was of course a strange mixture of different races. Chinese, Mexican, Japanese, Italian, Indian, Polish, German and British were more frequently seen than the ordinary white or black American, although of course they were all American citizens. The atmosphere around distinct quarters was of that of separate nations.

Much of Friday was taken up with visiting the various forts around the city. Grewe and I went first to Fort Baker over the magnificent Golden Gate Bridge, the largest single span suspension bridge in the world. We saw the notorious island of Alcatraz, which, coming so soon after the penitentiary at Leavenworth, made me almost an authority on prisons. It was quite a huge island really, although it seemed a mere pin spot in the magnificent bay of San Francisco. The number of forts around the bay was astounding[12]. We passed the Presidio, which is the HQ of the 4th Army Command, and then another Fort responsible for the coast defence of the San Francisco side of the bay. Over the bridge we got a distant view of the city and the harbour boom defences and then onto the rocky projectory, which formed the other side of the bay. There we visited one of Grewe's old Battery mates in hospital at Fort Baker[13]. While there we were able to get the passwords for half the other forts and so went on to Forts Cronkhite

Gertrude Lawrence watching a firing demonstration at Scorton Neck (see chapter 6). Cole is on the right of the picture

and Barry. A magnificent view of the Pacific (I felt like stout Cortez[14]) and of the beach, and so back to San Francisco.

On arrival back at camp, Dixie told me of a card that had been given him by Gertrude Lawrence, introducing him to one Dr Margaret Chung who was the only Chinese woman doctor in the US. He asked me to go along with him as the card read 'The Lonely Club for Blond-Haired Bastards'. We went along at lunchtime to find a most charming woman doctor, who had spent most of her time and money in making American airmen and submariners feel at home and

9   Sea Cliffs was the name of the restaurant at Cliff House, a famous San Francisco landmark built on the edge of cliffs and overlooking rocks treacherous for shipping. Although extensively modified, Cliff House still exists and is now part of the Golden Gate National Recreation Area.
10 Erected by Lillie Hitchcock Coit as a memorial to the efforts of firefighters during the San Francisco 1906 earthquake and fire.
11 The International Settlement was based on Pacific Avenue. It was neither international nor a settlement but more of a red-light district famous for its nightlife.
12 Forts Baker, Barry, Cronkhite, Funston, Miley, Winfield Scott and Fort Point all formed part of the harbour defences of San Francisco during the Second World War.
13 During the Second World War most of the buildings at Fort Baker were temporary, including the hospital. It was built near the beach at the foot of the parade ground, was completed in October 1941 and demolished in 1981.
14 Cole is quoting from a sonnet written by John Keats *On first looking into Chapman's Homer*: 'Or like stout Cortez when with eagle eyes/He star'd at the Pacific...'

looking after their wives and families if they got killed. She gave free medical advice to men in those two branches of the service and generally tried to make life easier for those who had given their service to the country in such dangerous pursuits.

She showed us a room full of every type of air souvenir; bits of planes, bombs, etc., from almost every theatre of war, and given by men who had taken part. She talked about 'my son sent this from so-and-so'. She had 620 'sons' in the air force, 27 sons in the submarine service and, as she said, the landlubbers fend for themselves. Each one went by the number she had given him, so she had letters from Bastard No. 421, etc., heavily censored but still readable. An amazing experience. She even had a bit of the plane that carried Churchill when he was shot at over France on his way to North Africa [probably in August 1942] – and we had never even heard of the incident.

Lieutenant Dix then went off to talk over the radio to China. As he said, he can't keep 800 million Chinese waiting. There were to be six radio broadcasts from San Francisco; my turn came on Sunday.

That evening all the officers had to attend a cocktail party given by the British consul at the Bohemian Club, usually the meeting place of most of the city's artists and sculptors. As many of the artists' work adorned the club rooms, we were almost more interested in the place itself rather than the party we were there to attend. The consul was ill and his job was being done by Mr Hillery, but we did meet Mrs Fisher, the consul's wife, and their daughters – twins 17½ years old – and some of the nicest girls I'd met, but very unlike; one is tall and thin and dark, the other is short and dumpy and fair.

We were introduced to Lieutenant-General Emmons, commanding the 4th Army[15], admirals, captains in the US army and navy, British naval captains, group captains from the British air force, and resident British civilians. I even met a lady whose husband owned two shortwave radio stations operating from the Mark Hopkins hotel, a Mrs Dunn. Also there was C. Aubrey Smith, the veteran British actor who was then appearing in the city[16]. It was the last, accompanied by his much younger wife, who claimed most of the British officers' attention; she was the most charming woman, but evidently 'wore the trousers'. Aubrey Smith was doing a show for a week, called *Old English* in aid of the war relief society and then was to move over to Los Angeles.

We had a great number of officers and men to witness the demonstrations in San Francisco and it was probably our most successful part of the tour. They were always so attentive and always on time and in position. But there was still a strange difference between American and British troops. You asked a body of American troops, what they were, guns or searchlights, and no

One of the many broadcasts Cole made when he was in America. This one is for The Army Hour *(see page 32)*

one answered. You repeated the question and everyone half looked at everyone else, but they seemed scared of getting up and saying anything. The sergeants never seemed to have the authority and the privates didn't answer anyway. It was the same trait as the officers; no one was willing to make a decision. Nevertheless we had the best complete demonstration, I think I'd seen on the tour. Everything went fine.

Lieutenant Colonel Metcalf arrived on Saturday 2 October, having been flown from an airport near Camp Irwin. The flight had been bumpy and uncomfortable and he was feeling somewhat exhausted, although pleased with the way things had been going. He mentioned that the detachment at Camp Irwin were in excellent heart, and that Roger Keys could not speak too highly of the arrangements there. Derek Scorer spoke with similar warmth of the detachment in Fort Knox. The barracks and colonel's quarters were located in San Francisco's winery district, where people got drunk on the products they made with alarming consistency. That being as it might, grapes were readily available and cheap – I bought two and a half pounds for a mere 38¢ (1/9); I hadn't seen a grape since before the war.

Once the Colonel had settled in we went around the equipment and I introduced him to the visitors, and so it went on

15 Lieutenant General Delos C Emmons was the Commanding General of Western Defense Command (WDC) from September 1943 to June 1944. WDC and the 4th Army both had their headquarters at the Presidio of San Francisco. WDC was responsible for defending the US's pacific coast. The 4th Army trained tactical units for combat. There was a lot of overlap between the two organisations.
16 Sir Charles Aubrey Smith was an international cricketer who captained Sussex and England and who took up acting when he retired from first class cricket. Regarded as the unofficial leader of the British film fraternity in Hollywood he founded the Hollywood Cricket Club and appeared in numerous films including *The Four Feathers*, *The Prisoner of Zenda* and *Dr Jekyll and Mr Hyde*.

The Battery quarters in San Francisco, on the corner of 6th and Harrison in the Winery District

until lunch. Saturday afternoon we had free. They'd arranged a football game (or rather a visit), for us. We were to go to the University of California to watch a game between them and the rival University of South California (the California Golden Bears versus the USC Trojans). I'd never seen an [American] football match, so I was very eager to see it. I was to take all the men and parade them during the half.

We moved in convoy; all the officers and all but ten of the men which was the biggest voluntary response we'd had. Arriving at the stadium we went into reserved seats. We got a real spontaneous ovation as we walked in and then I realised that the news had been spread around about our coming. I told Lieutenant Dix that he would lead the men onto the field and Colonel M and myself would wait for the Governor[17] who was to address us.

A band went through some of the most amazing and quick gyrations I'd ever seen a band do. Opposite to us were about 3,000 students all formed up under cheerleaders who were the rooting section of the home university. The cheerleaders, who must surely have been gym instructors or contortionists by the antics they went through, worked the 'rooters' into fanatical enthusiasm. The crowd were attended to by seemingly endless numbers of boys with candy, coke, and cigarettes, who were dressed in the most amazing uniforms.

The players, idols of the crowd, drew tumultuous applause as they came on. The dress for American football was really something out of another world. Knickerbockers were the chief leg wear and coloured sweaters the chief chest wear with every type and colour of hats – I picked up one as a souvenir – California's colours, blue and yellow, being predominant. Reserves were bigger in numbers than the team, coaches and attendants bigger in numbers than the reserves, and referees abounded everywhere. Of course, we couldn't understand what was going on but I was told it wasn't a particularly interesting game; with no killings or fights[18] (except a small one with a lot of booing), so we didn't see football as she was really played. For our part, we paraded at the half and Lieutenant Dix led the men with their usual precision and received tumultuous applause. The highlight was when the rooters, by means of coloured cards, flashed up a huge Union Jack while the band played *God save the King*. A tribute to another country that was more than just another ally. It was touching.

On Sunday I had intended to sleep in, but I was awake at the usual hour and thoughts of breakfast made me get up. I took things very quietly up to 1000 hours when Colonel Metcalf and I had arranged for a sedan to be put at our disposal so that we could see the sights of San Francisco. However, the colonel had been given an opportunity of going with Lieutenant Dix to the penitentiary on Alcatraz Island, so they departed at 0730. I arranged to meet them at 1100 hours at the Mark Hopkins Hotel. The use of the car was not to be sneezed at, so I went to the Golden Gate Park[19] to have a gentle amble through that famous beauty spot. The driver evidently knew that I was sightseeing and not going anywhere on business, so he took me the best way; along the beach, past the Seal Rocks and in by the western end of the long park.

There was everything anyone wanted in this great park: deer and buffalo enclosures, lakes, fishing, swimming, polo, a trotting track, a 'Rotten Row'[20], football fields and enclosures for every type of sport, memorials, music enclosures, Shakespeare garden of flowers, academy of science, African Hall, conservatory, rose gardens, arboretum buildings,

17 Earl Warren was elected Governor of California on 3 November 1942. He was responsible for improving the state's higher education using the University of California's network of small university and community colleges.
18 Cole is possibly using rugby terms here. In rugby 'killing the ball' is an attempt to slow down the flow of the ball or to destroy the opposition's attack, and is very much frowned on. A fight is exactly what it says!
19 A park in the city about three miles long by half a mile wide, its planting was planned by John McLaren the hugely-respected park superintendent who worked there for fifty-three years and died in the year Cole was writing, still in post at the age of 96.
20 A trackway within Hyde Park maintained for horse riding, Rotten Row runs east-west between Kensington Road and the Serpentine.

oriental tea gardens, yet more lakes, large and small groves and avenues, etc. All of these were laid out in a rectangular enclosure nearly sixty avenues long by nine blocks wide. On to meet Colonel M and Lieutenant D. They arrived a minute after I did and Dixie handed me an envelope which contained a note written, signed and sealed by the Associate Warden of Alcatraz, to say that Lieutenant R.E. Dix had been a voluntary inmate of Alcatraz. Colonel M had the same[21].

They told me of the trip, and how they went out in a boat to the island. They were met by the assistant warden and taken in through the gate which had a radio link for detecting metal. If you had a gun or file or hatchet on you an oscilloscope flashed red as soon as you passed through the gate. There were 250 inmates and the *average* sentence was 33 years; one man had the distinction of being in for 150 years, while there were several who were in for over one hundred years. To qualify for the prison, you must have been a bad 'un at one of the other prisons such as Leavenworth. The discipline there was just the world's strictest. The men were not allowed to speak after 5.30 in the evening until six o'clock the next morning. During the day they were only allowed to speak at certain periods. They got two periods of three hours exercise per week and earned about $10 per month, of which they were allowed two dollars for papers, etc. Cigarettes and tobacco were government issue. If they infringed any rule they got solitary confinement in a dark cell which was padded. If a man just looked wrong the warders gave him nineteen days in solitary. The assistant warden,

Half time at the San Francisco football match. The Battery parades before the Union Jack displayed by the crowd

so Colonel M told me, was just as mean as any man he'd ever seen; he would sentence a man for standing wrongly. He caught a man playing patience with a home-made pack of cards and gave him three months solitary. Gates were double locked, from the inside and the outside. Visitors were allowed once per month for one hour. They spoke through amplifiers set in the wall and looked through pieces of glass six inches by four inches. And that was all the contact with the outside world, those fellows had. All were in for major offences; rape, murder, dope pedalling, etc. Talk about 'how the other half lived', this was part of the other half that only existed.

I had a broadcast to do later that day so did some writing up to 1500 hours before leaving in a car with Major Haerst. He took me into the Columbia building, which was an annex of the Palace Hotel and introduced me to my compere, a William Winter[22], who was one of the most famous radio commentators in these parts. Winter was called by some people 'the Pollyanna'[23], because he had broadcast optimistically on every theatre of war and yet had never been out of California. The broadcast was being sponsored by Planters Peanuts, but the quarter-hour transmission was in the form of a news review.

I didn't quite know the form the interview was to take, but expected it to be along the usual lines. Winter wanted me to link up my answers with his news as far as possible, although his news turned out more often than not to be his views. We spent an hour preparing, most of which was taken up by me saying 'I'm afraid that's not quite true' or 'well, can't we put it this way?' or 'I'm sorry I'm not allowed to mention that,' etc., etc.

We finished our script by one minute before we were due to go on the air, I had a voice test for amplification, etc., which worked OK then 'on the air to the West Coast of America'. The Peanut announcer sat opposite me next to Winter,

21 Alcatraz is the Spanish for pelican and when Metcalf and Dix visited Alcatraz, Robert Stroud AZ-594, the 'Birdman of Alcatraz', had been imprisoned there for about ten months. The prison closed in 1963.
22 From 1941 Winter became the voice of America throughout Asia focusing on America's international relations and broadcasting low-key propaganda.
23 After the central character in *Pollyanna* by Eleanor H Porter, who invariably tried to see the best in everything.

Ack-Ack in Action

TO THE UNINITIATED, a gun on the ground fighting with a plane in the air looks like a sitting duck trying to cope with an eagle. The plane apparently has all the advantages of speed, maneuverability and power. But fortunately for groundlings the initiates have made the contest a good deal less uneven than it looks. The gun, according to the conservative estimates beloved of combat groups, has at least a fifty-fifty chance of bringing down the plane

Veteran British anti-aircraft men, seasoned at Sedan and Dunkirk, and the Battle of Britain, are helping U. S. soldiers learn how to wage air war from the ground.

By Carolyn Stull

they became aware of an unnatural quiet around them. Their supplies were supposed to come up in time for breakfast, but they did not appear. Sergeant

nected with the radio control started up and the crew working beside the gun checked the instruments and shoved a clip of shells into place.

crew of any nationality handling similar weapons. The important factor in the British method is the speed with which the unit goes into and comes out of action. This is accomplished partly through the simplicity of the commands and partly as a result of the discipline of the men.

THE UNIT that staged last week's demonstration has, on occasion, put a gun into action in 29 seconds. An

---

and we each had a microphone. It was just too easy, and I feel sure that Winter was relieved when he found that I wasn't either nervous or unused to this sort of thing. Afterwards I was shown round the broadcasting studios and told that the transmitter for the station was sixty miles away. Loss of power was alleviated by a series of thirty-two relays and transformers along the West Coast; Los Angeles also fed into this transmitter which had a 100 kW power output. Winter gave me a letter of introduction to his opposite number in the Columbia Broadcasting Service in Los Angeles so that I would be able to see the other side of the system.

Before leaving I autographed a sheet on the wall which already contained a very large number of people who had broadcast on these Winter programmes, including David Bowes Lyon, the Queen's brother[24], and the lieutenant commander who had sunk an aircraft carrier in Tokyo harbour[25].

From there I met Colonel Metcalf and Dixie and we decided to go out for a quiet evening (comparatively anyway, as we were tired out). Had food in a cafeteria and then, without any purpose in mind, except that sometime during the evening we wanted to see a burlesque show (American's own), we wandered out. We spotted *Victory through Air Power*, the new Walt Disney film based on Major de Seversky's book of the same name. It had had an exceptionally good press, so I'd been told, so we went in just in time to see the main film. It was certainly an interesting and unusual film. A combination of fact, propaganda, and well let's face it, fiction and wishful thinking. One or two downright perversions of the truth, notably the talk about air cover over Dunkirk. Still, an interesting peep into the future bombs and all the horrors that were likely to go with them. The film was making an impression on the people, the layman, and I felt it was rather a pity because it seemed to be almost synonymous with the clamour for the second front[26].

We left there to go to a burlesque [see also chapter 8] and, thinking to get away from the madding crowd, we went into a box, only to find it already half full of American sailors. San Francisco was of course just teeming with sailors of all nationalities. This was our first experience of a city where service people almost outnumbered civilians in the way that London, Liverpool, Southampton, etc., did. These particular sailors were in great form. They were ready to fulfil the audience's traditional function at a burlesque show and to boo (mainly to boo!), applaud, cat call, whistle, throw paper cups and balls – but not bottles – as the particular part of the show required.

The American burlesque was an institution for which there could surely be no comparison in other countries. The nearest approach was the fan dancer. However, we went along to see for ourselves. Well I'd felt nauseated quite a few times, but this was the first time at a theatre. The humour was filthy, the artists – 50th rate – should not have claimed the right to belong to the theatrical profession. The programme was a succession of filthy sketches and striptease girls, and the people who stripped did so at a supposedly pleasing rate, but unfortunately had neither the art nor the figures

---

24 Bowes Lyon, King George VI's brother-in-law, worked for the Political Warfare Executive which broadcast propaganda to occupied Europe; the station appeared to be operating from within Germany broadcasting German news.

25 Cole's comment here is interesting, as he seems to be referring to the Japanese supercarrier Shinano which was sunk in Tokyo Bay by the US submarine Archer-Fish (the hyphen in the name was dropped in 1952). The sinking took place on 29 November 1944, i.e. more than a year after Cole's US tour. Either he is mistaken in some of his details or has amended parts of his memoirs to include later information.

26 The second front refers to an allied invasion of France to relieve the pressure on the Russian forces bearing the brunt of Hitler's invasion of Russia. Although a second front had been mooted since 1942 and was certainly planned, neither Britain nor the US were prepared to begin an invasion until they were sure they had everything needed to support it.

and consequently just appeared like second-rate prostitutes. I got so nauseated, that I persuaded the others to leave and get a breath of fresh air.

In the morning Colonel Metcalf was shown about gun sites by that tireless showman Colonel Schlick. Lieutenant Dix went to prepare his script for his second broadcast, this time in the *Women's Magazine of the Air*[27]. Bob D took his band of trusty Bofors men out to Fort Funston to fire, accompanied by a covey of generals. The firing went well, they got nine hits on a target and took the generals by storm. Major General Gardner[28], commanding AAA WDC, was so impressed that he was the last to leave. He certainly was a glutton for information; he had sent a draughtsman to draw some of the equipment.

We all went out Fort Funston in the afternoon and to a crowd of about 400, including Lieutenant General Emmons, commanding WDC, the boys put on a grand show. The first round scored a hit, the third round tore half the 'sleeve' off. Six hits in three runs, the crowd were at our feet and Colonel Schlick was almost beside himself with praise for the boys. We had reporters and photographers as usual and a Miss Stull of the *Chronicle* reported on the show giving us an excellent write-up [see opposite].

We left the firing point, in itself a beauty spot overlooking the Pacific Ocean, and returned to San Francisco via the Portello Road. This passed such wonders as the Olympic Golf Club and the Fleishhacker Pool, the largest swimming pool in the world so we are told[29]. But the most magnificent view was opened up when we passed the Twin Peaks, and looked upon a panorama of the city. It was just such a sheer delight that it made you gasp. Perfect weather (we had nothing else there), perfect visibility (which was unusual in this spot, where mists predominated until ten or eleven in the morning and settled in again in the evening, besides rolling in during the day at any moment), perfect colour (a blend of white and the rust colours of the tiles and parts of the houses) and the background was staggering. I could have stayed for hours but unfortunately I had to get back. I'd arranged for the demonstrations to finish early and Lieutenant Evans to take the gunners who had not visited operational sites to one of the nearby sites I had visited. This meant that all our men had been to one or other of the sites, mixed with their boys, and really got down to exchange of ideas.

Colonel Metcalf had decided that he should go in advance to Los Angeles as there was much to do there, including organising a well-earned break in the form of a few days leave. Roger Keys and his detachment was to join the rest of the Battery in Camp Haan and there was only one full day left for the two detachments then in San Francisco to complete their firing and other demonstrations before we had to leave. At tea, his planning having been completed he asked me to join him for an evening's tour of Chinatown – a must for every visitor so we had been told.

We first called at the 'Dragon's Lair', where a huge dragon, terrifying to the eye, appropriately surmounted the entrance. We found a table for two near the wall, following my habit of finding a place where I could watch without being watched. The tactic didn't work however as we hadn't even had time to order a drink before a tall, slightly paunchy man sauntered over to the table. He asked whether we were part of the 'British Outfit' and then said:

'Saw you on your parade. Fine show it was too,' and then, addressing Tom 'But you were in charge weren't you?' Tom admitted it, explaining that I was in charge of the detachment but he in charge of the Battery. On hearing that, the man insisted on us joining him and his wife at their table, adding that she'd be delighted to meet us. He introduced

---

27 Launched on NBC in 1928 and presented by Ben Walker; a pirate radio station in Britain broadcast *Eve, the women's magazine of the air*, but did not start transmitting until 1965.
28 Major General Fulton Q.C. Gardner of the Fourth Antiaircraft Command was noted for being particular about personally checking AAA arrangements.
29 Certainly the largest swimming pool in the US, Fleishhacker Pool was 1,000 feet long by 150 feet wide and was built in 1924 by philanthropist Herbert Fleishhacker. Filled with heated seawater it was so large that the lifeguards patrolled in kayaks. Now filled in, it forms part of the car park for San Francisco Zoo, which Fleishhacker also built.

himself as Jim Rowell, his wife as Mame, and said that he was deputy sheriff of Phoenix in Arizona. Tom tried to explain why the British were in San Francisco and not in England or the Middle East and for the next hour we were cross questioned about British law, British customs, the war, the part the Americans were playing over in England. Mame chipped in with the odd question about British women and what they were doing for the war effort.

We had explained about a thousand times in San Francisco what our rank and nation was. They didn't see the British army here much; a few Royal Navy and quite a few air force, mainly Canadian, but quite a lot of Australian too. Escaping from the friendly couple we continued our tour of Chinatown, visiting several more joints until we thought it was time to go home. So we tried to get a taxi, and eventually had to share one with a Chinese worker and a drunken Chinese soldier. We were dropped back at barracks, where the cab driver flatly refused to allow me to pay saying that the drunken soldier would pay and adding 'it aint often I have limeys in uniform in my cab'.

Tuesday 5 October was the last full day of demonstration. Colonel Metcalf remarked at lunch that he'd been watching Ray Dix and his sixty men give a marching and rifle drill, and commented:

'Dix is a born actor. The crowd almost eat out of his hand. They laugh when he makes them, are silent when he wants them to be, they clap when he tells them to clap and leave when he's done with them. And they love it. It's really been fantastic the way the crowds of servicemen and civilians have reacted to all our demonstrations.'

'I've often wondered', I said as I watched the crowds' reaction, 'whether we're doing a better job here than we should be on an Ack Ack site in England or Africa.'

'There's no doubt in my mind,' Tom said, 'support for the British created not only by our gunnery but also by our mixing afterwards must be worth more than what these men by themselves could have done for their cause in England. But no doubt we shall find that out when we return home.' He said he was sure of it, and, after what I had seen and done there, so was I.

Reveille was early on Wednesday 6 October, at 0330 hours. Then it was cleaning barracks, getting personal kit packed and after that, breakfast; trucks and equipment moved on to the train at 0715 hours. Wiring and checking was absolutely completed in a total time of three hours – a marvellous job and a credit to Sergeant Howard and his trusty band. The trucks had all been painted, and I was really proud to be able to rejoin the battery with equipment looking as good as that did. I purposely didn't ask any of the officers to go down; I felt the Sergeant Major and Motor Sergeant Howard would work much better and much more quickly independently. Lieutenant Vyse went down after it was all over and checked to see everything was OK. It was.

I went to find Captain Crewe as I'd had word that one of the men who had had a minor operation in hospital, Gunner Rawlings, would not be able to travel with us. Permission had previously been given but staff had changed and the

Battery Sergeant Major Robert Green

message hadn't filtered through. Our own doctor, Doc Dykes, was with Roger Keys in Fort Knox so we had no qualified medic to talk with the hospital people. Only some splendid work by Gene Grewe secured Rawlings' release and Gene personally brought him to the train. The gunner was settled in one of the compartments with a medical orderly looking after him.

I'd sent all the men off for the afternoon and told them to be back by 1830 hours. The previous day I'd had to charge a bombardier for being in the town without a cap badge and improperly dressed. I remanded him to the CO at the CO's request. Earlier in the week I'd had to confine three of boys to barracks. That seemed to have had the necessary result of making the remainder of the chaps aware that I meant business. The only other incident was one of our men knocking one of the American escort boys down over a girl. That promised to be an ugly incident, but we aired it somewhat and then hushed it up and forgot it. I hoped that it wouldn't reappear at any time. Otherwise the conduct of the fellows throughout the trip was exceptionally good, and the spirit of the men that final evening was extremely good and very gratifying. They were all as happy as kids, despite an appalling shortage of money; I don't think they had a $10 bill between a hundred of them but they seemed to get around.

After picking up the letter of introduction from William Winter [see above] I joined Jack Van Noy, Rhys Evans and Bob Dunlop in the Palace Hotel. Lunch over we went to the theatre district and to do some shopping, or rather to gaze into shop windows. I just had time for tea at Bernstein's, the cafe that served and specialised in fish and seafood. I only went in for scallops, but had to content myself with half a lobster. The place was fitted out like a ship and doubtless attracted a lot of attention on that account[30]. Personally I thought the ship ought to be sunk or rebuilt because the taste seemed poor and the whole effect extremely artificial. And so back to the barracks, where we went through the usual anti-climax of packing.

As we went through the familiar events of getting personal kit onto the train. I could not help but feel that our stay in San Francisco had been the most successful period of our tour to date, with the possible exception of West Point which was in a totally different category. I felt that we had been better received both as individuals and as a body than we had been elsewhere, and that that in itself was well worth the time and money expended on this trip. I thought too that we got the message over better about the British war effort, not only to the military but to the civilian population. I'm absolutely certain that we raised the respect for the British people and the British army, both from the point of view of its human aspect, and from the war aspect. Rhys Evans spoke to a lot of the men and they were really chuffed at the enthusiasm of the people watching the demonstrations. That very gratifying air of happiness among the men pointed to their having had a successful and happy time. Our social life had been well planned, productive and we felt as though we had delivered the goods and left a good impression. Many people had given us unsolicited testimonials and I'm certain Tom Metcalf was pleased; for myself, I had every reason to be satisfied with the detachment.

---

30 The entrance to Bernstein's Fish Grotto was a reproduction of the bow of the *Nina*, the nickname of the *Santa Clara*, the most favoured by Christopher Columbus of the three ships which brought him to the New World. The restaurant was known as 'the ship that never sailed' as the bow jutted onto the pavement at 123 Powell Street; its interior continued the nautical theme.

CHAPTER 11

THE CITY OF THE ANGELS

Every man Jack was in bed on the train by 2200 hours. We had an excellent night's sleep and I needed it. A good breakfast and then, while the rest of the officers formed themselves into a poker school, out came my diary, and I found myself pursuing my favourite train pastime, writing. Philip Mollett and I were the only ones not actively connected with the pasteboards. Philip was probably the fellow who enjoyed the San Francisco show the most, and himself did an excellent job with his searchlight demonstration. Socially he found an exceedingly nice girl, with whom he spent every minute of his spare time. He was rather lovelorn on the train.

We were going on the coast route from San Francisco to Los Angeles. Again through mile after mile of nothing but scenery with its shortage of human infiltration. You sat up, however, when the streamlined famous South Pacific Railway train [see chapter 9] flashed past and you saw the shape of things to come.

After lunch we passed Santa Barbara. It looked beautiful with the same type of hilly, almost mountainous background that I first saw at Salt Lake City. Bathed in sunlight, as the posters were so consistent in saying, with the palms that were a traditional part of the western seaboard, it really looked as though it would be the ideal holiday resort[1]. It's a pity we didn't see more of it.

We passed that part of the coast where jetties had been built out into the ocean, and where oil was being pumped out from the ocean's bed[2]. The oil rigs out at sea brought us back to the reality of an economy becoming increasingly dependent on this black viscous liquid. The slightly mercenary flavour of oil created the image of fortunes lost and won, and yet when first you saw an oil well it all looked so peaceful from a train that your main impression was an extreme sense of disappointment that such a world could have been built around such an inanimate and structurally disappointing thing. Everyone was eager to expand on the often-told stories of oil but I for one felt a terrific disinclination to hear them.

The oil wells were in direct contrast to the mile after mile of unspoilt beaches where breakers such as I had never seen before were just rolling in. The beautiful coastal views we passed began to get almost monotonous. We had a good night and were then up at 0630 hours to leave the train for breakfast, after which we washed, shaved and changed into shorts. It was Friday 8 October and I went into the Battery office to be greeted by a storm of troubles, trials and tribulations. Light Ack Ack were the only demonstrations going on and it seemed as though we were in for a holiday in a big way. We had nothing at all to do until the following Thursday except entertainment. Still, that could be quite trying at times.

After taking over from Lieutenant Miles Salmon, who had been doing social secretary, I went with the two colonels for a swim. A real Hollywood bathing pool, with girls languishing on the sides, was located at the back of the officers' club. That of course sounded somewhat funny in World War II, but it was not quite what it sounded in this city so far away from war and so hot. We had an excellent swim and then went to the officers' club for tea given by the commanding general[3]. He was not there, although I did not hear an explanation of his absence, but his executive officer, a full colonel, was there, as well as about fifty other American officers on the staff.

Having changed for the evening we went to a Battery boxing match, whose highlights were barracking midway between the bouts, doubtful decisions which in the case of the last fight were definitely booed, and in my opinion quite rightly, a band to while away the time between bouts, and the extremely well built boys we have in the battery. This brought me to another of my observations on life in America. The percentage of fat officers in the US Army must have been about 100% greater than in our army and I

Crack British AA in Action

Blitz Busters Display Technique for Camp Haan Battalions

Moving with split-second precision, nine members of a British antiaircraft gun crew rolled out on the field at Area 3 Friday in their prime mover, unhitched the huge 3.7 inch gun (comparable to the American 90-mm. gun) and leveled it into firing position in approximately four minutes—near record time for this operation.

Another prime mover transported the director onto the field, followed by a third truck hauling the height finder and the BC scope, which were rapidly put into operation. Throughout the demonstration, Capt. Rupert Ledger, gun troop commander, gave a running account of the drill over a public address system.

British antiaircraft tactics which proved their effectiveness in the Battle of Britain are being demonstrated here by a crack English ack-ack battery now on the last leg of a nationwide tour of military camps.

VETERANS

The Tommies, all veterans of the blitz raids in the early days of the war when their embattled island stood off the once-powerful Luftwaffe, are members of the 1st British Composite Antiaircraft Battery visiting this country to exchange ideas on combating aircraft attacks.

The advance section of the battery, consisting of two 94-mm. guns and five searchlights, staged exhibitions of firing drill and tactical methods at Camp Irwin last week and moved to Camp Haan on Thursday for a two-week stay. Next Thursday they will be joined by their automatic weapons troop, now at the desert camp.

The British contingent, clad in their tropical uniform of khaki shirts, shorts and steel helmets, quickly won the admiration of the several hundred men from six Haan gun battalions who witnessed their first gun demonstrations.

IMPRESSED

The battery is commanded by Lt. Col. Thomas C. Metcalf, one of the outstanding gunners in

---

1   Sandwiched between the Santa Ynez Mountains and the Pacific, Santa Barbara is often called the American Riviera because its climate is similar to that of the Mediterranean.
2   The Summerland Offshore Oil Field was the world's first offshore oil field and developed in the 1890s. Wells were drilled from piers stretching into the sea from beaches along the coastline of Santa Barbara County. Production ceased about four years before Cole was writing.
3   Probably Brigadier General Townsend who was the commanding General of Camp Haan at about this time, although was transferred at the end of 1943. Major General Bruce 'Barney' Oldfield commanded the AAATC, while Lieutenant Colonel Russell Sharpe was the section's principal staff officer.

Battery headquarters in Camp Haan

wondered why. Did they keep in as good condition? Did they drink more? Were they as fit? Were they as healthy?

The evening finished with a dance at the Novco Naval Hospital; an invitation dance at a delightful hospital set in the mountains and with a beautiful artificial lake in the grounds. The nurses were all in formal dress and there was quite a mixture of officers of all types. For myself, I just mixed and listened, talked and drank a little. The bus went back at twenty past twelve arriving in camp at approximately 0200 hours.

Saturday brought a parade in Riverside[4] so out came the shorts and shirt. The drive with the colonel into Riverside reminded me of the country one saw in Technicolor films. The sun just blazed down in a clear blue sky, on country browned with continual sun. The mountains edging the plain on which Camp Haan and Riverside were situated, were of brown rock, sandy type. They were reputed to be 10,000 feet high, but looked only 3-4,000 feet, rising sheer out of the plain. There was no gentle rise, it was just as though they had been pushed up from underneath by a mighty hand.

Riverside itself was a central hub of four entirely different types of country. Within sixty miles you could have had the delights of the seaside and the sun, the sports of the snow on the mountains with skiing and ancillary snow sports, the arid wastes of the desert with its long pony trails, and the orange groves and Palmsprings. In peace days, when gasoline was not rationed, you could have done almost anything that you wanted to at any time of the year.

The road was lined with the type of palm that looked just like an oversized Brussel sprout stalk and made a very impressive entry into a beautifully clean and well laid out town. I had been given the job of talking to the chief air raid warden (civil defence chief), so I did not go on the parade, but waited at the city steps for the colonel. The usual type of army band led the parade and it was there waiting when the men arrived in convoy. Assembly and adjustment took about a

quarter of an hour and they moved away at 1030 hours. The pace was incredibly fast, and to start with wasn't so much marching as doubling. I dashed to the head of the column in a jeep to try and slow them down but only succeeded on my third attempt. The light ack ack troupe, under the command of Bob Dunlop failed to give 'eyes left' as the reviewing stand was not a stand in the accepted way, and not easily distinguishable, but otherwise the parade was normal and was well received by quite a sizeable crowd, who displayed the same interest in the arm swing, shorts and decisive step that had been observed elsewhere.

Before the Riverside parade

4   About 60 miles east of Los Angeles, Riverside is situated beside the Santa Ana River and is the county seat of Riverside County.

The parade at Riverside. The American band leads the parade of Tommies past the Mission Inn

I met Colonel Muirhead and Majors Steel and Logan on City Hall steps, and before we could say 'Jack Robinson' we were inundated with autograph hunters. I signed approximately seventy-six books, papers, backs of ration cards, pieces of brown paper, and season tickets, etc., in about half an hour. It really was the most amazing display. I was told afterwards that there was a large English colony here, which explains the number of people who came up to me and said they were from England, and where did I come from, and did I know so-and-so? I had to take two addresses and promise to write to the folk when I got back home. By contrast an American soldier approached me and asked me to sign his birth certificate. It appeared that he was an Indian – his name was Henry Jumping Eagle – and that the US gave each Indian a card saying that they were by nature of their birth fully-fledged United States citizens. This seemed rather a nerve on the part of the state seeing that the Indians were here before anyone else. He promised to send me a copy of his certificate as a souvenir.

The colonel and I went and had a coffee and then moved to the sheriff's office, where I was introduced to Mr Cash, the head of civil defence, and the colonel entertained the coroner. Plans had been laid for civil defence in Los Angeles and Riverside, but apparently Mr Cash was not happy that they bore any relation to fact and reality. So he asked me to vet them for him. First he gave me an outline of the situation, and from that I could see immediately that his main trouble was convincing citizens that there was a war on; they wouldn't display interest in civil defence because they didn't understand the meaning of the word. He couldn't get help from the services because they didn't want to commit themselves to anything that would mean hours of practice until the war, or rather the need for civil defence, became a reality. Consequently, any information I gave him was just irony; heaping coals on fire, etc. For example, when I pointed out the important role the fire fighting services played, and when I mentioned that one of our greatest troubles had been water supply and that we had got over that by erecting static water tanks, he retaliated by saying that the reorganisation of the fire fighting services to meet the type of blitz we had had would need far more authority than he had. The only thing he could do would be to recommend it and then, when the first bombing occurred, say 'well, I told you so'. He had a very difficult job, but I believed that he did want to have his organisation at least set, so that if and when it was needed, he could put it into operation backed by the clamour of the public for protection. It was a heartbreaking job though, for a keen young man who really did want to protect the people if he could.

The colonel had gone by this time, so Mr Cash took me round to the Mission Inn[5], which was rather a grotesque structure that had quite a history. It was built by a man in the days when California was just being developed. The missions were the linking spots along the main carriageway, and were the a nucleus of the towns which were then built

---

5   Despite its name the Mission Inn had little to do with the Spanish missions, but was developed out of Glenwood Cottage boarding house. Frank Miller, the son of the builder, changed its name to the Mission Inn and employed several different architects and many different styles to achieve the flamboyant building which still exists today. When Cole was writing, the Mission Inn was managed by Miller's daughter and son in law, Allis and DeWitt Hutchings, Miller having died in 1935.

around them[6]. The Mission Inn was a Spanish type of architecture, rambling for two blocks, but internally exceptionally well appointed and certainly much more the centre of the town than the City Hall. The ex-deputy-sheriff Cash told me that it was in this very place that liaison was so strong with the Japanese in an endeavour, pre-war, to form a really sound 'bloc'. But, as he put it, he always thought it was not only a waste of time, but downright bad form – almost a Munich[7].

We met Colonel Muirhead and his 'gang' inside the Mission Inn, and talked about the duties of sheriffs and the differences between English and American sheriffs, which was of course quite outstanding. The English sheriff being a social figurehead while the American was very similar to the Scotch sheriff and held quite a sway of power in the town or county. Then the colonel and I went out to Mr Cash's home. In the words of its owner, a typical Californian home was not anything to look at outside but was put together without any pretensions to beauty. However such houses were very clean, very tidy, and very well appointed inside. They had plenty of front and back garden space with twin lawns and paved entrances and were nearly all single storey buildings. Their only menace was fire, which seemed to happen all too frequently.

We missed lunch but went on to Corona instead, some fifteen miles from Riverside, where we were to meet Mr Chawndos, general manager of a water company out there. We met him at the City Hall (we seemed to have all our meetings at the City Hall) and then followed a whirlwind tour of ranches. I'd always imagined a ranch as being a huge grazing ground with corrals for horses and cattle, etc. But anything around those parts was a ranch. You got cattle, horses, sheep, chickens, orange, citrus fruit, dates, olives and grapefruit ranches. We went to a lemon ranch[8].

First we were shown around the packing house. Each packing house had its own air-cooled room where storage took place. A lemon was supposed to be better when it was plucked before being ripe, and then ripened in a house. We inspected air-conditioning equipment, sorting, cleaning, culling, drying, colouring and packing machinery and found it quite a simple process to get the right size of lemon in the right case in the right condition. A sample or two followed and then we learnt of the way that Sunkist[9] got its fruit from the various local growers up to a required standard and then shipped in Sunkist's name. On from there to a factory which handled surplus lemons (and a similar one handling oranges). The lemons were brought into the factory, which was owned by the growers themselves, at the average rate of 500 tons per day. They were tipped straight out of wagons onto an endless belt where they went through various processes until they became various commodities. I always thought that a lemon was simply a fruit, but when I saw the processes that this simple fruit went through there and the number of different products that were produced such as pectin, laxatives, plasma, juice, citric acid, fertiliser pulp, etc., etc., I changed my ideas.

The chief chemist, who had been with the firm from the start and was really the brains behind the concern, had been working on a product for four years, which was effective as a blood transfusion. It had the same effect as human blood, and was effective for twelve to fourteen hours. He had been experimenting on 800 rabbits, and hospitals had been trying the product out on incurables. So far it had been effective, but it had to have 500 clear-cut cases before the US government would accept it.

Leaving the lemon works we visited a grapefruit packing station, and so on to Mr Chawndos's house, where we had tea. A very pleasant gentleman called David, who was the manager

Cole inspects a banana tree and its fruit

of one of the groves, invited us to his house in Arlington. It had a glass verandah the whole way round, was set in the heart of the hills and groves, and had the most magnificent general view I'd yet seen from any house. Every type of tree imaginable was in a plantation nearby, and it was there I ate my first strawberry guava, a red sweet sort of soft fruit, a little firmer than a plum, but similar in appearance. Pomegranates and bananas (a few) were also growing in the area, while there were many groves of English walnuts.

We left Chawndos at Arlington and went on to Riverside to the Mission Inn, where we astounded the natives by appearing to book our dinner in shorts. We had to change in the gents as there was no room available. An excellent

6   The Californian missions were established by Spanish Franciscans from 1769 to 1823 to convert Native Americans to Catholicism. There were 21 of them stretching from San Francisco south to San Diego.
7   The Munich Pact was an ill-disguised act of appeasement to Nazi Germany in which Britain, France and Italy promised no intervention if Hitler annexed part of Czechoslovakia. It was signed in September 1938. One year later Germany invaded Poland and Europe was at war.
8   Probably the Corona Foothill Lemon Ranch which was the largest single lemon ranch in California. It is now the Corona Heritage Park & Museum.
9   A not-for-profit marketing co-operative owned and operated by California and Arizona citrus growers.

dinner and then we went up to El Mundo cocktail bar for a drink[10]. We were home at 2300 hours after a cool ride. The weather, so hot in the day, was usually very cool at night and you certainly needed a coat in the jeep.

The next day was Sunday and after going thirty hours with little food I felt I'd better get up for breakfast. Mr Chawndos had asked us to meet him in Riverside at 0915 hours and then he would take us in his car to see one of the colleges. We went through some beautiful country to a place called Pomona, where we located Pomona Co-ed College[11]. Mr and Mrs Chawndos's daughter met us (she was a very sweet girl aged about seventeen, but looking much older) and showed us round. The students almost ran the college themselves, arranging their own dances and having their own committees, and they seemed to make an exceptionally good job of it too. In addition to the college, there had been added a military college on West Point style, where student soldiers studied languages for various duties such as interpreting and interrogating.

On to LA via the foothills route; those hills seemed to be continually on our right-hand side and all looked alike. LA was a very rambling city, approximately thirty-two miles across, so we rode quite a while in a populated area and were surprised every once in a while to see an oil well literally in someone's back garden. Hollywood was a suburb of LA as was Santa Monica where we stayed, but the distance from the centre of the city was very great. The city part was not so big as San Francisco judging by the height of the buildings, nor so dense in population, but had quite a fine centre, especially the City Hall and the courts of justice and administration. The roads were good, four lanes and fast, and I reflected that I'd find difficulty adjusting to the usual two-lane traffic routes of England when I got back.

The next day I was up at 0530 hours to breakfast with the men at 0600. We were moving into the US Army Recreational Camp at Santa Monica that Monday for four days 'holiday'. That was a great place, the first organised army recreational camp I'd ever come across, where 1,000 beds were available for service men on leave. Handy for the beach, but seventeen miles from LA; however buses were frequent. Everything had been laid on and the men were going to be looked after like children.

Colonel Scott, who had organised the show, promised a better time than New York and certainly seemed to have got off on the right foot. The men arrived in convoy to be greeted by a band playing 'God save the King'. The Union Jack and Stars and Stripes were hung over the entrance to the camp, which was semi-tented with HQ buildings. Red Cross cars were at our disposal for any driving we wanted to do anywhere. A shuttle bus service was operated solely for the British other ranks and ran every hour twenty-four hours a day.

It was evident to me from the start that I should not be able to do in LA what I'd done in most other cities, i.e. get around to see the city, meet the head people, police, etc., and then have a tour of the clubs, etc. The city was too big.

Parade in front of City Hall, Los Angeles

10 The El Mundo was the first dedicated bar in the Mission Inn. Frank Miller had been a strict teetotaller so no liquor was sold in the Mission Inn when he was alive.
11 Pomona is a suburb of Los Angeles about half way between LA's centre and Riverside. Pomona College was founded there in 1887, but moved to Claremont two years later, although retaining the name. It is one of the five Claremont Colleges which share facilities.

Its suburbs, Hollywood, Beverly Hills, Glendale, Santa Monica, etc., are cities in themselves. I had to decide therefore, how I should occupy my time to the best advantage. We were supposed to have four days holiday, so the natural reaction for many was to see film stars. But I'd already met quite a few stars and could safely say that one film star was very much like another, simply because their mentors, the publicity men, followed the same patterns in handling their stars and the star's life. I knew we were going to be introduced to various film people, so I adopted the policy of leaving Hollywood entirely alone and concentrating on the environment which surrounded the people of the city.

Having arrived there, our first public function was to parade through 5th Street in LA. We got out the familiar shorts, our most publicised 'props', and got on board trucks. A fast ride gave us half an hour to spare at the forming-up position in Pershing Square. There we were besieged by a crowd of people, who asked the usual questions and clapped whenever a group of the boys were marched from A to B. We formed up and the band took the lead. We paraded with the 3.7 inch gun between heavy and light troops,

Sir Cedric Hardwicke acted as master of ceremonies in the reviewing stand (see footnote 15)

a 40 mm between light troops and searchlight personnel with a searchlight bringing up the rear. That arrangement proved bad; the pace slowed down and the band was not used to playing our cadence. The combination produced the worst parade we'd had, yet I don't believe the people really noticed it.

I felt most uncomfortable marching with the searchlight boys and I could see Bill H. was far from happy, stepping as he did almost continually, on the 40 mm gun which was never more than two to three yards in front of him. The march past the reviewing stand was spoiled because of the length of the column, poor music and changes in step. In the stand was the mayor, and the major general commanding the AA defences in this area, a rear admiral commanding the western approaches, and Cleugh, the British consul, as well as the usual hangers on. We mistimed the formation in front of the City Hall (which incidentally was a palatial building, dwarfing the nearby community), and as a result the national anthem was commenced before the searchlight troops were in position. Bill H. gave halt and we saluted; the band stopped and Bill tried to get his troop into position, but the band started playing our national anthem. Something approaching chaos ensued all because of a radio broadcast of the proceedings and because the timing had not been quite correct.

Colonel Metcalf made a good reply to the various speeches. The mayor, Fletcher Bowron, certainly made the finest mayoral speech I've heard so far (LaGuardia excepted). He gave us the keys of the city and remarked we were the first body of troops of any nation other than their own to parade in LA with their weapons of war. By now, we had two bands and they tried to outdo each other in drowning our words of command when we tried to move off. I never felt more humiliated in my life after that parade, as I felt that with such a fine welcome we ought to have trotted out our finest display. We really were becoming publicity conscious, especially in this city where publicity is the bread and butter of the populace.

We returned to Santa Monica, changed into service dress, and then went by Red Cross motor to the British consul's for cocktails. The troops went to the Hollywood Canteen[12], where they were entertained right royally by Bob Hope, Hedy Lamarr[13] and other stars. That must surely have been the highlight of their trip. Since the day they landed in the US most of the gunners said that the one thing they wanted to see in the US was Hollywood.

We arrived at the Cleughs at 1730 hours and were the first there. The house was small in comparison with some of the houses in Beverly Hills, but was very tastefully decorated with things everywhere to indicate that the owner was British. Being introduced to local and world-famous celebrities became monotonous. The only possible thing that could come out of this type of mass cocktail party was the knowledge that, at some later date, one could demoralise some lesser known celebrity at home or intrigue the family, or boast, by saying 'oh well, of course, I met so-and-so (mentioning a well-known film name) at such and such a time and he or she was a grand (or awful or sweet) fellow or girl'. In point

---

12 Hollywood Canteen was run by volunteers from the entertainment industry and provided food, dancing and entertainment for allied servicemen free of charge [see also Stage Door Canteen in Chapter 4].
13 Bob Hope was a British born comic actor who worked extensively to entertain military personnel; Hedy Lamarr was born in Vienna of Jewish parents. As well as being a famous actress she was also the co-inventor of frequency-hopping communication techniques to establish communications which resist interference. Originally designed to be used by radio-controlled torpedoes a modern form of such communication is important in maximising bandwidth today.

of fact that would be a scurvy sort of trick, because there was no sincerity about the party. It was purely a case of the chief American publicity agents in America meeting the chief British publicity agents in America because that was the thing that had to be done.

Little incidents of course stood out, for example Heather Thatcher, her monocle and her best British Oxford accent; Herbert Marshall arriving late and trying to make up for lost time; Greer Garson selling herself to the camera and all our glamour boys; Mrs Garson watching over her daughter as a good mother should; Basil Rathbone in good form; Sir Aubrey Smith as gracious as such melee in a small house and his deafness would permit and withal being the real gentleman[14]; Mrs Cleugh, our hostess, maintaining a wonderful calm in spite of all the difficulties she was having. The best I could say was that it was an experience such as one would never be able to get again, never buy, but never want to repeat. It was an astonishing thing that if you were to pay all the people for the time they spent there, the money would amount to over a million dollars.

On from there to individual houses, two, three or four British officers and American escort officers to each home. Ronald Colman had the colonels. Sir Cedric Hardwicke had Derek Scorer and Major Crocker. Doc Dykes, myself, Dixie and Greville Steele were at Sir Charles Mendl's[15]. What a beautiful home, they had, and yet how like all one heard of Hollywood, when the only description I could get in advance about Sir Charles was that he was a playboy who had married a rich widow and was living at her expense in the most expensive way. The dinner was excellent, and the party afterwards was very hazily remembered by many of us. Sufficient to say that everybody who was anybody drifted in and out during the course of the evening.

Dixie was terrific. He brought out his languages, which were such a wonderful stock in trade, and captured the hearts of a lot of people of foreign extraction. We were taken out to the house of Maximillian de Henckel, where so much chatter went on in foreign languages that I, like a good Englishman, and having the natural tendency to sleep at night time, decided to take a nap. This amused the populace no end, so I felt I contributed not a little to the party while satisfying my very earnest desire to catch up on some sleep. We arrived home at 0400 hours having committed that unforgivable sin of failing to find out

Hedy Lamarr and Bob Hope entertaining the British troops at the Hollywood Canteen

where we lived before we came out. We knew it was Santa Monica and the recreational camp, but that was not sufficient information in the early hours of the morning to a stranger to Santa Monica, as we found out after touring the streets looking for the place.

Tuesday 12 October was the first day of the holiday proper. I missed breakfast, which had become a habit, and didn't get up until 12 o'clock. Doc Dykes and I had decided to have a quiet day, but he remembered that he had been given a phone number the previous night so rang up and arranged for us to be picked up and taken around by someone we'd never met before. Doc kept bringing cokes. He certainly was a fine chap and *the* success of the escort detachment. He treated our boys like his own sons and was never too busy to give a helping hand. He must have spent at least a dollar a day giving cokes away and took a real delight in doing it. He said he just likes to hear us say 'cheerio'.

14 Heather Thatcher was a London-born screen actress who was famous for wearing a monocle to the wedding of James Cleason; Herbert Marshall lost a leg in the First World War and was an English actor and friend of Basil Rathbone; Greer Garson was also English and most famous at this time for playing the title role in the 1942 film *Mrs Miniver*; Basil Rathbone had been born in Johannesburg to English parents and is probably most famous for playing Sherlock Holmes; for information about Aubrey Smith see footnote 16 on page 95.
15 Ronald Colman was an English actor who served during the First World War with Basil Rathbone, Cedric Hardwicke and Herbert Marshall; Cedric Hardwicke was an English actor whose son Edward Hardwicke was also a notable actor; Sir Charles Mendl was a diplomat married to interior designer and actress Elsie de Wolfe.

At the Hollywood Canteen, clockwise from top left: Cary Grant, Reginald Denny and Basil Rathbone talk with the troops and sign autographs

The car drove up at 1445 hours and we were introduced to Esther Frommer and told that she was an artist. I thought to myself immediately, 'what, another? I've seen so many'. But here was a beautiful girl, petite, golden hair, well-dressed, driving a car, self-possessed but not forward, anxious to do something to help us see the city, but also eager to tell us that gas rationing made things difficult and appointments limited time. Anyway, she had had to come down to pick up some tickets, so away we all went to the University of California, Los Angeles. It was a branch of the university we went to in Berkeley, and San Francisco. A much younger branch, with the buildings still new; the ivy was just creeping up the wall with a long way to go.

We left Doc D looking at a football practice (he's crazy about football), while Esther and I went searching for some tickets for a visit of the Opera Company of South California. I found Esther so interesting, so informative, and so attractive that I really didn't want to find the tickets, just wander and talk. In any case, we were directed everywhere but the right place. She had travelled and studied in Italy, France and other continental countries. She had worked under Thomas Hart Benton in Kansas[16] (whose ardent admirer she was), studied in London, New York and worked in LA. She must have had quite a private income to have been able to do all that. She had been married for six years – her age I judged at 27 – so she must have packed some travelling into her short life. Her husband was a Bavarian surgeon specialist; I don't know what happened to him.

We eventually got the tickets and made our way back to the car and Doc. Esther took us to do a bit of shopping and then on to her apartment for a coke and to see some of her portraits. When I saw her work, I realised that she was a great painter, and that she'd probably become world-famous[17]. I was not an art critic, but I felt, after seeing works in most of the big art galleries in Europe and America, that she had something that really was something. She worked in tempera with a light oil covering. A portrait of a girl Elizabeth[18], in a white dress, was something I could have sat and studied for hours.

From there, much as I regretted leaving, we went to the Beverly Hills Hotel, which was managed by a friend of hers called Ronny Burke, up to three weeks ago an Englishman. He immediately put the facilities of the hotel at my disposal, and, while Esther went and fulfilled a duty by visiting the art gallery situated in the big hotel[19], Doc and I had a swim in the pool. A real refresher; I needed it. I had had no breakfast or lunch and was feeling a little faded. A cup of tea, made from the usual screwball (with apologies from Ronny), a couple of martinis and a lot of chatter on many subjects, particularly on LA's outlook on the war by Ronny. He had felt for some time that LA just didn't know there was a war on, a view I heartily endorsed. Esther had a good sense of humour, and it was altogether a very happy party which I enjoyed and felt was more real and genuine than anything I ought to have expected in the city and in particular in that hotel, which

---

16 Painter and founder of the Regionalist art movement, Benton taught at the Kansas City Art Institute from 1935 to 1941.
17 It is possible that Esther Frommer was the artist Esther Burger O'Keeffe.
18 Possibly later to become Elizabeth Keck, wife of Howard B. Keck, oil tycoon and racehorse breeder.
19 When Cole was writing, the art gallery in the Beverly Hills Hotel was probably managed by Francis Taylor, actress Elizabeth Taylor's father. Elizabeth herself was twelve at the time and just about to star in the film *National Velvet*.

Left: at Mary Pickford's house Pickfair. Left to right: George Burns, Colonel Tom Metcalf, Harpo Marx and Gracie Allen. The colonel appears to have lost, if not his head, at least his hat to Harpo Marx

Below: The Battery as guests of Mary Pickford at Pickfair. Half way up the stairs flanked by two ladies is Nigel Bruce, Dr Watson to Basil Rathbone's Sherlock Holmes (see footnote 14)

was the meeting place for stars off duty. Many stars even lived there: Arline Judge, Spencer Tracy, Walter Houston[20], and others. The hotel, in addition to having a main building also had bungalows which people rented and which were fully booked up, mainly by those connected with the movie star business.

Esther left us to get changed; she was going to the opera. Doc had never been to an opera before and was somewhat scared. He seemed to think that opera was 'beyond the pale' and 'a resort for intellectuals', but I persuaded him to have a crack at it.

We took a taxi and eventually got our seat – a good one – in Royce Hall, University of California, Los Angeles. It really was amazing what beautiful theatres and stages they put in the universities. I couldn't see how they got the money for such ventures. That opera, a one-night show, must have cost quite a lot to put on, and I'm sure the box office couldn't pay for it. However, I didn't grumble. The baritone, Geoffrey Hives, was supposed to be on view for the Metropolitan Opera Company of New York. He was certainly good but the tenor stole the show.

Next day we'd been told to parade to visit film stars' homes, culminating in a tea party at Mary Pickford's home Pickfair. However Dixie and I decided that we didn't want to tour the film stars' homes, so we skipped off about ten o'clock, and arranged to be in Pickfair at four o'clock. Dixie met the Mayers, Jewish people with an interest in 20th Century Fox and exceptionally nice and hospitable folk[21]. They put a car at Dixie's disposal, and he took the daughter all over and thoroughly enjoyed himself. On this particular occasion, he took me into town in this De Soto two-cum-four-seater. We did some shopping, visited the finest department store I'd ever seen in my life, which is Bullock's in Wilshire and had been in the family for two or three generations[22]. From there we went to pick up Delphine Mayer, the daughter, for lunch. She was an exceptionally brilliant girl, an attorney at Law, president of a number of societies, attractive, young (only 27), and an excellent conversationalist.

---

20 Arline Judge was a seven-times married American actress in largely B movies; Spencer Tracy is considered one of the best American actors of all time; Walter Houston was a Canadian-born American actor and father of actor and director John Houston.

21 Cole appears to be referring to Louis B. Mayer and his family, who was the Mayer in Metro-Goldwyn-Mayer (MGM) and was also a financial backer of 20th Century Pictures which became 20th Century Fox. However, Mayer's daughters were called Edith (Edie) and Irene, not Delphine (see later in the text). Perhaps Cole misheard or misremembered?

22 Opened in 1929 the Art Deco building was one of the first to be designed to welcome shoppers arriving by car, and the first department store to have a porte cochere.

Her secretary-friend, Sylvia, came out with us for lunch. I found her a very pleasant companion, almost equally brilliant, just waiting to take her Bar examination. I had a long conversation with Sylvia about the Mexican problem. That seemed almost as important, if not more so, to the people in California as the Negro problem did up north in the shipbuilding and industrial cities. Apparently 'imported' in large numbers as unskilled labour – almost slave labour – Mexicans had since been used and used and never had a say in their own ways of life. The city administration had kept them penned down, so the story went, and even at school they did not get the same facilities as the American people. The result was a hatred that had been developing for some time and was almost at bursting point then. How true that all was, of course, was something I would not venture to comment on, because I had come into little contact with the Mexicans, but the fact that there was some talk of a problem was interesting. That seemed to indicate another little sore that the US government will have to clear up. They were becoming almost as numerous as our own Dominion troubles that everyone seemed so intent on airing. Sylvia was intent on helping the oppressed, maybe because she was herself a Jewish girl and had known only of a history that was full of cases of oppression.

Dixie and I left them to go to Pickfair, the home of Mary Pickford and named after herself and her late husband, Douglas Fairbanks. She was then married to Buddy Rogers, a younger man, and they had two very sweet children, a boy and a girl. That home was the showpiece of Hollywood (or rather Beverly Hills) with its fine gardens, lawn, swimming pool, outhouses and summerhouses, as well as being a fine house in itself and was well deserved being known as a showpiece. Half the Battery were there, the other half, less the officers who were all there that day, came on the following day. The USO sponsored the visit, serving tea and cakes (cookies) outside in the grounds, while the American Red Cross provided the transport.

A pianist played British and American popular songs and a crowd soon gathered around the piano. Photographers by the score, reporters, etc., made this into just another publicity stunt and after half an hour I was bored by the chatter and the sight of the same scene that we had viewed so often. My boredom was soon dispelled when I was one of the few who had an opportunity of visiting the inside of the house. It was beautiful indeed, with painted ceilings and delicate tracery. It even had its own projection cinema; the first house to have it in LA. Two portraits of Mary Pickford were interesting, one was taken from photographs when she was nineteen and the sweetheart of the world, and one was done recently. And they were both done by the same artist[23], who was a friend of Esther's – who incidentally posed for the hands, as there were no photographs of hands so I discovered later. They insisted I have my photograph taken with Mary Pickford, pointing to her portrait.

The resulting photograph (see text on this page). It's a pity that Mary Pickford and Captain Cole are not more visible!

Dixie and I skipped off then, and went round to the Mayers' for a drink and then dancing with Delphine and Sylvia. Landed back at the barracks with the help of a lift from a civilian, it being too far for Delphine to drive back, and the car being needed for the next day. The civilian was interesting. He was English but had lived on and off in America for thirteen years. He was aiming to make enough money to return to England, buy a pub and semi-retire and expected to go back any time. He was a little bitter about Hollywood and LA; he had found that you couldn't take a holiday if you wanted to preserve your business. Altogether, I was surprised he spoke so. He wasn't army age, but at least if he liked England so much and disliked the people here, he might have had the courage of his convictions and gone back to share the troubles and trials of the people he liked.

On Thursday I'd arranged to meet Esther for an afternoon of shopping. It was already 14 October and I wanted to get some presents, a duty I had long delayed. Dixie and I got a lift to the Beverly Wilshire Hotel, where he was to meet Delphine at twelve. We fooled around in a drugstore first and Dixie bought a bottle of scent which cost him $13 for Delphine. That was really expensive when you considered his pay[24], but he told me he hated giving cheaper presents. He liked giving presents and in this case, because of the exceptional hospitality, he wouldn't have dreamed of giving her a cheap present. He really was good that way; his gift of roses to her mother the other day was typical. We went well out of our way to get some really nice flowers – and there were some magnificent florists' shops around there.

For lunch I had a most excellent meal of ham and eggs, with ham which reminded me of a slice of real home-cooked ham at home. I ate in the company of four American officers who invited me to their table. They told me they were

23 Possibly Christian von Schneidan. He also painted 'Esther with Violin', who is just possibly the Esther of Cole's memoir.
24 Depending on skills and seniority, $13 could be as much as a third of a week's pay for Lieutenant Dix.

fighting the battle of Hollywood, had been here six months paying £95 a month for a very small apartment, and were making training films. This training film business became so big that private firms in the non-film world could not handle it, hence they came to the heart of the industry. They never seemed to have two dollars to rub together, so they told me. However, we had this excellent lunch for 80¢, which would easily have cost $2.50 in the Biltmore Hotel. Esther, along with two companions, Eve and Jean, were half an hour late, but the carload of beauty more than made up for it.

We went and bought twenty-four pairs of rayon stockings, which I am told on good authority were the only type one could then buy. The woman's touch most certainly came in handy here. I found everything beautifully displayed but correspondingly expensive, so decided to wait for other presents until Fort Bliss [see chapter 12], and over the Mexican border where things were cheaper. Then I helped Esther buy a blouse or at least I said it suited her, which it did. Arranged for the stockings to be sent on – to my sorrow, as I learned afterwards. From there we dropped Esther (she had an appointment) and went on to Eve's house, a magnificent home near Pickfair, in fact overlooking it. There we met Eve's mother and Eve's husband, a naval lieutenant, just back from Florida – which he described as the worst place he'd ever been in – and two very delightful children. I did not realise how much you missed children until you went on trips like these.

Next day Colonel Metcalf told me he'd made arrangements for us both to go out to Arrowhead, a well-known beauty spot some ninety-five miles from Santa Monica. The colonel wanted us to start at 0915 hours. It was inconvenient as I'd made other plans which I had to cancel. I also found that the stockings I had bought had not arrived, so I had to chase them up and Saks didn't open until 10 o'clock[25].

The lady who was going to take us out arrived at 0915, and I found that she was a Red Cross volunteer driver, wealthy, who did this sort of thing as part of her war effort. I thought it quite a sacrifice to use four of her gas coupons to take us out almost 200 miles. She thought it an honour; it's a strange world. We had to pick up a Mrs Lind from some hotel as she was to go with us. Both these delightful people were aged about fifty, but their chatter and company was that of young girls.

I persuaded 'Judy' to run me round to Saks to chase the stockings. Went around to the back door and found there was an air raid practice on, so I fumed on the doorstep for fifteen minutes. It was really the funniest thing, but in the event of a real raid would possibly have been tragic. Eventually I got inside to find, after minutes of searching, that the stockings were in the hands of the delivery men. At 1000 hours I was just about to depart when the national anthem was played. I had to stand still and think about those people in the car already half an hour late and waiting for me. Still, all was well that ended well, we picked up 'Gertrude' and went on our way to Lake Arrowhead.

Two miles of flat road through orange groves, vineyards, ranches, and twenty miles of hill and mountain. We got up to 5,300 feet in height and got a magnificent view of the surrounding flat country. Lake Arrowhead was deep blue water surrounded by wooded and hilly slopes with the edges of the Lake literally covered with boats, motor cruisers, boathouses, and the usual impedimenta connected with boating, fishing and swimming. It was with regret that I left Arrowhead, I could quite happily have bathed in its delightful waters, rowed and swam to my heart's content for at least a week without requiring the so-called delights of city life. Judy did once spend holidays there, but it had been two years since she came out to see it. We had a meal en route at George's place, which looked unpretentious from outside but served excellent food. Judy insisted on paying. In fact our day did not cost a single bean; which while in a way good, owing to our financial straits, was nevertheless somewhat embarrassing to manly pride. However, one could only protest about twice without seeming ungracious.

That day, 15 October, was our last in Los Angeles so we went back to the city to catch our train. We had taken our luggage with us and arranged to meet Lieutenant Malcolm and Colonel Hunter on the station. I realised as I was leaving why I did not want to get too familiar with LA and only to meet its people. It was that dread of getting to like a city too much which obviously had everything to like; climate, space, people, business, glamour, cleanliness, money, and then having to leave it knowing full well that you would have to return some day. I didn't want to come back here to live. I knew and loved England and its people too much, yet how the English ever achieved even half the happiness they did, with only about half the facilities that the people over there had I couldn't tell. It must be something in our character. Yet that same something which made the horrors of Dunkirk into the strengthening of a nation by welding them much closer than they probably ever had been before in history; that same something which made Britain the cosy place that it was; that same something which had approved and applauded Lord Woolton[26] for restricting food, causing ration worries, dictating needs, wants and what was available; that same something which made England into one huge vegetable garden while the people paid among the highest taxes in the world; that same something was the something which made me proud to be British.

---

25 A chain of high quality US department stores still operating today.
26 Frederick James Marquis, 1st Lord Woolton became Minister of Food in 1940 and was responsible not only for food rationing but for encouraging people to eat as well as they could with what was available.

CHAPTER 12

TEXAS AND MEXICO

The train was not crowded. The bedroom we had been allotted didn't exist, but the porter found us another. It was much nicer to travel on a passenger train than on a troop train, but of course, more expensive. Sergeant Dermady, Sergeant Bauer (this was my first contact with him in three and a half months), Lieutenant George Malcolm (who was also a comparative stranger to me, although he'd been with the escort detachment since it was a detachment) were all gathered together in a few minutes. We ate and went to bed early; I was sharing with Malcolm and we needed sleep.

Lieutenant George Malcolm

The following day was Saturday 16 October. The country was again developing into rugged desert country and I got my first view of the large type of cactus films of cowboys were so lavishly decorated with. We were travelling on the famous Sunset Route[1], and had passed through such world-famous towns as Palm Springs, Yuma and San Bernadino, none of which we saw as we were asleep. The first stop we made was at Tucson where we stretched our legs on the platform. I talked to a man on the station. He was full of the 'Ole Southwest', as he called it, and I thought his words worth recording:

'Wherever you go in the Southwest, you will find a land blessed with natural grandeur, touched with the glamour of an age-old history, and teeming with romance; here the ruin of a prehistoric dwelling of the red man, there a mighty dam, conserving the waters of the river, or a vast desert plain stretching for limitless miles towards the setting sun; maybe a rugged mountain range, its spires pointing to the blue vault of heaven or a cluster of quaint adobe shacks, or a metropolitan city.

'You will find good roads over which you may drive with safety. Above all, you will find the courtesy and hospitality of the old West in the people you meet.

'They say that he who once breathes deeply the pure air of the south-western desert will never again be content to live elsewhere; that those who once get a taste of the glamorous, sunny Ole Southwest always want to come back, sometimes to remain for the rest of their lives.

'To eyes accustomed to huge cities with sprawling suburbs, to orderly, fenced farms, to the compressed restricted manner of life in the North and East, there is an impression of vastness, even of emptiness in the Ole Southwest. This majesty of spaciousness affects people differently; some feel keenly at first the absence of numerous cities, of ever-present man-made improvements; others experience the sense of glorious release from their previous cramped existence. But almost without exception, people soon learn to love the Ole Southwest. For here is a natural, unaffected land with mountains and open desert as they were in the days of the pioneer and the red man.'

We wanted a fast drink, so, with the aid of a civilian – we were not allowed to buy liquor before 1700 hours – we managed to get a bottle at our next stop. From that moment on we had pantomime. The civilian, who turned out to be a Southern Pacific railwayman, quoted the song of the Southern Pacific to me:

'From bridges – no rust,
Rock ballast – no dust,
Oil burning engines – no smoke,
No money – no trust.
Friendly SP all the way.'

I couldn't vouch for the authenticity or correctness of statement, as I observed no bridges, no ballast and never saw the engine close to, but the SP did seem very friendly. The railwayman was quite

The Texan feeling about the 'Ole Southwest' was amply expanded and explained in the song they sung around there. Simply called the Cowboy's prayer, it expressed most of the feelings that are not normally expressible:

'O Lord, I've never lived where churches grow;
I've loved creation better as it stood
That day you finished it, so long ago,
And looked upon your work and called it good.

'Just let me live my life as I've begun
And give me work that's open to the sky;
Make me a partner of the wind and sun,
And I won't ask a life that's soft and high.

'Make me as big and open as the plains;
As honest as the horse between my knees;
Clean as the wind that blows behind the rains;
Free as the hawk that circles down the breeze.

'Just keep an eye on all that's done and said;
Just right me sometime when I turn aside;
And guide me on the long, dim trail ahead
That stretches upward towards the Great Divide.'

---

1   Part of the Southern Pacific, now Union Pacific Railway, the Sunset Route was originally the nickname of the Galveston, Harrisburg and San Antonio Railway, but became the name of the line running roughly west to east through Arizona, New Mexico and Texas a little north of the border with Mexico.

blotto at that hour (about 1400 hours), having consumed as he said, about four quarts of liquor since last evening, and invited all and sundry into our bedroom. We had lieutenant commanders in the navy – also well on the way – lieutenants in the marines, coastguardsmen and civilians. The SP man was foolishly getting his wallet out, boasting that he had $3,500 on him and saying that he was paid $800 per month and was generally acting like a fool. Eventually we had to move him, gently but irresistibly, into his own compartment.

The party habit grew; others had their bedrooms full of strangers, parties kept moving in between the various compartments and the climax came when the MPs who travelled on trains came and warned all the service personnel to behave themselves.

Colonel Scott was at El Paso to meet us with a sedan. The other officers went and ate, but I went with Sergeant Dermady and Sergeant Bauer so that I could get a glimpse of Saturday night in town. The 100,000 inhabitants of El Paso were mostly Mexican as, in 1836, Texas revolted against its Mexican rulers and set up its own republic. In 1845 Texas joined the United States of America[2]. El Paso was right on the border; just over the immigration bridge you were in the town of Juarez[3].

The place was absolutely full of soldiers who were having a fine time. Apparently Saturday was the only night they were allowed to stay after 2330 hours, and by the time we left at 0045 hours the place was still full. We finally arrived at our barracks at Fort Bliss, a peacetime cavalry camp now turned over to AA training[4] and about four miles from El Paso, at nearly 0200 hours.

On an advance party, you had the advantage of becoming more familiar with the area than most people in the unit. The US camps were all self-contained and built on the same principle to house from about 20,000 to 80,000 troops. They were in effect small towns. Fort Bliss seemed to be miles from anywhere on three sides, but near enough to El Paso to cause that town embarrassment by the large numbers of floating population. The camps were laid out in areas, streets, avenues, stadia and motor pools. For example, Blank Battalion would have its HQ facing so-and-so Avenue in between 4th and 5th Streets. It made it fairly easy for getting around, but no one dreamt of walking; all movement was by vehicle. Camps were never enclosed and the public had access to nearly all parts, but certain areas were guarded. PXs [see footnote 5, chapter 8], generally with a chapel nearby, were sprinkled evenly throughout the area.

Next morning we first had food and then went to present our credentials to the commanding general. We didn't really present anything, but the escort detachment introduced us. The general commanding the AAATC HQ, Brigadier General Hinman[5], seemed a hard worker, energetic and forceful. At least that was my first impression and I had no reason to change my mind afterwards. The general told us that they had had 360 days of fine weather, hadn't seen a cloud for four days, could see a plane quite clearly at 32,000 feet, and generally gave us the impression that we should have no difficulty in firing there. Everybody was ready to help, schedules were worked out (presumably on information supplied by other camps) and all that remained to be done was to decide where to fire the 40 mms and to approve the schedule. That wasn't difficult, so by 1000 hours we were ready to visit the firing point on a reconnaissance. Oro Grande[6], as the firing point was called, was forty-seven miles away. We had authority from the general to travel at 50 mph and actually arrived in fifty-three minutes[7].

The road was dead straight over flat, sandy country and hills were clearly visible although fifty miles away. Mesquite,

2   El Paso was in what is now New Mexico and not part of the Republic of Texas, but was claimed when the USA annexed Texas in 1845.
3   El Paso and Juarez face each other across the Rio Grande which forms the American/Mexican border at that point. Juarez has approximately twice the population of El Paso, but both were and are large conurbations.
4   Most cavalry units had converted to infantry and field artillery during the 1920s and '30s. The last of the 1st Cavalry Division's mounted units converted to infantry formations on 28 February 1943, the year in which Cole is writing. A special ceremonial unit, the Horse Cavalry Detachment was re-established in January 1972.
5   Commandant Anti-Aircraft Training Center Fort Bliss during 1943, Dale Durkee Hinman retired in 1944 with a heart ailment, and died in 1949.
6   A very small town 3,000 feet up in the Mojave Desert, its limestone quarries make a major contribution to the cement industry.
7   Speed limits in America are set by the state legislature and not federally, so the same road can often have a lower speed limit at night or in different directions, different sizes/weights of vehicle may be subject to different speed limits and military speed limits are usually lower than civilian ones. Texas also has *prima facie* rather than absolute speed limits, i.e. speeding motorists may have the charge dropped if they can prove a valid reason for exceeding the stated speed limit.

scrub, no water, coyotes, cattle, an odd ranch house and corral, were the only things visible. We crossed the Texan border into New Mexico after about ten miles, but the land didn't change. Desolate was the word to describe the country. A few road signs advertising places like 'Tom's Place' were conspicuous, but as the colonel said the place itself was probably 500 miles down the road, which gave an idea of the vastness of the place.

The firing point, the first I'd seen over land, was just as desolate as the country. In a quarter of an hour we'd found out all we wanted to know and headed back to camp. We arrived back in time for lunch. I couldn't imagine setting out on 100-mile trip at 1000 hours in England, and being back for lunch. Still when you saw oil wells in the middle of the street (as there were in LA) it was hard then to imagine an acute fuel shortage nor any real necessity, apart from tyres, to worry about travelling distances.

In the afternoon we inspected the arrangements for the men and found them OK. I went round to see the demonstration area, which again was a baseball field. We'd also managed to get an area usually used as a cavalry jumping course, so we had plenty of space. In the camp we were constantly coming across mules driven or ridden by coloured troops, while the smell of mules and horses was still very prevalent around there, from the camp's cavalry days. Most of the mules were destined for places like Burma[8]. I showed my ignorance of the mule by not realising that it didn't breed. They are supposed to be even more intelligent than horses – I wouldn't know[9]!

Just as I got back from inspecting the demonstration area, a windstorm started up and it began to rain. It caused consternation in the camp after what Brigadier General Hinman had said earlier about the weather and clarity of the sky. Someone was heard to blame the British!

We had tea early and then drove into El Paso where we had a tour around the city, which was a very straggly one, at the base of the Franklin mountain range. The driver informed us that 60% of the population of El Paso was Mexican [the correct figure is now 75-80%] and some of the districts were real slums. I couldn't help overhearing a discussion going on in the front seat. One of the sergeants was saying that Mexicans were very lazy and, apart from making as much money as possible from tourists, were reluctant to improve their way of living.

---

8   Mules were used as pack animals in the Burmese jungle where British, American and Chinese forces fought the Japanese and their allies.
9   A mule is the offspring of a male donkey and a female horse (the offspring of a male horse and female donkey is called a hinny). All male mules and most female mules are infertile. Mules are sure footed, hardy and capable of carrying heavy loads on less food than a horse of similar size would require. And Cole is right; they are considered to be more intelligent than either horses or donkeys.

I hated to see only one side of the picture. Consequently I asked several local people where I could find and be introduced to a representative middle/upper-class Mexican family. I wanted to talk to them, listen to their views in order to wipe out of my mind the not-so-beautiful first impression. To my horror, I was told that no one would be able to recommend, or even knew of such a family, but maybe if I went to Mexico City, I might find someone. I reminded them that doctors, priests, etc., must surely exist, but the answer came back that these people had mainly practiced or been trained in America or elsewhere and would not be unbiased. So over to Juarez I went to see what the Mexican in Mexico looked and talked and acted like. But I was warned that Juarez was a border town, a tourist town, an unrepresentative town, and so I found it. I had my pass checked, changed my money into two dollar bills – a regulation necessary owing to the flood of counterfeiting, alleged to be work of the Nazis that has gone on[10] – and paid 2¢ to the American government, presumably for the use of the bridge. Within three minutes of getting inside the town I was accosted by three taxidrivers, who wanted to introduce me to girls. One, who seemed to be no more than seventeen, wanted me to see an exhibition in a private home between two girls the mere description of which almost made me sick.

It was not a good start.

The further I went into the town, which did not appear to have any private residences in the part I saw, but was all hotels, souvenir shops, low clubs, liquor shops and dance halls, the more I felt that this was not the sort of town by which I ought to judge Mexico. It reminded me so much of the descriptions I had heard of Algiers, Cairo, etc., with their bazaars and clubs, that I could hardly credit that little more than twenty-four hours before I had been dining in a beautiful home in Beverly Hills.

The stories I heard about the crookedness of city officials were only hearsay, but to me they were interesting. One of the things I heard was that a taxi driver took a man to a girl's home and left him there and went to the police; the police took the man before the sheriff who fined him so many dollars; the taxi driver and the policeman and the sheriff then shared the fine. A nice racket, if it was true, but that I never

Marching into Mexico over the Immigration Bridge (see footnote 18)

knew. The only good thing I discovered in Juarez was the metal jewellery, which was peculiar to that part of the world. I bought some of it at a reasonable price, the rate of exchange being favourable to us.

Scent with London and Paris names was available everywhere, as were silk stockings, but the variation in price was astonishing, and the fact that the customs officials told us that no scent had been imported from France for three and a half years, made us a little chary of Chanel, Soir de Paris, etc. Malcolm and I did visit the 'best place in town' for a drink, only to find ourselves spotlighted by the management and treated to a drink while the band played *Anchors' Away* in our honour. We had no difficulty with the immigration authorities, but we were afterwards told some humorous tales about other people's experiences. One rather clever man, when asked his nationality, said 'Nazi', so he was left for eight hours in a cell to prove that he wasn't. Another took three days to be allowed over because he had said, facetiously, that he was Chinese, and so on. We had to warn our fellows, or they would probably, in fun, have given somewhat similar answers.

I spent Monday morning in a very leisurely manner, writing out the few orders that were likely to be needed for the incoming troops. Everything seemed to be well organised – there were so many officers working on the thing that it should have been well organised. There were literally hundreds of officers and men there with nothing to do. Major Peyton, whom we'd met at Camp Davis [see chapter 3] told us of the many officers who were just idling their time at Fort Bliss waiting for work and appointments. That sort of thing seemed prevalent in AAA in all camps. They'd gone so far as to put sergeants on guard duties because of the vast numbers who had been returned from cadres – OTU [operational training units] – overseas, etc. We had a squad of ten men, a sergeant and two corporals, cleaning out our one officers' barrack room; it was humorous to watch them. No one seemed to be in charge, so no one would give a decision; when there was nothing active to do, they just dropped onto a bed and daydreamed. I felt sorry for them,

10 Two-dollar bills are legal tender in the US, but are very scarce. Counterfeit British banknotes had been detected by the Bank of England in 1943, the year Cole was writing. Counterfeit US currency was scheduled for production by the Nazis early in 1945 but none was produced.

116

because I had never found any worse way of passing time than having nothing to do. The changeover in the camp from cavalry to AA seemed to have left a lot of people high and dry. Result; we had two captains as liaison officers, neither with anything to do, and the prospect of about half a day's real work in ten.

I went to find out about the ordnance supplies. REME [see chapter 1] had complained so many times that the advance party people did nothing for them, that this time, I felt I ought to refute that statement. A trip round the barracks, a visit to the PX, a visit to the unloading point, to the AAATC and a conference with the officer commanding the firing point (he wasn't there yesterday when we went) before going to the officers' club for supper. It was an exceedingly nice officers' club, on a ridge overlooking the polo field and the town, with facilities for eating, drinking and dancing. The main picture on the dance floor, was a painting of a scene we'd by then seen scores of times; the Indians, surrounding and killing one of the old wagon trains. This particular painting was hand done on an old wagon cover and should, I think, be preserved in some museum[11].

I met a lieutenant in the Army Air Corps. He had just come back from Bedford, England and was extremely friendly. It was quite illuminating, the remarks he made about planes and operational trips. He said the Mosquito[12] was the finest plane in the world, deprecated the American fighter, was positively rude about the pilots he was training, whom he said 'thought they knew everything, but were lucky if they lived to tell the tale'. He was obviously nervous and keyed up. His one desire was to get back to ops, but you could tell he was afraid by the remarks he made about being lucky to be back, about the number of planes lost on the first daylight bombing trips, about the lack of success of the Thunderbolt[13], about the superiority of the Spitfire IX, about the poorly-trained gunners in the Fortresses[14] and how they were having to be sent back for further training because they had definitely been responsible for the high percentage of losses. Altogether he presented a very gloomy picture of the daylight bombing efforts, but I felt that he was suffering more from nerves than giving the correct picture. Still, I was very pleased that he'd enjoyed England. He did say that there was more friction now between the Americans and the RAF than there had been in the early days of the daylight bombing offensive. I felt it was a pity he come back to the USA with stories like this, as they were, to say the least of it, unfortunate propaganda.

George Malcolm and I were driven into town by two friends of his and we spent the evening in El Paso trying to find a decent shop for buying presents for the folks at home. It wasn't until about 2230 hours, just as we were about to go home, that we found anything like a decent shopping centre. We came home in a taxi owned by a Texan, who had some very derogatory things to say about the police in El Paso, and how they would victimise a taxi driver who would not slip them a $50 bill every now and again. From the many times that I have heard of this bribery of the police I began to believe it, as also the corruption of the politicians and the heads of city councils.

The following day we checked again on the barrack arrangements and found that the motor pool was rather a long way from the barrack area, but felt that it would work. The waiting for the trains to come in was the worst part of our work but it gave us a chance to get a few

Close up of one of the 3.7 inch heavy guns; the photographer is crouching under the barrel

11 Called 'Custer's Last Fight' the canvas was painted by Cassily Adams in 1888 and was 16' 5" long by 9' 6" wide. After various vicissitudes, it was hung in the Fort Bliss Officers' Club in 1938. Cole was remarkably prescient about it needing to be preserved in a museum; the canvas was destroyed by fire on 13 June 1946. We know what it looked like as it appeared in adverts for the Anheuser-Busch Co who once owned it.
12 Built by de Havilland, the Mosquito was a British multi-role combat aircraft and one of the fastest planes in the world at the time.
13 Built by American company Republic Aviation, the Thunderbolt was the largest and heaviest fighter bomber with a single propeller engine.
14 The Boeing B17 Flying Fortress was a four-engined heavy bomber. The crew of ten included six gunners.

orders out about bounds, sick parades and Battery formations, write a few letters, catch up on the diary, and generally sort ourselves out. I added up my correspondence and found I had written 105 letters home since I arrived, 100 of them using V mail[15]. I didn't know how quickly they had been getting there, but I did know they had been arriving. For myself, correspondence had been relatively poor; I didn't suppose I'd had twenty-five letters altogether.

By that time it looked as though we should be unloading in the dark. I hated late arrivals. It seemed so unnecessary when sleeping accommodation was provided on the trains, and yet I suppose we had to keep expenses down to a minimum. Of course the worst happened. The trains arrived at 2200 hours and 2400 hours. We had four searchlights in position so that the troops could disembark without losing all their gear in the dark. The scene was reminiscent of the Blackpool floodlighting. I wondered how we should have thought of this nine months previously with the possibility of Jerry [German bombers] paying us a visit. Anyway, things went smoothly and we were all settled down in our barracks by 0100 hours. A meal had been arranged and the men enjoyed it. All the officers were living in barracks, which was the first time we'd not lived in rooms, but was reminiscent of England to some extent, even though the comings and goings in the night disturbed some of the more 'gentle' officers.

The day after the trains' arrival was the usual scramble to get equipment washed, livened up and sorted out for demonstrations. Those mornings were best not recorded because they invariably contained bad tempers, order, counter-order and disorder. There was always some snag which cropped up which threw a spanner in the works. The colonel gave a very humorous talk to the troops at 1300 hours. He described the horrors of Juarez, El Paso, etc., etc. Told them that their hour of play was over and we were back to work. Informed them that he was trying to make sure that on the disbandment they would not be subjected to the horrors of the depot at Woolwich[16] and generally put them in the picture as to what was going to happen as far as he knew it. He also warned them not to cheer the bull at a bullfight to be given in their honour; that it was considered 'infra dig', which amused the boys no end, and warned them not to be funny at the expense of the immigration authorities as it didn't pay. More cleaning, etc. in the afternoon and then the chaps were free for the evening.

Thursday 21 October was the start of another period of demonstrations. We were to be visited by Mexican generals and other high ranking officers so there was much to do and, on Friday, I had had to go into El Paso at lunchtime to do a broadcast. This time it was for the 'Women of the South West', and I was to have a spontaneous interview with Mrs Alice Barry, who turned out to be a pungent lady with lots of ideas. She broadcast that programme at the same hour, five days a week for Popular Dry Goods Ltd.[17] She was also one of El Paso's biggest entertainers and a lady about town who asked me lots of questions about women at war. She told me before we started the broadcast that she was most concerned about the part women were playing in the war. She felt that they were doing about one tenth of what they should do. She was firmly convinced that the fault lay with the politicians and said that drafting ought to have taken place and that would have solved the problem, but her opinion of the politicians in the matter was not a very high one.

Leaving the studio, I went round to a branch of Woolworth's, and introduced myself to the manager. He was very kind and promised to help me in any way he could as I couldn't decide whether to send presents home or take them. The souvenir position was getting sticky. For example, the El Paso Chamber of Commerce presented the Battery with a pair of Texas Longhorns. These were placed in the mess of AA Command. We hadn't room for many more souvenirs, but I hated the thought of jettisoning the things I'd collected as they seemed to be of definite value, at any rate, as far as long-term policy went.

I went back to camp with Sergeant Dermady via the CBS studios as he had had to arrange a forty-five minute broadcast. The studios were the nicest I'd seen outside Radio City. They were small, the main studio hold-

At the Mexican banquet. Left to right is the Governor of the State of Chihuahua, the Mayor of El Paso, Colonel Muirhead, Brigadier General Hinman

15 V or Victory mail was designed to reduce the weight of posted mail from overseas. The sender wrote on special letter sheets which folded into a distinctive envelope. They were then photographed and the image reduced to fit onto microfilm which was what was transported. In the country of destination letters were printed from the microfilm at about a quarter of their original size and delivered to the addressee.
16 The Royal Artillery Barracks where many of the men would have trained.
17 A large department store in El Paso which, after the war, expanded into a local chain.

ing an audience of 125, but the setting was so neat. Shortly afterwards I listened to the broadcast our men were doing from KROD (CBC). It was quite good. The colonel spoke extremely well and the songs, etc. were quite representative.

Reveille was early the following day, at 0430 hours, as we had to go out to Oro Grande to set up the equipment. Unfortunately I wasn't called, so it wasn't until the convoy was lined up that I woke. I dressed hurriedly and caught the last jeep in the convoy – whew! The ride in was cold. The weather there was so unusual to us; during the night it was cold enough to freeze you, during the day it was hot enough to boil you. We were all frozen in the jeeps, but we got to Oro Grande in one and three quarter hours. That was a fast ride with 3.7 inch guns, PF [see chapter 3], etc.; too fast in fact, but the road was dead straight and dead flat so no damage was done. The morning was the most magnificent sight I'd seen. Starting out in the dark, we watched the sun rise, saw the marvellous effect of the red sun on the hills to the west, and the rainbow effect in the east. What a pity we didn't have a colour camera handy. We set up equipment prior to firing on Monday and also bedded down the guns by firing a few rounds. There was no difficulty in firing any time except between Saturday 1200 hours and Monday 0800 hours when the area was used by local farmers for grazing. Consequently we had to finish by lunchtime.

That afternoon I went into El Paso with Lieutenant Chambers by streetcar. He was a peculiar man, didn't mix, seemed bad tempered most times, had no friends and no conversation. I felt sorry for him that day; he'd got the worst job in the escort detachment as he looked after messing, and there had been more complaints recently about the poor way that food had been served and also the lack of it in certain cases. As a result a great deal of attention was being paid by both sides to the question. Fort Bliss was definitely an anti-climax in the food world. When we arrived in America it was a novelty to have different foods and the different ways food was served. After nearly four months the men were not getting enough solid food to eat and were naturally very apprehensive about it. The American mess sergeant just didn't understand. I never got to like squash, sweet potato, corn (except on the cob), hash, corn dogs, or the corned brisket the enlisted men seemed to like. The steaks were excellent but almost always too

Colonel Metcalf shakes hands with the Carmenita at the bullfight

big. The bacon was too fat and the eggs almost always overcooked, particularly in the mess hall. As a result, and without having rationing to worry about, I ate out most evenings as many of the other British officers did.

While in El Paso I met Dixie who had been broadcasting. We got a taxi back to camp, picking up an American soldier who had been badly beaten up. One of our escort sergeants was beaten up the other day and lost $31 and his watch. Attacks like that happened every day and were typical of the type of towns Juarez and El Paso were.

There was a conference of troop commanders at 0900 hours the following day – much too early for Sunday morning – to discuss firing at that camp, the move to the next camp and advance details. At 1145 hours we moved off in jeeps for a banquet and bullfight in Juarez. Spent a lot of time deciding the order of priority for travel but eventually arrived at the Immigration Bridge[18], to be met by a guard of honour, and the usual speed motorcycle cops. There were forty three of us; officers of our unit, the escort unit and the AAATC HQ staff. We had free passage over the bridge at the expense of 'Reddy Kilowatt', the mascot of the El Paso Power Company[19].

Arrived at the banquet hall, the Casino de Juarez, where we met and were individually introduced to the mayor and then many high-ranking officers of the Mexican army. Introductions were interminable as civilians, heads of the various civic departments, schools, hospitals, etc., were also there to meet us, but so few spoke English that from the word go we had a lot of language difficulty. I found myself placed opposite three Mexican colonels, not one of whom spoke a word of English, but one of whom spoke halting French. We at least could converse basically in French, but the meal was quiet one. We sat for two and a half hours – one hour over two opening drinks – and as a banquet it was a fine snack. The Governor of the State of Chihuahua [Juarez is in the Mexican state of Chihuahua] arrived and we all stood up; he was the biggest of the big shots there, but couldn't speak a word of English, so he kept in the background. The mayor delivered

---

18   Probably Zaragoza Bridge which appears to have been the only international bridge crossing existing when Cole was writing.
19   An anthropomorphised character made up of lightning for limbs and a light bulb for a nose, Reddy Kilowatt was licensed to North American companies looking to persuade customers of the efficacy of electricity production.

an inspiring speech first in Mexican and then in English. He spoke kindly of Winston Churchill, President Roosevelt, and his own President, and in glowing terms of the fortitude and courage of the British nation in 1940. Altogether a very amusing banquet, and quite historical as Colonel Muirhead said in his responding speech, which incidentally brought notice to the fact that the Mexicans and English had never crossed swords. The occasion was however too long and with too few interpreters.

From there we went to the bullfight in our honour. That was to be the highlight, the big moment. We had been publicised a tremendous amount over it. El Maestro des Maestros Carmenita, 'the highest-paid bullfighter in the world', was the sole performer against four picked bulls. These were strangely described as never having been killed before.

We were billed as the heroic defenders of London, the capital of Great Brittany. Our colonel was the commander-in-chief and sundry little misrepresentations and poor spelling permeated through the advertisements. The arena was full, the men having marched through the streets under the BSM and were all seated on the shady side. The timing was good and when we were all seated the show began. Matadors, toreadors, picadors; in fact everyone but the bull paraded in the arena. Dressed in the brocaded uniform made familiar by Eddie Cantor[20] in his picture, they paid the usual homage to the crowd and to the patron saint of bullfighters. The crowd gave El Maestro a very good welcome and then, to a fanfare of trumpets blown by civilians on rusty old instruments, the show began.

The first bull, a three-year-old, pranced in seemingly in real bullish form. To add to the joy, it was stabbed with a six-inch knife to which were attached ribbons, just to make the show festive. The picadors and the matador played with their

red capes, to make the bull mad. Skill was needed by the toreadors for them to place the barbs in the bull's broad back, and also by the matador for him to put the sword in just the right place to kill the bull – a spot only about one and a half inches square. But no skill was needed by the picadors who rode a blindfolded horse padded on one side, purely so that the bull could occasionally get the satisfaction of a real job with his horns. Poor horse. It didn't know what was coming until suddenly it got a real wham in the side. The picador stuck a prod into the bull to let it know that the game was really one-sided and, to clarion notes on the rusty bugles, the game continued. It all went to form, the bull didn't have a chance, but the Mexican element didn't seem to mind.

There were four bulls and all went the same way. Blood spilled by the bull – its life's blood – was nonchalantly smoothed away in the sand of the arena by paid help. Two horses came in and dragged the bull away in turn, and so it went on. The matador was booed on the last show, because it took him three stabs to kill the bull. We were told afterwards that it had been a poor afternoon sport.

We had been warned not to cheer the bull so we contained ourselves in deference to our position as guests. On questioning some of the men afterwards, however, I couldn't find anyone who thought anything of this so-called sport. The only satisfaction we got out of it, was that it wasn't every Englishman who could say he'd been to bullfight in Mexico.

Monday was a major day for firing so we were up at 0430 hours and out to Oro Grande again. Setting up having been completed on Saturday, we just went ahead and fired nearly all day. Next day was quieter. I managed to do a bit of studying of new radar techniques and facilities before going into Juarez with a group of friends. As we sat down to dinner, Mrs Alice Barry, who'd been my questioner on the broadcast programme, came in with a member of the press and got all our names and ranks, etc., for the gossip column. To my astonishment Captain Johnny Richards [see chapter 3] from Camp Davis arrived en route for Camp Haan. He was in exceptionally good form and introduced me to the party he was with. Then we went to another friend of Johnny's where the conversation drifted to England and the English,

---

20 American comic actor and songwriter whose 1932 film *The Kid from Spain* featured bullfighting.

rationing, etc. The lady of the house was so astonished at our clothes rationing that she asked for my sister's address so that she could send her some dresses she had no further use for. It was a nice gesture and one which I feel my sister will appreciate. Crossing the bridge on the way back children underneath it made great play of catching pennies in large cups on long poles.

The advance parties all left for the next stage on Wednesday 27 October; Colonel Metcalf went advance with Colonel Hunter to Camp Hulen [near Palacios, Texas] and I was due to leave that same evening for Fort Stewart [Georgia]. An interesting sidelight; the services of supply corps had previously inspected a complete set of our uniforms and were very interested in our socks, battle dress, angora shirts, service dress, etc. On my final day the recognition department photographed all the different uniforms as they said that the details were different in their 'Recognize your Friend and Foe' series.

I packed my bags, held a conference with the sergeant major, inspected the equipment, and spent some time in the Battery office arranging final details of the marching drill demonstration.

I had lunch with Colonel Muirhead who had become exceptionally decent towards me and insisted on buying my lunch and treating me to beer, cigarettes, etc. That was the last I saw of him for quite a period as, two days later, he rejoined his staff at Washington. It had been a pleasure having him with us. Included in the lunch, because he was at the table, was a chaplain, just newly in the army. Roman Catholic, he had been ten years in

Marching demonstration at Fort Bliss

the States, and his home was in south Germany. He apologised or rather gave the impression that he was fearful about telling us this information but, despite the promise of a very interesting story, it never materialised.

Johnny Richards came and picked me up and ran me and my baggage into town calling in at various places on the way. Firstly we called at Mrs Ransome's, where we had had a drink the previous evening. We found a hen party or rather a bridge party going on. Those young wives of officers on the post seemed to have a lot of time on their hands. I thought that every post commander's wife should really organise these young wives into something useful, if it was necessary that they travel with their husbands. Most of the time I considered it entirely unnecessary as it distracted the men from doing a real job. While we were at one house asking about something, the wife thought to ring up her husband on the post. She did so, asked him some trivial thing, asked him to be home early to dinner as she has guests coming in and rang off. Both these people must want something to do if that was the best they could get out of life supposedly dedicated to winning the war. In addition, the business of wives following husbands led to congestion, dislocation of food services, wastage of time and distraction; the only thing good about it was that it kept both their morales up to a higher pitch than would otherwise be possible. When the husband got overseas the break was harder. Seeing the luxury houses provided for the army men and their families on some of the posts left me aghast and somewhat sceptical of the efficacy of their effort.

Catching my train at 2130 hours and seeing the gaunt country from the train I regretted that I hadn't seen more of Texas. For anyone wishing to start a new life, I was told that Texas was the place. Good climate, a young and virile people, untold opportunities for pioneering, a wealthy country, rich in minerals, plus its agricultural possibilities, as well as its traditional cattle grazing and herding. I'd been in it and travelled through it, but my only experience was El Paso, which all true Texans disowned, and I'd had no chance of seeing such towns as Houston, Dallas, etc., about which I'd heard so much and wanted to see for myself. I felt I ought to do Texas the honour of quoting from a brochure:

'Texas was part of the Spanish territory of Mexico until 1821 when the Mexican Republic was established. In 1835 Texas revolted from Mexican authority and the Mexican President, General Santa Anna, with 4,000 crack soldiers attached San Antonio in 1836, capturing the Alamo in March. There were about 182 Texans defending the Alamo and no one survived to tell the tale, but for every Texan killed, the Mexicans lost thirteen men. The next month, however, Santa Anna was defeated in San Jacinto, and surrendered to General Sam Houston, who was in command of a small company of raw volunteers. In September 1836 General Houston was elected President of the new Republic of Texas. The city of Houston, settled in 1837, was named in his honor. In 1845 Texas came into the Union.

Riding with the equipment on the flatbed of the train. It was cooler and gave a better view. Far left: Lieutenant George Malcolm. Front: Lieutenants Leslie Colborn (left) and Robert Cross

'The area of Texas is 265,896 square miles, is larger than the states of Illinois, Iowa, Indiana, Michigan and Wisconsin combined. It is almost six times the size of the state of New York' and about twice the size of England.

'The official state flower is the Blue Bonnet, which blossoms profusely in the spring, forming a veritable dark sky-blue blanket over the hillsides. The Pecan tree is the official state tree, and its crop is an important source of revenue to the owners.

'The Rio Grande Valley during the winter months ships to every part of the USA spinach, lettuce, onions, beets, carrots, cabbage, oranges and grapefruit, also lemons.

'Water for irrigation is pumped mainly from the larger streams to irrigate the Rio Grande Valley. Near San Antonio, impounded waters from Medina Lake furnishes the lands adjacent thereto. The El Paso Valley receives its water from Elephant Butte Dam located in New Mexico. In the northwest part of Texas irrigation is furnished by Lake Kemp located near Wichita Falls. In other sections artesian water is used for irrigation.

'The noted longhorn cattle are about gone and now the blooded Herefords and other fancy breeds have made Texas the ranking beef producing state in the Union. Fort Worth is the largest cattle market south of Kansas City and St Louis.

'Texas produces about 30% of the cotton, 75% of the mohair and 15% of the wool of the US. San Angelo is the largest wool concentration and shipping point in the US.

'Dallas, "a bit of New York" metropolitan atmosphere, skyscrapers, over 1,000 manufacturing plants, and $15,000,000 permanent State Fair site, part of which is the civic center, a group of museums including historical, natural history and fine arts museums and aquariums. 73% of the nation's crude oil is produced in Texas.

'A fifty mile deep water ship channel, extending from Houston through historic Buffalo Bayou, thence across Galveston Bay to the Gulf of Mexico, connects Houston with the gulf where eighteen railroads meet sixty-three steamship lines, plying to all parts of the world.

'Ships flying the flags of all nations, cargoes of all descriptions, use the ports of Texas, Galveston, Houston, Port Arthur, Beaumont, Corpus Christi and other ports along its coastline. Only one state, New York, surpasses Texas in ocean commerce.

'The largest oil refinery in the US is located at Port Arthur.

'Two Gulf Coast counties – Brazoria and Matagorda – produce over half the sulphur output of the US. Millions of bushels of wheat are exported annually from the rolling plains in the north and northwest section of the state.

'More than half the state's annual budget is expended for education; its treasury maintains the largest school fund and supports more institutions of higher learning than any other state.

'The greatest collection of horns in the world are housed in the Buckhorn Museum where the visitor is inspired and awed by the atmosphere of the famous old Buckhorn Saloon.'

Ahem! So *that* was Texas. I seemed to have missed quite a lot!

CHAPTER 13

THE DEEP SOUTH

I got the usual stares on the train from people unable to recognise my uniform. I felt that the British government had sadly neglected this side of propaganda as about a twentieth of 1% of the people could tell me the meaning of my insignia, 20% approximately told me that they thought I was British, but a four-star general, 50% were just flatly ignorant and asked and the remainder classed me as a Canadian, Australian, or New Zealand officer. The American people were so eager for news and so eager to learn, that I was amazed at the work our government had done to increase relations, despite what might have appeared the case at home.

I met a captain in the Air Corps. A very interesting man who seemed to have ideas about conditions in America. In an attempt to get him to talk, I advanced certain theories, such as 'that America at home doesn't know there is a war on', etc. He was in entire agreement with that sentiment, and suggested that the finest thing that could happen to America right now was two or more bombs on every big city. It was a strange thing, this acknowledgement of a nation's laxity by so many of the members of that nation. And I felt that it had been told me too many times not to be a genuine cross-section.

The captain got out at San Antonio, but not before he had pointed out to me Randolph Field, the second biggest airport in the US – or so he said – and told me to look out for the biggest, Kelly Field[1], just on the other side of San Antonio. San Antonio itself seemed a very interesting city. It was a great pity I did not have a chance to wander among its people.

The country changed after San Antonio. Where we had been having mesquite, there were green fields – not the rich green seen at home, but still fields of green instead of wild scrubland. Steve Dermady of public relations was remaining in Texas but travelling as far as Rosenberg [near Houston in Fort Bend County], and that evening he and I worked on a radio programme for Savannah, Georgia. I wanted a script this time, if I were to broadcast on Women at War, so we started to prepare one. It took us about an hour and a half for a fifteen minute programme, but I felt it would be the best we had put on yet.

After a night on the train, Friday 29 October saw us in the state of Louisiana, making the twenty-seventh state to date. We were rapidly getting into the area where French influence was strong, as evidenced in the names of towns such as Baton Rouge, Napoleonville, etc. I understood that New Orleans was the centre of gravity of the French section, so I hoped to see as much as possible in the ten-hour stop we had scheduled there.

Over the Huey Long Bridge[2], a most awe-inspiring structure, five miles long and crossing the Mississippi. A tug boat, nosing along a small warship which looked anything but warlike in the placid waters on that very sunny day, reminded me of some of the songs and stories celebrating the river. And so to a view of my third ocean, the Gulf of Mexico.

We were an hour late into New Orleans, arriving at 1100 hours. I had to pick up a reservation there for the remainder of my journey, and also change stations to join the Louisville and Nashville railway. The stations were both crowded with service folk. A really cosmopolitan crowd, they were too; army, navy, air corps of quite a few nations. I didn't feel

> I include the 'blurb' I managed to get about San Antonio from a bookstall on the station:
>
> 'San Antonio, with over a quarter of a million inhabitants, was settled in 1689 by the Spaniards. It is the oldest city in Texas. The present city limits are the same as those established by the King of Spain in 1731.
> 'The Alamo Cenotaph, a sixty foot shaft recently completed, stands on Alamo Plaza, just outside the walls of the famous shrine, The Alamo. It rests on the site where the bodies of the Alamo dead were heaped and burned by the Mexican General Santa Anna.
> 'The "Shrine of Texas Liberty", The Alamo is located in the heart of San Antonio, where it is viewed by thousands of tourists annually.
> 'San Antonio boasts fifty-two beautiful parks and plazas, with gorgeous horticultural effects, which are second to no other parks in the country. Brackenbridge Park covering four hundred acres of virgin forest is one of the principal parks, and a leading tourist attraction. The Sunken Gardens are unrivalled in their beauty and enchantment. There are many beauties of nature in natural San Pedro Park with its groves of ancient oak.
> 'A thriving modern city in every respect, San Antonio's mellow background is preserved with all its romantic history, and old World atmosphere. Skyscrapers and modern buildings rub elbows with ancient cathedrals and missions in this city of revered landmarks and bustling modernity.
> 'The historic missions, founded by the Franciscan Fathers for worship and refuge, and later used as fortresses, are a mecca [!] for thousands of visitors every year. They are The Alamo, built 1718; Mission Conception, built 1731; Mission San Jose, built 1720; Mission San Juan de Capistrano, built 1731; and Mission San Francisco de la Espada, built 1731. The Spanish Governor's Palace recently restored to its original condition is another interesting landmark in San Antonio.
> 'San Antonio was an important city in Mexico, after Mexico secured its freedom from Spain. After the Texas War for independence, which ended in 1836 with the battle of San Jacinto, and after nine years as the Republic of Texas, the Lone Star State was admitted to the Union and has been under the Stars and Stripes ever since, except during the Civil War when Texas joined other Southern States in the Confederacy. It has been under six flags: Spain, France, Mexico, the Lone Star Flag of Texas, the Flag of the Confederacy and the Stars and Stripes.
> 'Fort Sam Houston, the largest fort in the United States, is the army headquarters for the 8th Corps Area, which comprises a large part of the western United States. One of the largest military establishments in the United States is Randolph Field, "the West Point of the Air".'

---

1   Randolph Field was named after Captain William Randolph, who was on the base naming committee at the time of his death in a crash. It was established as a training base for pilots in 1930 and continues as the Randolph Air Force Base today. Kelly Field was used during the First World War by the Army Air Service, the precursor of the US Air Force. In continuous Air Force use from March 1917, it closed in 1995.
2   The Huey P Long Bridge (Jefferson Parish) was named after the governor assassinated in September 1935; the bridge was opened in December of that year and so had only replaced the ferry for eight years when Cole crossed it.

so strange there where obviously they got a big influx of strangers through the port.

A lady in distress needed my help. She had been taken off the plane in which she was travelling to Greenville, North Carolina, because of urgent traffic necessities, and was having to continue the journey by train. Reservations were her difficulty, so we stormed the citadels of the ticket office together. I managed to get reservations for both of us, one on the 19.55 and one on the 21.30 train, so for the rest of the time we could meander around.

The lady, a Mrs M.K. Ross, was the wife of an air corps surgeon. She told me that she had nothing left now but time and money. New Orleans was divided into two parts by a street called the Canal. On the one side was the American quarter, the other the old French quarter. It was to the French quarter we made our way intending to visit the Old Absinthe House Bar, which I had heard was a famous old French drinking house. We got a taxi, but my first glance at the place made me doubt very much whether it was the place to take a lady, and so we moved on to the equally famous Pat O'Brien's Bar[3]. It was said that everybody who was anybody had at some time or another been in the bar and, if you stayed there long enough, you'd see everyone in the world. [Note: usually said of the Old Absinthe House, not Pat O'Brien's.] That might have been true, but I could think of fifty bars more famous in London and a hundred more historical in appearance. The only things that created any sort of unusual impression were the electric lights – wall lights – encased in old wine bottles, and the number of old drinking mugs and skins on hooks on the ceiling.

On from there we did a little shop gazing, in the quaint curio shops and not so quaint tourist shops. Pecan pralines sent anywhere in the US were intriguing[4]. I arranged to send some to my mother, but was unsure whether they would arrive. (They didn't.) From that time I always associated New Orleans with pecan pralines, because every shop sold them.

We lunched at Arnaulds[5], a restaurant tucked away in a back street, relying on its good food and reputation, interior cleanliness and service for its trade. That was my first experience of 'Volaille' [similar to chicken supreme] creamed in a paper bag and served in the bag now browned by heating. Seafood appeared to be another New Orleans favourite, and so it should be, but the Trout Meuniere that I had was anything but a credit to a seacoast town. A glass of sherry failed to arouse my appetite – the day was too warm – and the rather humid atmosphere seemed to have lowered my resistive powers. My one wish was to go to the museum to see the costumes worn by the locals at their festival Mardi Gras, which was probably the most

I got quite a lot of information about the Mardi Gras, which I write down in the same form that it was given to me:

'1827 was the beginning of what is now called Mardi Gras, when a small group of about a dozen exuberant Creoles, just back from their studies in Paris, dressed themselves in fantastic costumes on Shrove Tuesday morning and startled the colonial guard with a street procession. In 1837, the first group of floats appeared. Since then Mardi Gras has developed into an annual celebration, when half a million human beings throw off their shells of restraint and freely express their festive feelings. Bankers to dusty roustabouts doff the habiliments of reality and don the fantastic regalia of a worldwide make-believe and, with the children, resign themselves to wholesome expression of the spirit of play. The carnival season begins shortly after Christmas each year and extends until Ash Wednesday.

'Momus, the Greek god of mockery and censure, is the first of the major processions, and is followed by King Nor, Proteus, Rex and Comus. Mardi Gras day presents a spectacle of miles of glittering floats, miles of packed streets, thousands of persons clamouring for favours and yelling at those on the floats. Thousands of red and white flares and gasoline torches in the hands of marching, gaudily-costumed Negroes, illuminate the coaches. Each float carries from four to eight maskers – who are members of the secret order – and they are costumed to depict the characters in the theme being presented. Small souvenirs, such as fans, necklaces, flowers, thrown from the floats as they pass, acknowledge the applause of the thousands whose eager faces line the route of their parade.

'On Mardi Gras day, scores of popular marching clubs and maskers from every part of the city emerge in an endless variety of spectacles. Merchants' Associations review the maskers and award prizes to the most original. The morning of Mardi Gras day, Rex parades; in the evening Comus, who for three-quarters of a century has led the oddities of Mardi Gras in the final celebration with its grand concluding pageant and ball. And then comes the solemnity of Lent, with the solemn, dull thud at midnight, when the tolling of chimes of the ancient St Louis Cathedral, like the beating heart of New Orleans, call the faithful to prayer and the discarding of the gaudy trappings of their carefree world.

'Torchlights of one year's pageant are scarcely extinguished before work is started upon plans for the coming year.'

famous celebration in the States, and which was visited by people from all over the country. The festival took place in mid-January, so we were not able to witness it. I did want to see the costumes and read the history of it if I could, but unfortunately it was so hot that in desperation we had to commit what I considered an awful slight to New Orleans; we had to go into a movie to get cool.

Only just sufficient time was left to catch my train, although I did see a linen shop that attracted my attention. Some beautifully embroidered linen handkerchiefs were in the window. We went in to price them and the average price was $2.50; 12/6d for one handkerchief! That seemed a bit dear, but that was nothing to the disappointment I had in finding that they were made in Portugal and embroidered in China. I'd travelled almost the whole length of the USA and the only time I'd been really attracted by gifts, I found they come from England (at Bullock's in LA), Mexico (Juarez and El Paso), and China and Portugal (New Orleans).

---

3   When Cole was writing, the Old Absinthe House Bar was actually housed in a warehouse and not in the Old Absinthe House itself which might have explained its insalubrious appearance. The bar had been moved from the Old Absinthe House secretly to save it from being destroyed at the start of Prohibition in 1920. It was returned in 2004. Although founded in 1933, Pat O'Brien's had only been at the location where Cole visited it since 1942. It is still there today.
4   Pecans are used instead of almonds and held together with sugar, butter and cream. The pralines are a fudge-type biscuit.
5   Founded by Count Arnauld Casanave in 1918, and specialising in French/creole food, Arnauld's still exists. When Cole visited it, the Count himself was still managing the restaurant; he died in 1948.

On arrival at the train, I thought that it would be best to go to bed, as I had to change trains early in the morning. During the night we went through Mississippi, Alabama, and arrived at Montgomery, Georgia in the early hours of Saturday morning. That brought the total number of states we'd visited to thirty out of forty eight.

Despite the early morning – it was 5 o'clock – I managed to get my shoes shined by a real shoeshine showman, who did 20% shoeshine and 80% showmanship. Still, I enjoyed watching him. Breakfasted in the restaurant on the station, and then got onto the train to Waycross [Ware County, Georgia], where I had another change of railway. By then I would be on the Atlantic Coast Line, so I'd almost completed my coast-to-coast tour. The train I was travelling on was a local and stopped at every station. It was the first time I'd travelled on such a train in America and was very reminiscent of home. We got short stops with market

Left to right: Lieutenant Hicks, Lieutenant Randall, Captain Gene Grewe

people getting on and off in ones and twos. There was no dining car on the train, but I'd had no warning and consequently had no sandwiches or food of any sort with me. However a 'Butch'[6], as they appeared to call him, came round selling sandwiches, coca cola, potato crisps, etc. While they were expensive, at least they filled you up.

By this time we were in extremely fertile country where the main occupation seemed to be small-time gardening, although I saw evidence of the cotton picking industry. The land was swampy forest land, one of the staple industries being the cultivation of the pecan nut for fertilising. Negroes abounded around these parts and, at every stop, the percentage of black folk to white was about 70% to 30%. Since entering Georgia, we had not passed through a decent town, and had been travelling for seven hours. There appeared, from the train anyway, to be nothing but badly built, unsightly shacks, something similar to North Carolina. An excellent opportunity after the war would be to replace these with the well-built army huts which abounded at the big camps. Certainly a lot of progress was necessary if one of the worst features of American countryside was to be cleaned up. It seems senseless pointing with pride at New York's skyscrapers while condoning the thousands of terrible shacks which dotted the countryside for thousands of miles.

I got into conversation with a naval lieutenant who said he had been in the battle in the Indian Ocean, where the British lost the *Cornwall* and the *Dorsetshire*[7]. He paid striking tribute to the RAF and said that the Spitfires got fifty seven out of seventy five Japanese planes. I was struck by the remarkably good conduct of the American enlisted men travelling on trains. On this train they were all probably strangers, but they had so far sat in their places, watched events with interest, and failed to be either restless or unruly. Their seats and places were much cleaner than mine; their coats were neatly hung up on hooks and their luggage stowed on the racks.

It was just 2100 hours when we steamed into McIntosh [near Hinesville, Georgia], a place which comprised sidings and that appeared to be all. Lieutenant Hicks and a Lieutenant Ruske were there to meet me with a sedan car. We ran into Camp Stewart in about ten minutes, during which time they gave me a brief history of the camp. It appeared that almost everything was set up already and it only needed us to check over things. There were also four letters waiting for me which I could hardly wait to read, it had been so long since I'd had mail.

Having failed to wake in time for breakfast on Sunday 31 October, I had to do without. Major Croker, Lieutenant Hicks and myself started in to work right away. Went to the AAATC HQ, where we met Major Brassel, who had charge of our arrangements, and where we ran through the proposed schedule. They seemed exceptionally eager to see our work and I felt sure that this was the one place where we had to really put on a first-class show. The camp appeared to be exceptionally well laid out, although extremely large. Sand, of course, abounded everywhere. The firing point was over uninhabited, marshy land, and the post would have been as dismal in appearance as Davis, were it not for the few trees. These were mainly turpentine trees, which seemed to abound around those parts. I heard that the price paid per tree

6   'Butch' was an abbreviation of 'butcher', one American definition of which is a vendor, particularly on trains and in theatres. Butches were usually boys selling wares on a freelance basis and, although not employed by the railroad, were often tolerated and allowed to ride free of charge as they were offering a service.
7   In the Indian Ocean Raid of April 1942 the Imperial Japanese Navy routed an allied convoy to claim superiority in the Indian Ocean. The convoy was escorted by heavy cruisers *HMS Cornwall* and *HMS Dorsetshire*. Both were sunk with the loss of 424 men.

I managed to get to know a little of the history of the State of Georgia from published pamphlets:

'Georgia, the Empire State of the South, was founded in 1733 by General James Edward Oglethorpe and a band of English settlers. Chartered by George II for whom it was named, originally the territory included the land north of Florida, extending from the Atlantic Ocean to the Mississippi River. Today Georgia is the large state east of the Mississippi River.

'Georgia's richest resource appears to be her infinite variety.

'Her topography is varied. North Georgia is mountainous, middle or Piedmont area is rolling upland and the south, level or gently rolling. Of the nine climatic zones into which the United States is divided, seven are in her boundaries. The average year-round temperature is 63.6 degrees; average rainfall is less than fifty inches.

'Georgia's products are varied. If her peaches and watermelons are typical, so are her cotton, marble, granite and forests. The state produces or can produce forty four of the fifty two commercial minerals, nearly every character of fruit or vegetable, lumber, livestock, poultry, in fact, practically everything needed for the comfort of life.

'Georgia seems to lead the nation in the production of naval stores, peaches, watermelons, peanuts, pimentos, sweet potatoes, pecans, and in the mineral field, ochre, barytes and fullers' earth.

'One of the original thirteen colonies, Georgia was one of the first four states to ratify the constitution. Among other notable Georgia firsts are supposed to be: the invention of the cotton gin; the first woman United States senator; the first long-distance telephone call; the first state-chartered college for women; the first state-chartered university; the first baptism in America; the foundation of the Girl Scouts; the first time ether was used as an anaesthetic.

'Atlanta, the capital city, is the commercial, industrial and financial dynamo of the Southeast. A great distributing centre, the city is also a great industrial centre. Nourishing all the charm of the old South, Atlanta has a well-deserved reputation for true hospitality.

'Savannah, the mother city of Georgia, ranks second in size and abounds in points of never-ending interest and historic value from colonial days to the present. Other large and progressive cities include Augusta, Macon, Columbus and Athens.

'The leading industry is textile manufacturing and the 240 mills make Georgia rank fourth in size among cotton manufacturing states. Fully 75% of all tyre cords and fabrics used in automobile tyres in the United States is manufactured in Georgia.

'Miles of sea coast, hundreds of rivers and lakes and millions of acres of forest provide breeding places for a variety of wild creatures and fish. Sixteen miles from Atlanta is Stone Mountain, reputedly the largest solid body of exposed granite of the world.

'Georgia's state song, with words by Robert Loveman, goes as follows:

From the mountains to the sea
Where her rivers roll
There I ever longed to be
O' my heart, my soul.
By her meadows, let me lie
In her vales remain
Underneath her roof-tree sky
Watch the shadows wane.

Georgia land of our delight
Haven of the blest
Here by happy day and night.
Peace enthrones the breast.
Georgia, Georgia dearest earth
Underneath the blue
Clime that ever giveth birth
To the brave and true.'

for collection of the sap (turpentine) for one year was 1¢. That seemed ridiculously low, but when I saw how many trees there were to an acre it was astonishing how it would mount up.

Stewart itself was forty-two miles from Savannah, which was the nearest town. The civilian transport to and from Savannah was almost reminiscent of English camp transport and the petrol rationing appeared to be really strict. It was strange how each camp in America had its own 'advertising agency', known of course as the public relations office. The information they produced was both frank and interesting:

'The Anti-aircraft Training Center at Camp Stewart, nestled in the coastal piney woods of South Georgia less than a mile from the historic village of Hinesville, was created by Congress in the latter part of June 1940.

'One of the largest firing and camp areas in the nation, it embraces approximately 280,000 acres in five South Georgia counties.

'The original tract of approximately 5,000 acres was acquired about July 1, 1940. First actual construction work started on September 17, 1940, with the arrival of six carpenters and six labourers to erect a temporary office structure. By February 1, 1941 all housing and troop facilities at the camp were virtually completed, with some 5,000 workers having been employed, hundreds of buildings and tent structures erected and miles of paved roads laid down. The entire campsite was literally carved out of the almost virgin pine and cypress forests of South Georgia.

'The first actual anti-aircraft training programme for the camp got underway in the early December. On January 10, 1941 the first beams of anti-aircraft lights from the camp stabbed the night sky in a practice manoeuvre.

'The first actual firing practice started April 8, 1941, at Fernandina, Florida, a tiny isle just below the

Sergeant Helmsley eating watermelon

Brigadier General Clare Hibbs Armstrong, Commanding Officer 109th Coast Artillery Group and in charge of Camp Stewart. From November 1944 to April 1945 General Armstrong commanded the AAA defence of Antwerp for which he was awarded the Army Distinguished Service Medal. He retired in 1952 and died in 1969

state line. The island and the Okefenokee Swamp of South Georgia were used as firing areas pending securing of the camp's regular firing areas, now in daily use.

'The post's miniature anti-aircraft range, using rifles on moving targets simulating attacking aeroplanes, opened in the middle of the summer of 1941.

'The camp was named after General Daniel Stewart, revolutionary war hero and native of Liberty County, in which the main part of the camp is situated. Born December 20, 1761 in St John's Parish, now Liberty County, Stewart joined the revolution at fifteen years of age and served in battle under Marion and Sumter of South Carolina. Taken prisoner by the British he escaped from a prison ship in Charleston harbor. After the revolution he served in several Indian wars and was made a Brigadier General. He served many years in the State Legislature. Stewart married Sarah Hines, a sister of Charlton Hines, for whom the nearby town of Hinesville was named. Stewart died at the age of sixty nine on May 17, 1829 and was buried in Midway Cemetery, about nine miles from Hinesville, on the highway to Savannah, about forty-two miles distant.'

Having spent the day, moving from one place to another, inspecting the area where the men were to be quartered (a hutted area again), checking on this and that we went into Savannah to contact a Mr Groves about the parade we were going to hold in the town. Unfortunately, he lived a further twelve miles out, at Beaulieu, so we contented ourselves with a tour of the town.

The town itself was a small seaport, its main occupation those days being unloading weapons of war from various camps. After the style of Wilmington, it had one unusual feature; a twenty-three mile long avenue of palms to the beach. It was supposedly the longest palm-lined avenue in the world. Otherwise, it was essentially a local town living its own life.

The negro quarter was, as usual, a series of hovels and lowered the whole tone of the town. This holding down of the negro, while seeming to prevent riots, etc., also had the opposite effect of keeping down his standard of living. To me, the section provided striking contrast to the town of Teaneck, near New York, which was so beautifully laid out and had so much local pride, that in consequence it looked something worth being proud of. Both towns were of equal size, but the North-South divide couldn't have been more striking.

The major, Nelson Hennessey, Lieutenant Ruske and I went along to the General Oglethorpe Hotel[8]. It was named after a general who was granted a king's charter in the early days of settlement there. The hotel was a magnificent

---

8   Oglethorpe was a British General who founded the colony in Georgia as a refuge for the British poor. In 1998 the hotel building was converted to condominiums and renamed Wilmington Plantation.

affair. Built, of course, for the tourist, it had one of those incomparably blue-watered swimming pools, so inviting that no matter what time of the day or night, you felt like swimming. The hotel also saw quite a hectic sort of night life apparently. One lady, rather under the weather, advanced on Nelson H and told him that she'd fallen for him, that she had some four-star Hennessy in her room and would he like to try it. We nicknamed him four-star Hennessy for the remainder of the night, and the name stuck, causing him great embarrassment.

Monday 1 November saw us up early and we went to work in earnest. A final check up on the programme, and then it was put out to duplicate. The 'soldier's friend' next took our attention, namely mail. There was a terrific amount for the men and a very welcome sight indeed. Next I contacted all sorts of people about all sorts of things, such as messing, laundry, billeting, telephones, beds, sheets, social activities. That was followed by a run around the demonstration area. It was an ideal location, being a long rectangle of grassy land flanged with trees. Then we had a tour of the firing point. They fired over twenty miles of land, uninhabited except for wild horses, boars, hogs, fowls, reptiles etc. It certainly didn't look a very exciting spot to visit without a 3.7 inch gun, a couple of Bofors and a bulldozer. But the firing point was well appointed, and that was our main worry. Back to the officers' club for lunch – an excellent lunch and well served. I enjoyed my food there in direct contrast to Fort Bliss camp.

After lunch we went into Savannah to meet the mayor, Thomas Gamble, as we had to make arrangements for the parade. Met his secretary who spoke with a real southern drawl and who asked me to come back later as the mayor wasn't in. City Hall had on the wall a commemoration tablet of the arrival of the first iron ship in Savannah. It came from Liverpool[9]. The mayor was not a young man. He certainly seemed to have an eye for publicity, however, his chief concern being that he should get his and our names in the paper as having been in committee over this affair. We didn't keep him long, but told him what we wanted and left.

We next went to find the representative of the British war transport department, who lived at Beaulieu, Mr Robert W. Groves. He lived on a delightful Plantation in a house, which although reasonably small, had been modified and modernised. Mr and Mrs Groves made us feel really at home and wanted to do so much for the boys that it almost hurt to have to say no, because of difficulty of transportation, etc. We spent an hour and a half with them and could have spent more.

The following day the Battery came in. There had been the usual crop of rumours as to time of arrival and we spent the morning checking final arrangements. I went along to the quartering bloke to try and ensure that the men's food was going to be all right. I told of the wastage of good food owing to our not eating or liking such things as frankfurters, coleslaw, etc. I never thought I should be on the side which had to have their food adjusted. At home, I'd seen the occasions when continental and Indian troops had had to have special feeding arrangements made for them, and it had always rather astonished me that they couldn't eat our food, but then I understood. Not that American food was much different, only the American army's way of cooking and serving it.

A band was placed ready for the reception of the 'notable visitors'. This band business always made me feel as though the occasion was a special one, but I soon discovered that whenever troops came in the band went to meet them, whoever they might be. That took some of the spice from the gingerbread, especially when I found that there were four bands, each doing nothing else but provide music, and having their own HQ, etc., etc.

The Battery arrived and order was soon established. Unloading was accomplished in a record time of one hour fifteen minutes which, for thirty-four flat cars, each sixty feet long, was good work and astonished the camp people there.

Next day Derek Scorer wanted me to go with him to Savannah to check about the parade. There was a very interesting church on the way in; the oldest church in this old district. Silhouetted against a background of tall trees, it stood proud but small, its history recorded on plaques set in the church grounds.

We first made a few enquiries about USO [see chapter 4] activities for the men. The USO wanted to give a party and dance for them, so we told the hostess of our no compulsion rule, but said we would publish it in Battery orders. Then we went on a tour of the parade route with a police lieutenant. I had originally asked for a mile and a half march, but the one scheduled was nearer four miles. At least we were warned.

Thursday was a quiet day. There was a conference of AAATC officers at 1400 hours which was the worst possible time, especially when it got stuffy in the lecture room and the speaker failed to see that half his audience were going to sleep. We woke them up by a break and then Dix kept them awake by a very good talk on practice camp procedure.

They were 1,000 officers over strength in that camp alone. It was a strange thing that over-officering in AA. It had been so noticeable on the tour, with second lieutenants doing point duty, in charge of a single mess hall, etc., etc. One battalion whose normal strength was twenty three officers, had fifty six on its strength. The thing that discouraged me about it all was that officer material who passed through Officer Candidate School (OCS) were being given certificates to say they had passed and then returned to their unit in their original rank, to be called upon to take a commission 'sometime when there is a vacancy'. That must have had a very lowering effect on morale and they surely must have needed officer material in other arms of the service. Or if the ratio of officers to men was so high, then surely the standard for an officer should have been raised much higher. The whole standard of training was jeopardised too by the soul-destroying waiting for something to do that officers were having to contend with. I should have liked to understand

---

9   The paddle steamer *John Randolph*, built by John Laird at what became the Cammell Laird shipyard in Birkenhead. It is interesting that Cole comments on the memorial and not on the grandeur of the Renaissance Revival building.

an economic system which could stand such a big monetary drain on its resources as the wage bill must have been in AAA gunnery in the American army.

Guy Fawkes Day – although not celebrated in the US of course – was a day of demonstrations. The address system was so set up that you heard your own voice coming back at you; it was quite strange and most distracting. The audience was the strangest we had yet encountered, being composed of clerks and office boys with not the slightest knowledge of or interest in AA gunnery. The lack of knowledge was very well evidenced by the questions asked, such as 'why do all the privates wear black shoes?'

As well as demonstrations some of the men from a cruiser in Charleston came along to play us at football[10] in the afternoon. They arrived complete with colours, in the form of the chief petty officer dressed in yellow and blue bowler hat, with a large rosette of yellow and blue. Comments about the Arsenal and George Allison[11] flowed freely with our fellows getting on magnificently with the navy, a terrific amount of leg pulling and finally the crushing defeat of the army by the navy, seven goals to three. At 1500 hours the officers had to dash away to Savannah for the cocktail party given by the British consul and his wife, Mr and Mrs Henderson.

6 November was not only the day of the parade but also a day of organisation to get all things in. Demonstrations in the morning until 1100 hours. Cease firing, lunch and change, and then in by convoy to Savannah, where we assembled in the parkway extension for our long march. A last coke in a nearby drugstore, then formed up and, with a band playing an exceptionally good cadence, we moved off.

We were getting so nonchalant about these parades that you could almost see the look of boredom in the men's faces. What a difference to that most successful of parades, our first, at Wilmington. Instead, on this parade, we *expected* clapping, we almost insisted on wailing police sirens, were almost as critical of the crowd as they were interested in us.

Midway Congregational Church. Founded in 1752, this building dates from 1792

We swung along mechanically but regularly.

In point of fact, it was a good parade, and a good finale. And after it came a cup of tea, so welcome on that hot day. The British consul and his wife were host to the officers, and the exceedingly kind lady helpers of the British merchant navy club hosted the men. Free cigarettes for the men were indicative of the kindness of these people, who went out of their way to make them feel at home, not for publicity's sake but as a real homely gesture. How pro-British people seemed to be. They knew much more of our habits than we had encountered in other towns and cities – mainly of course through contact with merchant navy seamen.

One Georgian expressed his opinion of the duration of the war by saying: 'I think this war will last five years more. One year to lick the Germans; one year to lick the Japs; and three years to get the goddam yankees out of the South.'[12] After four months in the country I felt I really did know what was meant by North and South in the United States. This town we had marched through was my idea of a typical southern town, judging on my experience of the southerner so far. Dreamy, badly planned, badly organised – in some instances it literally smelled – but above all there was that air of charm that the smells, the slums, the bad planning could not dispel or overawe. The society column, the pride in character, the tradition, meant much more to them than the means of living. Even the newspaper, whose owner we met at the cocktail party, devoted three columns of society news to every one column of advertisement. If Mrs Brown sneezed, it was recorded for everyone's information.

Back to camp after tea. We had been specially invited to the Saturday night dance at the officer's club, which that

---

10 The visiting team were apparently from the Royal Navy and were playing soccer, not American football.
11 Allison was the BBC's first sports commentator and manager of Arsenal football team.
12 For many English speaking countries Yankee or Yank is a colloquial term for any American. However, during the American Civil War the army of the south used Yankee as a derogatory term for their Northern enemies.

week was in our honour. A terrific amount of Scotch had been procured from somewhere and the party was thus assured of success. In fact, it was an exceptionally good dance. Lieutenant Bob Ruske, who had done such stout work for us there, spent most of the evening with us. He told me a story for which he apologised, if, as he said, it offended – but he felt sure it wouldn't. It didn't. He told me that Franklin D. Roosevelt died and went to heaven. He had to wait at the gate. Winston Churchill died at the same time, went to heaven and also had to wait. FDR turned to WC and said 'you batter the gate down and I'll pay for it'.

I was very tired after many late nights and slept late next day. It was a Sunday and we were to go to our first barbecue. Colonel Metcalf, Rhys Evans and I set off for the scene of the barbecue, while Colonel Hunter in another sedan raced away to fetch a general who was going to be there. I felt it might be a really staid party, so I was delighted when I found that there was quite a festive air on our arrival. The barbecue was held at a plantation called Folly Farms, formerly Myrtle Grove Plantation, twenty-eight miles from camp. The hosts were Mrs Rotan, who was reputed to have a fortune of $50 million[13], her brother, and Lieutenant Colonel Buie and his wife. Apart from Mrs Rotan's two big plantations, Henry Ford owned 90,000 acres of land around the area. Ford tried to prove that the land was fertile and capable of producing good crops, and lived there on a farm for approximately two months of the year[14].

The setting was magnificent; a clearing in a wood, with a house, a huge white balustraded and pillared affair of

The barbecue at Folly Farm Plantation. Colonel Buie is seated in an apron. On his right is Colonel Metcalf. Seated and visible between them is Captain Cole. Mrs Rotan is, presumably, in the centre on the top step. On her right is Lieutenant Colonel Hunter

typically Southern architecture, in the background. Tables and chairs were scattered around, enough to seat about thirty people, and a temporary bar had been set up in a hedged nook with a Captain Moss and his wife doing bartenders. Colonel B was the barbecuer and chickens were being barbecued. I must say that the chickens presented a fine sight as they lay over a slow wood fire out in the open, opened up, looking very crisp and beautifully brown.

It appeared that some form of barbecue was held weekly at some place in the neighbourhood, much as we would hold a bridge drive. I mentally dubbed that afternoon the '$150 million party', because I was told, unofficially, that two members of the party between them controlled interest in property and money to the value of $150 million.

13 Mrs Allie Ludlow Rotan had been the widow of Mr George Elkins, an extremely wealthy capitalist. Mr Samuel Rotan had been Mr Elkins' legal counsel.
14 Henry Ford lived at Richmond Hill during the winter months and built the Ford Farms along the Ogeechee River. Ford died in 1947, but still owned the land when Cole was writing. His plantation is now a private sporting club.

After eating until I almost felt I would burst, we all formed in a circle, sitting on stiff-backed wooden chairs and commenced to play silly games. It was amazing how much fun we got out of them and time flew by until, after about three hours, the party broke up. Afterwards Colonel Buie and his lady, Metcalf, Evans and I went out to Captain Moss's house where we were joined later by Mrs Rotan and her brother. A drink or two, an invitation to stay and have boiled shrimps and the evening soon passed by. We arrived home by midnight after a funny but excellent afternoon and evening.

Gun and searchlight demonstrations occupied the whole of the next day and one captain had travelled 200 miles to see us. He was an instructor in small arms, so I didn't really understand what he expected to get out of an AA unit, but at least he was keenly interested and asked a lot of questions.

Tuesday was also a day of demonstrations, winding up with a demonstration of infantry drill by Lieutenant Dix and about sixty men. This had been arranged for the hard ground in front of the AAATC HQ. Dixie had some funny remarks about never having demonstrated to screaming children before, as some mothers had brought their children, and they had taken this opportunity for crying.

Colonel Metcalf, Rhys and myself hurried to change and went to meet Colonel Buie and three young ladies he had invited to join us. We all went off to the 'skeet range'[15] where we were to have a shrimp roast given by the dental and medical officers in the camp. A crowd of about sixty were gathered around a huge log fire. It was extremely cold and the fire was very welcome, as was a bourbon and coke served in a coke bottle (no drink was supposed to be allowed at the party, except bottled beer, which was much too cold). 150 lbs of shrimps were on the boil in a huge pan, Colonel Buie in attendance as usual; he seemed to like cooking or perhaps merely put up the least resistance. Not only shrimps were in the pan, however, as apparently one of the more important things was the amount of seasoning used. Lemons, peppers, tomatoes, spices, etc. were liberally used, and the shrimps when they were served tasted less like shrimps than any shrimps I'd ever tasted. One peculiar sidelight was that the 'gentlemen's' and 'ladies'' [i.e. labelling on the WCs] were renamed *Esquire* and *Vogue* after popular men's and women's magazines.

Searchlights had a night mission which helped to illuminate our shrimp roast. They had been doing exceptionally good searchlight work ever since they went over to America and that night's was no exception. The plane was illuminated the whole time.

More demonstrations took up most of Wednesday 10 November, particularly light AA. They were working those boys hard because there were at least thirty battalions at Fort Stewart to which to demonstrate. The heavies also had a trial shoot, which was very successful.

Next day was Armistice Day and was the first 11 November that I could ever remember when no siren sounded at 1100 hours. It had been decided that no official arrangements would be made for Armistice Day celebrations in the camp, although in the town some such arrangement had been made. In consequence I for one missed the hour. Lieutenant-General McNair came down again [see chapter 3], this time on a visit to the camp and not to the Battery. However he did watch the Battery's shooting, which was quite impressive. We also had some exceptionally good unseen shooting the following morning and brought the target down.

That night the men gave a boxing exhibition. Heavy AAs versus Searchlights, resulting in a draw. The Americans were interested in our methods of Army boxing, which differed in many ways from theirs.

Monday 15 November was almost my last day but I had to do what I felt to be a very big job and that was to address the Rotary Club of Savannah. Rotary was a very extensive movement there, as I had discovered, and the businessmen, what I would call the middle-class people, were nearly all members of the movement. Consequently, I decided to spend some time preparing a short, controversial opening speech, in the hope that it would lead to some really sound questions and answers afterwards. Lieutenant Bob Ruske had been asked to introduce me and had said he would buy a $100 war bond for the 'privilege'. Captain Primrose, who was staying with us for a short while on a business holiday from the army staff at Washington, came in with us to support me if necessary, but he flatly refused to speak.

By 1100 hours we were all set to go in to Savannah. We stopped at a cafe en route where the proprietor told us of his British relations, and of his son in the air force in Britain. He substantiated this by giving us a bottle of Californian wine as a present, and insisted on showing us over his place. There was a pool at the back containing a huge black bass that was almost a pet. It came to the side of the pool and the proprietor fed it with cold ham scraps. They made my mouth water and made me think of the waste campaign at home where most people didn't see such scarce food for months at a time.

On from there to Savannah, where we arrived well in time for the 1400 hour start. We were the guests of honour and were introduced as such by the President. The President's secretary read out a list of distinguished guests, all of whom stood up and remained standing during that part of the proceedings, and then it came to my turn to be introduced. Bob said that I was a Dr Jekyll and Mr Hyde, a man with sealed lips on the one hand and a Yorkshireman who loved to talk on the other. He told of his pleasant associations with the Battery and paid us many compliments. Altogether, I spent about an hour on my feet, mainly answering really intelligent questions. My notes indicate the lines along which my speech lay:

---

15 Skeet is an American sport designed to test the skill and marksmanship of shotgun users by firing at catapulted clay targets.

'Gentlemen, some short time ago, our Mr Anthony Eden [Secretary of State for Foreign affairs] said:

' "I think it is a mistake to try to base Anglo-American relations mainly upon sentiment as we may not always like each other very much. I think it is a mistake to try to base them on common origins, common parentage, even common language, because there will occasions when we differ. Therefore it is desirable to base them on their true foundation, which is a common interest in peace and in preventing a repetition of these catastrophic world conflicts every twenty years."

'Much has been said and written about Anglo-American relations. Only last week our Prime Minister, in a speech at the Lord Mayor's Day luncheon at the Mansion House said:

' "I'm sure I speak for all those on both sides of the Atlantic who mean the same thing – and they are numbered by scores of millions – when I say that the supreme duty of all of us, British and Americans alike, is to preserve that goodwill that now exists throughout the English-speaking world, and thus aid our armies in their grim and heavy task.

' "Even if things are said in one country or the other, which are untrue, which are provocative, which are clumsy, which are indiscreet or even malicious, there should be no angry rejoinders…

' "Not only the fortunes of this fearful war, but also the happiness of future generations, depend upon the fraternal association of Great Britain and the United States, without prejudice to the larger world structure that will be erected to secure the peace and freedom of mankind."

'That speech I consider to be most opportune. Furthermore, I feel the Prime Minister would expect people like myself to dispel as far as it is possible within my power, any doubts or wrong ideas that may exist. *But*, as Anthony Eden quite rightly says, do not expect us to have to match up individualities with yours, rather realise that we can have different ways of doing the minor things, while yet achieving the same object. Rather, let us think of our idiosyncrasies as relieving any monotony that might be created by our having a firm and mutual understanding for peace. *And above all*, let us remember *first things first –*

'There can be no doubt about it that the sooner we win this war, the better opportunities we shall have to formulate the peace. Consequently, our first task is winning the war.

'I am a member of a Battery of 346 men over here to contact American AA officers, and our primary duty is to help get the maximum amount of benefit for both our countries in our war task – AA gunnery. It is incidental that I'm a human being and that during our tour, which has taken us into thirty states in your vast country, I have been free to observe your daily life and your common task. It is incidental that I've been comparing your life with ours. Nevertheless, it is a great pleasure for me to diverge from my task and meet the people of America – yourselves – who through the great work of the Rotary movement are making certain of the welding of public opinion into the right frame; who are doing so much to foster that spirit of friendship which knows no geographic, political or economic boundaries; the spirit of the sermon on the Mount and the brotherhood of man.

'It is a great pleasure, because it helps me in my task-to-be; the task, or should I call it duty, of endeavouring to put before the British people with whom I come in contact at home, a more representative picture of the American and America.

'How little I really knew about you before I came to your country. How little the people at home know about those little things which make life what it is; your pleasures, your pains, your food and drink, your hygiene and habits, your poise and bearing and the countless other things that go to make a home and a life.

'What countless harm can be done by misrepresentation by films, by plays, by newspapers, by radio and by other forms of publicity which play such a big part in our everyday lives these days. And yet what countless good can be done by physical contact, by seeing for yourself and by talking among yourselves.

'Conversely, what does the American know about England? The American who travelled in Great Britain before the war was never representative of the people and sometimes quite bad propaganda, in much the same way as our tourists could be over here.

'I would rather that you yourself endeavour to solve your problems about my country by asking me questions. My answers, if I can answer, will be off the record, but I hope correct. Please don't hesitate to ask me what you will, but please remember that in answering questions about my reactions to America, I reserve the right to be as light-hearted as was the American officer who, when asked what his opinion of the people of Great Britain was, summed them up as follows:

' "There are four distinct peoples in Great Britain:

' "The Scotsman keeps the Sabbath and everything he can lay his hands on.

' "The Welshman prays on his knees on Sunday and on his neighbours for the rest of the week.

' "The Irishman doesn't know what he wants but is prepared to fight and die for it.

' "The Englishman thinks he is self-created and absolutely adores his creator.

'I may add that I am an Englishman and could feel most offended, but don't.'

After I had finished so many people came up and shook me by the hand that I really felt I had said the right things.

The President was pleased, so he said, at the reference to the good work of the Rotary, and especially pleased to hear it come from a member of the old world.

That was my last evening at Camp Stewart as I rose at 0500 hours the following day to go to Camp Davis. I was slightly late so in haste I gathered my things together and then got myself into the jeep muffled up as best as I could, for what was to be a long and tedious ride. No breakfast, just a fast glass of milk and away we went in the darkness. Mile upon mile, through Savannah and on, watching the daybreak and not appreciating it, unwashed, unshaven and feeling numb, we still kept going and going and going. It wasn't until we reached Charleston after 168 miles that I began to be myself and then my hunger started to become evident.

Colonel Hunter wanted a run round Charleston and as he was not only historically minded but historically knowledgeable, I don't think we could have had a better guide in our party. We first went to the battery where, looking out into the day, we saw the seat of the Civil War, Fort Sumter[16]. Menacing the bay were the weapons of war, cannons with

Captain Cole (left) and Captain Primrose in less than serious mood!

the usual pyramids of cannonballs stacked neatly next to them, but their muzzles filled with cement.

A large tramp steamer in the Bay reminded us of the value of this port in peace time, and a cruiser and some small patrol boats told us of its vital mission in war. The rest of the tour round Charleston was only disappointing because it was done in a jeep. And my main impression was of old shacks – Negro quarters – dirty areas and roads and occasionally a quiet country-type road lined with trees and bounded by large antebellum mansions of the kind I had got so used to seeing in the south. We picked up Major Croker here. He had set off the day before and stopped off for one day in Charleston to meet his sister.

On from there we made good time hoping to find some eating place outside the town, but not a place did we find in 100 miles, until we came into the town of Georgetown, South Carolina. It was my first time in the state of South Carolina, but we only saw this one town throughout our whole cross-state tour. The country certainly seemed quite nice in places, where autumn had got the trees into its clutches, and the multitude of colours belied the sunniness of the day but, generally speaking, swamp predominated, and the parts which had been cultivated then presented only the ugly remnants of a corn harvest, like gaunt fingers sticking up from the earth.

Lunch in Georgetown was southern fried chicken. A wash, a brush up and a strong cup of coffee and I was myself again; feeling by now, however, a little tender around the rear quarters, after 260-odd miles in a jeep. Lunch took us approximately an hour. Glaister Primrose, complaining bitterly of his lumbago, was feeling somewhat sorry for himself as he remembered a date he should have been keeping in a Savannah hotel, with a very charming girl. He saved his conscience by sending off a wire from the Western Union[17]. I don't believe it had ever been forcibly brought to my notice before that you could not send telegrams from a post office over there; they went via a telegraph office, which was a separate entity.

On our way again, on the last hundred-mile lap. Uneventful as before, we eventually rolled into North Carolina and on towards Wilmington. To me it was a historic moment as I came to the place where I had been before, thus completing approximately 22,000 miles around America. Into Wilmington and through without stopping and on to the well-travelled Wilmington to Camp Davis road, arriving in Camp Davis just after 1700 hours. Eleven hours to do 360 miles, with about two hours' stop on the way. Such was my return to North Carolina and to our last camp before returning home.

16 Built to guard the entrance to Charleston Harbour, Fort Sumter was where the first shots of the American Civil War were fired.
17 US communications and financial services company, Western Union was formerly most famous for its telegram service. Although the company still exists it ceased handling telegrams in February 2006.

CHAPTER 14

NORTH CAROLINA AGAIN

It had been decided that we spend a few days at Fort Fisher, which was the other half of the AAATC camp and some sixty miles away. Major Bede, who was to be attached to us as liaison officer, gave me a lift there. It was like coming home to be travelling on the Wilmington Road again.

Fort Fisher was near Carolina Beach [New Hanover County, North Carolina], a place I'd heard a lot about, but never seen before. All the huts were set in amongst the trees, and the sand and the dirt didn't strike me as presenting anything but a workplace. Details of the programme, inspections of the points, arranging public address systems, mess halls, barracks, was becoming by now so familiar to me that the morning and afternoon passed quickly. I lunched with the officers of the post and so we concluded our mission there.

I had arranged with John Lane that I would see him that evening in Wilmington, so I went into the town with Major Bede. He persuaded me to have a drink with him at his home as it was early for my appointment. He was newlywed, and very much in love. His wife was out when we arrived, so we had a quiet drink and chat, and I managed to get a wash and brush up. The old house was lovely and full of souvenirs. One of the more interesting was a copy of the signal from the US Signal Corps in 1918 telling a battalion commander to cease firing. Coming so soon after the twenty-fifth anniversary of the armistice, in the midst of another war, while I myself was in the US, I thought it was quite a coincidence. Other old scraps of paper told of money transactions in pounds sterling, and the family tree.

Mrs Bede came in at that stage so they ran me into town. I was about twenty minutes late but Major Rousseau was with John, and it was nice to be with him again. We all went to the Governor Dudley, where we met the owner of the house, who started to tell me of its traditions when I pointed out that I'd been there before [see chapter 3]. Met General Townsend and his wife who seemed as pleased to see me again as I was to see them; strange to think that I was once nervous of being in their company.

After dinner we went round to Mrs MacMillan's. I was disappointed to find that Helen was portrait painting in Georgia and that Mrs Fletcher was finishing her book in Washington, while Mr Fletcher had been called on by the government for a special job in or near Canada. Still, it was simply grand to be able to sit around a coal fire again and chat. It appeared that they were cutting down on the number of employ-

Major V.P. Rousseau, Post HQ Camp Davis

ees in the shipyards. Commissions of investigation had been finding so many people wandering about doing practically nothing that they had sliced nearly 5,000 people out of the shipyards. Running parallel with the terrific reduction which had taken place at Camp Davis, that had made Wilmington almost habitable. There even appeared to be the possibility of people getting a house then.

On Thursday I was again up early and went round to the men's quarters to find that the three trucks had arrived four hours late the previous night, due to a breakdown which was fixed on the road. After that I waited around HQ to try and get a schedule for Camp Davis worked out, but we waited and waited and waited. Waiting around headquarters was always an interesting occupation. You could usually see more 'lead swinging' [time wasting] and also more hard work going on than in any other comparable place. The people who always seemed to have the least to do were the multitudes of majors who seemed to congregate around the place[1].

At 1130 hours I got tired of waiting and left. I intended to go back to the barracks to write a letter, but spotted the Q [quartermaster], so went instead to the new battery area to see where we could park the equipment that the men had

1   Slightly ironic as Cole ended his army service with the rank of major!

brought in with them the previous night. I found that our store, which we had left intact, had been forced open but nothing appeared to be missing.

I then went to listen to Secretary Hull's speech on the radio; an historic occasion in that it was the first time that any secretary of state had addressed the congress. He talked about the Moscow talks, and I thought it a most opportune speech. Anyway, the applause he got, definitely indicated an end, at least for the time being, to isolationism[2].

We fixed the schedule, went out to the firing point and finally rounded off plans for Camp Davis. The people of Wilmington also wanted another parade, I heard. We were delighted to give them one if they wanted it. In addition I heard that there was a possibility of Lord Halifax, the British ambassador, coming down on the last official day of our tour. There was an atmosphere of closing down. People were asking 'what are you taking back?', etc., etc., which caused me to feel that our tour was nearing the end and all the vicissitudes of packing up had to be gone through. It was strange that when we got near the going home period, probably the biggest pointer to the success of our tour was that we hardly wanted to go home. We wanted to delay it, especially if there wasn't the possibility of Christmas at home.

That afternoon I met Colonel Adam E. Potts, the camp commandant. He was a delightful gentleman who simply adored making Camp Davis look good. He remembered it when, to build the barracks, the carpenters had to float the logs along the swampland. He talked of the nine million cubic feet of earth necessary to reclaim the land, and of his experiments to make the camp pleasant to look at by planting shrubs and flowers. He told us of his efforts to reclaim a portion of land on which to cultivate seedlings and shrubs, and how he had to dynamite the subsoil to allow drainage, clear the shrubs, clear the weeds, break up the earth. Then he had to irrigate, plough and harrow, and then plant, and how it took a small fortune to do it before any return was made. When we were there, in order to pay for the project, they planted a certain proportion with vegetables, and had 20,000 cabbages and cauliflowers ready to use by the camp.

Met Frances Campbell in the evening after a visit to the movies to see *Guadalcanal Diary*[3], my only sight of war since I came over to the States, five months ago, and that an unreal one. Frances was leaving Camp Davis, after two and a half years as a secretary. She told me she earned $220 per month, which, according to my reckoning, was nearly £14 per week, at present rates of exchange[4]. Despite my liking for her, and she was a very charming girl and a good conversationalist, for a moment I had extremely mixed feelings about a girl earning that much money in wartime; probably a natural reaction to our own poor wages.

The following day was 19 November and the Battery moved in from Camp Stewart. They had a 356 mile journey, and were doing it in two convoys: one heavy and one fast. The fast convoy, which meant all the men, stores, light AA guns and searchlight generators was due in that day. The heavy convoy, consisting of the heavy guns, etc., was staying the night at Georgetown. The fast convoy left Stewart 0400 hours, the heavy convoy two hours earlier.

Colonel Metcalf arrived early and went through to Camp Davis where he went through the programme and settled small points. In the afternoon we moved over to Fort Fisher, Glaister Primrose coming there with us. As the convoy was not expected to arrive until 1900 hours we spent the remainder of the time checking to see that all arrangements were complete. Lieutenant Mollett, with three American officers, arrived at 1700 hours and then at 1815 hours the fast

convoy came in. The men were cold, weary and saddle sore, but in good spirits. They soon parked their vehicles and equipment and got down to a good hot meal, drew blankets, and before long had settled into bed. It's no fun doing 360 miles in a two and a half ton lorry in fifteen hours, but they had no setbacks, and as the escort said, 'we just kept rolling'.

Next day, the Saturday, we got our equipment sited and bedded down ready for shooting on Monday. The firing point was not a good one for heavy guns, normally being used only for light AA, so we had a conference in the morning in which the Colonel went over the programme and pinpointed difficulties. The heavy convoy arrived at 1100 hours and reported all correct with no troubles.

I had arranged to spend the weekend with Mrs MacMillan, with whom I've had so many pleasant evenings at

---

2   The occasion was indeed historical as Cordell Hull was speaking about the Moscow Declaration which, among other things, paved the way for establishing an international organisation dedicated to maintaining peace. The organisation became the United Nations, and Hull was awarded the Nobel Peace Prize for his role in establishing it.
3   The film concentrated on the personal lives of those US Marines involved in the Battle of Guadalcanal. It was released in the US in late October 1943, only one year after the battle (see footnote 38, page XX).
4   Cole is quite right. In 1943 the exchange rate was $1 for around 5 shillings; there were 20 shillings in the pound.

Wrightsville Beach. After an excellent meal as guests of John Lane at the Governor Dudley we had a late night and so were late up next morning and had one long rush to get to church. Mrs MacMillan made some wheat cakes which were nicer than the ones we usually get, but still not my taste for breakfast. We arrived at St James's Church, with one minute to go before the service commenced; it was the oldest church in Wilmington, and one of the oldest in the diocese.

The rector was famous for being, amongst other things, somewhat of a pacifist, a thing which was not looked upon with a favour by his parishioners. He was also noted for irrelevancy in his sermons, and this one was no exception. He took as his text the message given to Titus by Paul when Titus took over the diocese of Crete in those very early days now so distant from this latest occupation of Crete[5].

We arrived back at the house, after a brief visit to a Mrs Macrae whom I have only noted down here because of two things. One, she owned a beautiful house designed by the architect who designed the Lincoln Memorial[6], and two, she had such a lot of money.

Thursday 25 November was Thanksgiving Day and was not supposed to be a holiday in the army that year owing to war conditions. It was felt in Camp Davis that recreational training was the best type of work for the afternoon of probably the most serious holiday of the year. The training was to be 'liaison physical culture' in the schedule, which took the form of the traditional football match between Fort Bragg and Camp Davis with the usual festivities. Before the game the British were asked to give a demonstration of drill so Lieutenant Dix took his band of trusty men, sixty in all, and gave the same type of demonstration that has been given at Fort Bliss and Camp Stewart. Quite a neat get out!

Everyone ate turkey at Thanksgiving. It was traditional, and that day was no exception. It was obvious that Thanksgiving Day was almost as reverent and quiet a holiday generally as was Christmas Day. I was most impressed. Nearly everyone went to church on Thanksgiving Day to offer thanks for the first harvest garnered by whites and Indians after the landing of the Mayflower. It was something similar to the church's harvest festival in England, but whereas ours was a thanksgiving for a present-day blessing, that was a thanksgiving for an original plus a present-day blessing.

The following day we moved back to our American home, Camp Davis. We were billeted next to a battalion of negroes. Their drill and moving about was, or seemed, much smarter than the average GI, probably because they took great pride in their appearance and were out to show that they could be as good or better than anyone in the army. It was a sort of psychological issue and most noticeable to us all.

In the afternoon we sorted out equipment. I went out with Captain Key to Holly Shelter, pointed out the firing range and the position for the 40s, and then went on to site the equipment at Topsail Firing Range, which was about twelve miles from Davis, on the coast of the Atlantic[7]. It was strange to talk about Atlantic and Pacific. They looked alike and if you were taken blindfold to either it would have been difficult to tell the difference, but what a difference there was strategically between the two oceans. To us the Atlantic equalled German enemies, the Pacific Japanese enemies.

The final weekend of our official tour began with preparation of equipment, arrangement of programme, a conference and a talk by the Colonel. A few days ago I had suggested it was time for another of the Colonel's intimate talks to the Battery. My reason for saying that was because we had been for months as guests of the American people and its army, and above all else, the hospitality had been tremendous. We were at the stage where we should be returning soon to England, and it was not only our duty, but should have been our privilege to spread only good propaganda on our return. Something expressed in a silly manner by a gunner, all even by officers, might have done more harm than good expressed in the wrong quarters in England. Consequently I asked the Colonel to talk about this and broaden the men's ideas on the subject. He did so, most excellently, by asking the men to put themselves in the American army and then see how they would think about things 4,000 miles away from the scene of any fighting. He asked them to try and work themselves up into red-hot enthusiasm without the goad of the bombings and the proximity to warfare. He also gave us the latest information he had on troop movement and read a few congratulatory extracts from letters received. He congratulated the searchlight troops, the light AA troop and heavy AA in that order on a job well done, and also thanked the Battery for their cooperation in what he considered to be a very difficult job well and satisfactorily concluded. A very excellent pep talk.

We had received an invitation to spend Sunday lunch at Orton House so we all went to the Governor Dudley to meet the other guests going out to Orton. I rode along with a Colonel and Mrs Bealer and Lieutenant Colonel and Mrs Blaney. Unfortunately the car broke down, but a negro passing gave us a lift. He wouldn't go into Orton by the main entrance, as he had always had impressed on him that the main entrance was for white folk. Despite telling him we were guests, he still wouldn't go in the front, but went all the way round the back. The colonel gave him two dollars for the ride.

There were three generals at the party. Major General Henry L. Larsen of the Marines; Brigadier General Milburn, of the School [see chapter 3]; Brigadier General Samuel McCroskey, whom we had just heard had succeeded Brigadier General Townsend, in command of the AAATC [see chapter 3]. General Larsen had more medals than any man I'd ever seen. Five complete rows. I was dying to ask him what they were all for but didn't want to show my ignorance. The party

---

5   St Paul's letter to Titus, chapter 1, verse 5: 'For this cause left I thee in Crete, that though shouldest set in order the things that were wanting, and appoint elders in every city, as I gave thee charge.' *American Standard Version*
6   More renowned for designing public buildings and statuary, Henry Bacon designed only a few private residences. The Lincoln Memorial was his final and most famous project.
7   Sears Landing on Topsail Island was used by the army as an AA firing point until late 1944. In early 1946 it was taken over by the navy to test ramjet-powered missiles; the allied equivalent of the V2.

Catering at Camp Davis. John Lane is at the front on the right

loosened up quite a lot and soon we were all chatting merrily. The astonishing thing was the entree that John Lane had to such high society. He was the only enlisted man within miles, yet he never looked uncomfortable or out of place.

The host and hostess, Mr and Mrs Sprunt[8], made us very welcome and champagne flowed freely. Lunch was of barbecued pig, which had been barbecued since midnight, cut into shreds and highly seasoned. It was almost the colour and texture of the outside of a coconut but tasted delicious. Then we had a walk in the magnificent gardens. They were reminiscent of the pre-war gardens, belonging to some of the older-established mansions in England, when gardeners were available. The spring was really the time of the year for Orton, with the azaleas and gardenias in full bloom, but at least we could see pictures and paintings and use our imagination. There was a terrific amount of duck shooting available at Orton, and organised parties went out and brought in anything up to 100 duck in the morning. Many famous people had stayed at that house in recent years, as evidenced by the guestbook. Orton was so famous around those parts that it had its own brochure from which I quote:

'Orton's romantic past is closely interwoven with the stirring events of the lower Cape Fear region, where the first recorded settlement was attempted in 1640 by a company of New England seafarers. They were after a milder climate and pasturage for cattle, but their location was ill chosen and they fell on hard times.

'A year or two later, King Charles II at his restoration gave all the land now North and South Carolina to a group of his adherents, known from then on as the Lords Proprietors.

'In honour of the King, the Proprietors called their grant Carolina. The first settlement was known as Charlestown on the Charles River, later to be known as Cape Fear. Only one of the Lords Proprietors ever came to Carolina, but rivers, counties and plantations remain named for all of them to this day.

'Their governor, Yeamans, sent the good ship *Adventure* to explore the Carolina coast and the Cape Fear section was chosen for the first settlement in 1644. This venture too, was ill starred, and when the relief ship was wrecked at the mouth of the river almost within their sight, the unfortunate settlers deserted the Cape Fear and made their way to colonies in the North.

'Thereupon, the proprietors closed the Cape Fear to any new settlers and this ban was not lifted for fifty years. It became headquarters for pirates, and it is said that as many as twenty pirate ships lay in Southport's harbour under the leadership of Richard Worley and Stede Bonnet. They took a heavy toll on the commerce of the successful colonies of Carolina. Finally, in 1772, an expedition commanded by Colonel William Rhett caught up with these worthies and decisively defeated them. Bonnet and twenty others were brought back in chains and ceremoniously hanged at the yard arm in Charleston harbour.

'No great stretch of imagination is needed to account for the name Cape Fear, and Cape Fear River, for at its mouth a line of dangerous shoals stretches twenty miles out to sea. Over this waste of land and water the ocean waves make and break and send up geysers of spray when they meet head-on over the sand lumps. When the menace of the pirates was added to this natural hazard, it indeed became a place dreaded by all seafarers. Nowadays a lightship marks the beginning of the shoals and beacons outline a safe channel.

---

8   The Sprunt family purchased Orton Plantation in 1894. In the 1930s James Laurence Sprunt and his wife Annie (first cousin to poet Ogden Nash) enlarged the existing garden to cover twenty acres, and opened it to the public. The gardens remained open for the next eighty years until, in 2010, the Sprunt family sold Orton to Louis Moore Bacon, a direct descendent of Roger Moore who built the original house. The new owner closed the gardens to the public.

'While pirates held sway on the Cape Fear, the number of white settlers to the north, in Albermarle as it was called, grew steadily. The increase of white strangers and the consequent encroachment on their hunting ground caused the Indians to go on the warpath. Led by the fierce Tuscarora the various tribes began a war of extermination on the white man in 1711, and would have succeeded had it not been for the prompt assistance of the Southern Carolina Colonists. Expeditions of whites and friendly Indians, tempted by the white leaders' promise of many captives to be sold into slavery, were successfully led by Colonel Barnwell and Colonel James Moore, eldest son of Governor James Moore of the southern colonies. The Indians were defeated and a large part of the Tuscarora were forced to leave Carolina.

'On another occasion when Indian warfare threatened, Major Maurice Moore, second son of Governor James Moore, came to the aid of the Albermarle settlements. He lived there for a number of years and played a prominent part in breaking up the disgraceful partnership between the pirate Blackbeard and a number of prominent officials.

'When, in 1715, the southern Yamasee Indians took the warpath against the whites, the northern settlers sent Colonel Maurice Moore in command of troops to take part in the fight, which was successfully concluded.

'In his travels and campaigns between the southern and northern Carolina settlements. Maurice Moore became well acquainted with the Cape Fear region, and on one journey he had to fight his way through the section. Its great river with

Captain Ledger, one of the officers in charge of publicity

a deep entrance to the sea, the fertility of the soil and its abundance of game and fish impressed him so favourably that he determined one day to settle it. Fortune favoured his plan, for the last of the propriety governors, George Burrington, appointed in 1723, took a large share in lifting the ban on the Cape Fear and asked Maurice Moore to head an expedition of settlers.

'Maurice Moore had already been granted lands on the Cape Fear for his public services. In his plan of settlement he was joined by his brothers, Roger and Nathaniel, who gathered a selected group of friends and relatives from around Charleston, while Maurice picked a company from Albermarle. They met at the Cape Fear in 1725 and after selecting a favourable site of the town to be named Brunswick in honour of the royal house, Maurice Moore, settled thirty miles up the river.

'Roger Moore however chose his estate immediately north of the town site and named it Orton for the home of the Moores in the Lake District of England. When, at the outset, the Cape Fear Indians attacked his settlement, he annihilated them on Sugarloaf, the sand bluff just across the river from Orton. He built his fine house on a bluff with a broad meadow and the wide sweeping river in the foreground. It was a fortress as well as at home, for its thick brick walls were loop-holed for firearms to repel Indian, pirate or Spanish raiders. They still remain as the central part of the existing house.

'Orton rapidly became a famous plantation. Its rice fields and forests made Roger Moore, a great slave owner and a lavish host. His success as a leader and the dominant part he played in the affairs of the colony earned for him the title "King" Roger Moore. So active was his and his son's opposition to the arbitrary actions of the proprietary and royal governors sent to rule the Cape Fear that King George III referred to them as "those pestiferous Moores"!

'King Roger died in 1750 and his sons, William and George, succeeded him. William died in 1757. In 1766 George led the armed Brunswick contingent up to Governor Tryton's Palace in protest of the Stamp Act.

'When Cornwallis and his British regulars in eighteen ships sailed up the Cape Fear in 1781, they landed a raiding party and destroyed King Roger's famous Mill.

'Richard Quince, George Moore's brother-in-law, owned Orton for a number of years and sold it in 1820 to Benjamin Smith, Colonel in the Continental Army, aide-de-camp to General Washington, Governor of North Carolina and Grand Master of the first Masonic lodge in North Carolina. Governor Smith was one of the founders of the University of North Carolina and gave to it the 20,000 acres of Tennessee land devoted to him by Congress. General Washington's visit to him in 1795 and a duel with Morris Moore's grandson are two episodes in his varied career. Governor Smith died heavily in debt in Smithville, now Southport, and to prevent the seizure of his body by creditors, friends buried him secretly and hastily in St Philip's churchyard.

Demonstration firing at Scorton Neck. Secretary of War Mr Stimson is the civilian with the field glasses (see chapter 6)

'Dr Frederick Hill next owned Orton in 1840. He added a storey to the colonial house and the four imposing columns.

'During the Civil War Orton was close by the scene of stirring and important action. The Confederates built breastworks on its southern boundary and made Fort Anderson around the walls of St Philip's Church. These were auxiliary works to the all-important stronghold of Fort Fisher across the river and a few miles south. Fort Fisher guarded the entrance to Cape Fear, and held the blockading fleet at bay for years so that the swift and daring blockade runners had the chance to run the gauntlet of their guns. When Fort Fisher finally fell, and with it the last hope of the Confederacy, in 1865, the Federal fleet steamed into the river and for two days bombarded Fort Anderson so heavily that the Confederates were forced to abandon it. Then Orton was overrun with federal troops who used the house as a hospital for their smallpox cases.

'Blighted by the memory of this pestilential disease, and by the economic upheaval of the Reconstruction era, Orton was abandoned and deserted for many years. The great domain of King Roger Moore was on the verge of obliteration when it came into possession of the present owner's family, Colonel Kenneth M. Murchison, a Confederate veteran who was succeeded by his son-in-law the late James Sprunt LLD.

'Orton was the scene of James Boyd's novel *Marching On*; in it the Plantation house is the home of the heroine.

'The site of Governor Tryon's Palace is only half a mile distant from the garden. Here the colonial dames of North Carolina erected a stone marker which states that this was the home site of colonial governors Dobbs and Tryon and that on February 10, 1766, a body of armed patriots led by George Moore of Orton and Cornelius Harnett of Wilmington demanded that none of the odious requirements of the Stamp Act be enforced in this province. The same Governor Tryon became royal governor of New York state, some years later.

'Another half mile on the same road brings the visitor to old Brunswick. Only the aged and massive walls of St Philip's Church and a few tombstones, battered by the shells of the Federal fleet in 1865, remain to commemorate the great expectations of the high-spirited pioneers who founded it. But in its relatively short span of life Brunswick saw more dramatic action than many of its successful contemporaries. In 1748 a Spanish expedition captured it, but after four days the intrepid settlers drove them off. After destroying one of the Spanish ships, twenty-seven prisoners were taken and sold as slaves and the proceeds were used to complete the church. The prominent citizens of Brunswick, Quinces, Drys and others, were among the leaders of the revolutionary faction of the Cape Fear, and Cornelius Harnett, a signer of the Declaration of Independence, spent his boyhood there. Lord Cornwallis's landing party was resisted by local minute men and the place where they fought, just west of Brunswick, is still known as Liberty Pond. When the Confederates abandoned Fort Anderson, they left their dead within the walls of St Philip's, a climax to its usefulness.'

Monday morning was miserable; raining heavily and cold. Such a surprise to us to have had rain, in fact to have had anything that interfered with our demonstration. For only the second time on the tour, we had a demonstration cancelled.

We had only three more days of official tour left and that morning and most of the following day was spent writing reports. The whole report was to be in six chapters, showing the phases of our tour; I was writing the social activities chapter.

Thursday 2 December was the last official day of our tour. Our last demonstration was notable for two reasons. Firstly, the audience was entirely negro, and secondly the times for going into action were a record. There were no scenes nor any trumpet blowing at the close. The thing just quietly terminated and we went back to barracks, in many ways satisfied, in some ways glad, but with that sneaking feeling of sorrow.

Next day, after a conference at 0830 hours on the following week's training programme, everyone poshed up and cleaned up for the parade in Wilmington. Lord Halifax was to visit Wilmington to look at shipbuilding and view other activities in the town. We were to put on a parade which was to terminate with an inspection by the British ambassador.

In order to get the number of men to fit comfortably in troops in front of the City Hall only 300 men paraded and all supernumerary officers were not required. So I spent all the afternoon in my barracks quietly getting my things sorted out. Saturday was much the same as we commenced packing for our return to wherever we going. All the radar equipment we brought with us was going back to England. The guns returned to Canada. Dix, Ledger and Battery Sergeant Majors Green and Shrives were going to Canada for a six month period, during which time they were going to instruct in gunnery. Captain Scorer, Lieutenant Vyse and the Battery Quartermaster Sergeant and his stooge stayed as the rear party. Where the rest of us were to go we didn't yet know. A busy morning with a deadline of 9 December for packing to be finished.

After a quiet weekend the training programme started on Monday. It had the following objectives:

1   To train the men in those arms with which they might have to become proficient; searchlight men on Bofors, etc.
2   To revise men's knowledge on basic subjects which had been neglected on the tour; gas, the bren, rifle drill, etc.
3   To occupy the men, so that they didn't have time to think about the end of the tour and the return.
4   To commence a 'back to normal' movement.

In my own case, I arranged to have instruction from the American AAA School on their equipment. So we spent a busy day.

In the evening the searchlight troop gave a concert, which was an unqualified success. I realised that I had been entirely right about my original idea of a Battery concert party, but that I hadn't had the courage of my convictions and let myself be talked out of it [see chapter 3].

Training continued for the next couple of days, but Tuesday evening was taken up by the officers giving a farewell party to friends and officers of the post. It was a mammoth affair and pronounced a huge success; mainly because we'd taken the precaution of buying in 144 bottles of scotch whisky some two to three months ago. Everyone was extremely enthusiastic and said it was the finest party ever in the officer's club. Boiled ham, cheese, etc. was served in sandwiches, and we didn't notice, with time passing so quickly, that the band failed to turn up until 2130. I was so profoundly sorry to say au revoir to all those people. They were so grand, so charming, that I missed them more than I could say. I gave my address to so many people that, even though I didn't hear from them all, I had quite a huge correspondence. The evening ended after midnight with me going home with the band after having speeded the parting guests.

Wednesday was another day of packing and farewells. I was invited out to dinner by Mrs Corbett and to lunch by Doc Dykes. Doc just loved to take people along to his Officers' and Nurses' Hospital Cafeteria and they certainly served excellent meals. At seven o'clock we arrived at the Corbetts, the first of the guests. The other guests arrived shortly, first Major and Mrs Jones. It wasn't until we'd been together for about half an hour that I realised that Major Jones was the famous golfer Bobby Jones[9]. However, apart from asking him whether he liked England on his tours (which answer was definitely in the affirmative), we did not talk golf at all. In point of fact he had given up the game for the duration. He said he had not the capability of doing two jobs well, and consequently preferred to do his war job of being a major in the Army Air Corps.

The Battery office was a beehive by that time. The Colonel had, for the previous ten days, been sitting writing. He'd had to complete a huge report on the tour, try and analyse each person's work for recommendation or otherwise on the disbandment of the Battery, arrange the move back, get out an *Au Revoir America* book on the lines of *Hello America* [see chapter 3], send letters of thanks to every one of the people who helped in any way on our tour – a vast job – and arrange for photographs, cuttings, etc., to be listed, edited and got together for AA command. His biggest job, probably, had been writing individual reports on the men and the officers. With none of this could we be of any help except getting skeleton data and submitting it to him for him to have a basis for his opinion.

On Thursday we all had our photographs taken. We had no large panorama camera, so had to be taken by troops. We also completed packing. We were then completely ready and waiting to move back to where???

Our boys threw a stag party that night for the escort attachment. 7,000 bottles of beer had been ordered between 500 of

9   Bobby Jones is still the only golfer to have won all four major golf tournaments (the open and amateur championships in both the UK and the US) in one year (1930). Jones was a lawyer and never became a professional golfer, but co-founded the Masters Tournament and was involved in the sport throughout his life.

Two of the Battery's formal photographs
Left: the seargeants with BSM Green in centre front
Below: the officers. Lieutenant Colonel Metcalf was away; Captain Cole is centre front

them. That made it a *real* night! I had been trying to organise some form of mild entertainment, but passed the main responsibility over to Dix as he asked me to. The evening went with a terrific swing. Doc Dykes was given a tremendous ovation by everyone and made a reply which was typical of this lovable man to the delight of everybody. The only quiet that was obtained during the evening was when the searchlight troop put on two of the scenes used last Monday at their true concert. They were a real success again. Judging by the reception I thought we'd certainly have to do a ship's concert.

It was the strangest thing but on our farewell night there was a blackout practice in the camp with orders that all lights were to go out at 2130 hours until 2215 hours, with ALL people to vacate buildings. We issued a protest about this and got permission to stay in our building. So we arranged for Derek Scorer to show his colour films during this period. He had a most magnificent collection of colour films and they could be projected onto a screen to make an even better lantern lecture[10] than any I'd witnessed.

On Friday I rode into Wilmington and went for lunch to the St John's Tavern[11] for a change. That restaurant was probably the oldest Masonic lodge in the area, being constructed in 1789. Some of the original painting of Masonic signs were still on the walls. After lunch John Lane and I launched into an orgy of shopping, but all I managed to buy after three hours travelling from shop to shop, were some razor blades and angostura bitters. At five o'clock we rang up the MacMillans to see whether they had arrived home, and were delighted to find that they had. I was so glad that I could see them before I left. We bought some beautiful carnations en route; I had been captivated by a greenhouse full to overflowing with poinsettias in bowls and nearly bought some, but realised that they would not be a novelty to anyone but myself.

Helen and Jane Wright with her husband had all arrived, so we had a happy reunion. We took them out to dinner and, as Laurence Wright had not been to the St John's Tavern, we went there for the second time that day. Mrs MacMillan reminded me of our distant relationship through Constant Southwark. I promised to send her a copy of our lineage just for fun. She was most kind to me and I just hated leaving. I certainly hoped to be able to see all those good people again sometime soon.

On Sunday 12 December we were notified that we were to move for an unknown destination. Security to the last! That morning we changed our money into English notes, so we knew we'd almost had our tour. It was an awful feeling now that its full significance was on us. Despite the many hectic occasions when we felt that we would have been better back home, we certainly regretted having to leave. Our only compensation was the knowledge that we might be home for Christmas. We were scheduled to leave at 1800 hours but actually got onto the train two hours later with little or no difficulty. Both Camp Davis generals came to see us off. Colonel Potts, the camp commandant, on behalf of the boys in the stockade (i.e. the military prison or glasshouse) presented us with holly in the form of a Victory V sign. They said they'd watched us working and it had given them a lot of pleasure, confined as they were.

And so it was goodbye to North Carolina, goodbye Camp Davis, and on our way.

---

10 The magic lantern was the forerunner of the slide projector and used a portable light source to project images from glass slides onto a screen; the term 'lantern lecture' was often used generically to indicate an illustrated lecture.
11 In partnership with Gar Faulkner, James McKoy established St John's Tavern as a restaurant in 1943, the year in which Cole was writing. McKoy was the nephew of Henry Bacon the architect (see footnote 6 above).

POSTSCRIPT

The Battery arrived back in England on 21 December 1943 and disembarked the following day. While we were waiting to go ashore, we were visited by a major general representing General Sir Frederick Pile, Commander in Chief of AA command who, in a speech of welcome, was kind enough to refer to the success of our visit in most flattering terms. We had received many letters of appreciation prior to leaving the States from such notable people as Mr Stimson, the Secretary for War; Mr Patterson, the Under Secretary; Lieutenant General McNair, commanding Army Ground Forces; Her Majesty's Consul General, Los Angeles, and many senior officers in the US army. It gave us great satisfaction to feel that our efforts were appreciated.

The anti-climax, the disbanding of the Battery, was soon on us however but I do not propose to go into that question at all. Instead I shall bring the book to a close by a short, personal analysis of events.

I recorded events as they happened. I made clear that this was to be no treatise on Anglo-American relations, no official view but, on thinking things over after the tour was completed, I felt I ought to try to analyse my impressions and make a coherent whole of a series of jumbled events and circumstances.

Without question, my most lasting memory of the American tour was connected with the American's broad definition of democracy. It appeared obvious from the start that I would be unable to get a clear picture of normal American life. It was equally obvious that what I should get would be an insight into America under conditions imposed by a war which had not at that time touched on their doorstep. Soon I was forced to asked myself the question 'What are the Americans fighting for?' The question was answered in theory, time and time again, by the use of the magic word 'democracy', that being the quickest way of dealing with a difficult question and that being the accepted answer and/or slogan. So all that remained for me to do was to define democracy as seen through American eyes. I say all...

After my momentous tour, I was no nearer supplying this definition, than when I started. I could only go so far as to say that America's definition most assuredly differed from Great Britain's definition. In every town, in every house, in political life and in business life, far more stress was laid by the Americans on the right to preserve their independence of thought, far more work was done in committee, far more decisions reached by submission to a group than we experienced in Great Britain. To such an extent was this so, that there seemed to be evidence that the American was danger of losing the willingness to be led, losing the desire to become a member of a team with a captain having powers consistent with his standing. No individual seemed to relish the idea of standing up and saying 'you will do it this way', no one seemed to want to risk the possibility of a rebuff or the likelihood of being accused of dictatorship. Although laudable in theory it tended to create confusion rather than increase initiative.

I found examples time and time again, where an individual was most knowledgeable but refused to make a decision for any number of people greater than two. I spent many hours holding a watching brief on committees, while members wrangled and argued and debated for endless periods with no-one seemingly in a position to, or desirous of, giving a decision. It nearly always became a case of too many cooks spoiling the broth. Everyone, being far more politically minded than the Englishman, and far more voluble in political matters, was far more suspicious of a leader's decisions and consequently far less likely to back him up.

In theory discussion seemed sound in that it tended to ensure that no irresponsible person would commit the people irretrievably on a wrong project. In practice, however, as I experienced many times in a small way, I could rarely find anybody in authority who would answer yes or no, and say it as though they meant it. I wondered whether in fact America doesn't carry democracy too far? That to my mind, was a fundamental difference between our two peoples.

Regarding other questions I'd asked myself regarding my personal relations with the Americans I have met, I prepared a series of questions and supply my own answers in light of my own experiences:

Do you want a union between the two nations which would weld them into one?
No. I like the feeling of stability that 1,000+ years of history gives me, in comparison to the feeling of elation that goes with vastness and power.

Do you like the American people?
YES.
It was a strange thing, but almost every person I had met, talked to, or had dealings with in my whole tour, had been most kind, most anxious to help and eager to learn. I appreciate their friendliness and shall ever be grateful for their hospitality. I admire their youthful approach to life and like their exuberance.

Would you like to live in America?
In my present frame of mind, no. I fear an anti-climax. This tour or anything approaching the magnitude of this tour, would be an impossibility in everyday life. If I were to become a member of the community, their problems would become my problems, and I feel that there are as many problems to be faced in America as there are in Great Britain.

What particular problems are you thinking of?

I feel that the after-effects of this war are going to be felt in America in equally as big a way, if not bigger, than in England. Without touching too heavily on a topic that needs no aggravation whatsoever from outside, I feel that the negro situation is going to come rapidly to the forefront after the war. In addition, wages which during the war are high will, in my opinion, drop, and this decline will see the rising of many petty problems that are clouded over normally by the rosiness of a good wage. Finally, I doubt whether in my present frame of mind I would be sufficiently confident in the leaders that are now in power or likely to be in power.

Life in the United States of America will, in my humble opinion, be extremely volatile during the next generation.

Would you like to revisit America?

Most definitely, yes. Because I would not want to take a share in the type of burdens that I think are likely to occur, doesn't mean that I couldn't be a very sympathetic neighbour. I have many friends, whom I shall feel honoured to visit again, if they will have me, but I wouldn't want to become imbued with the drug of competition so prevalent in America. I recall to mind the words of the Englishman I met in Los Angeles [see chapter 11]. His one desire was to return and buy a small public house in Cornwall, where he could live without that seven-day-a-week, twenty-four-hour-a-day battle that is necessary to fight for a livelihood in the US.

Is this fight for existence then prevalent throughout America?

I think so, but feel that it is more evident in the north, and in the industrialised belts, than in the south. But many eyes appear to be turning to development in the south, and that will, in my opinion, create the same set of conditions that exists in the north.

Did the Americans teach you, anything?

Most definitely yes. They taught me that they were jealous of the British calm, but preferred their own 'push'. They showed me that they would be glad to infuse some of our steadiness into their own system, but that they would like more enthusiasm from us for their

Lieutenant Colonel Metcalf greets a young supporter welcoming the British visitors. Colonel Muirhead (right) and BSM Green (behind the flag) look on

own undeniable achievements. They taught me that by confidence they were able to achieve many things we should hesitate to undertake. They taught me that there are two ways of handling almost any question, and that is not always the British that have the right one. They taught me that they could be great friends, but hinted that they could be great enemies. But above all, I learned that they were human, and that under the hard-boiled exterior which many choose, and some have to adopt, was a warm heart, a human understanding which could not always be allowed to show.

Clifford Cole, 1944

MORE PUBLICATIONS FROM LOAGHTAN BOOKS

If you have enjoyed *Invading America, 1943*, why not try some of our other books? All are available to order through our website www.loaghtanbooks.com. Postage and packing is included within the British Isles.

Dear Ray...

A collection of WW2 letters written to a serving Royal Artillery gunner by his ATS fiancee, his mother and other members of his extended family. Background information places the correspondance in context, while contemporary and often humorous anecdotes shed sidelights on the difficulties of maintaining ordinary life under wartime conditions.

As Ray's fiancee writes, the letters 'make you realise that you are not just dealing with bits of paper but with people'.

Colour illustrated throughout, 192 pages, softback, £13.95.

ISBN: 978-1-908060-01-3

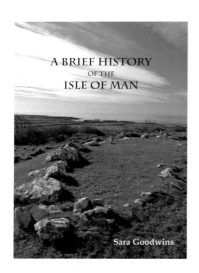

A Brief History of the Isle of Man

Doing exactly what it says on the cover the book describes the history of the island from its creation to the present day. In addition the short final chapter covers selected Manx myths – the island's 'alternative history'.

The publication is aimed principally at visitors to the island, but will also interest those who just don't have the time for a more in-depth look at the history of Mann.

Colour illustrated throughout, 152 pages, softback, £9.95.

ISBN: 978-1-908060-00-6